EMERSON'S
ROMANTIC
STYLE

EMERSON'S ROMANTIC STYLE

By Julie Ellison

PRINCETON UNIVERSITY PRESS

PRINCETON, NEW JERSEY

1 · 9 · 8 · 4

Copyright © 1984 by Princeton University Press

Published by Princeton University Press, 41 William Street,
Princeton, New Jersey 08540
In the United Kingdom: Princeton University Press, Guildford, Surrey

Library of Congress Cataloging in Publication Data will be
found on the last printed page of this book

ISBN 0-691-06612-4

This book has been composed in Linotron Goudy

Clothbound editions of Princeton University Press books
are printed on acid-free paper, and binding materials are
chosen for strength and durability.

Printed in the United States of America by Princeton University Press
Princeton, New Jersey

TO MY MOTHER
Miriam Train Ellison
AND
IN MEMORY OF MY FATHER
E. Jerome Ellison

CONTENTS

ACKNOWLEDGMENTS

I am indebted to the teachers and colleagues who have been creative readers of the various sections and stages of this book, particularly to Harold Bloom, Geoffrey Hartman, Barbara Packer, Richard Brodhead, Bryan Jay Wolf, James McIntosh, and Tobin Siebers.

I am especially grateful to my husband, Mark Creekmore, for his patience, humor, and radiant sanity throughout. And I take this opportunity to welcome Peter Ellison Creekmore, the "radiating, jaculating fellow" whose arrival coincided so happily with this book's completion.

An earlier version of material in Chapters 1, 2, and 4, "Emerson's Sublime Analysis," appeared in a special issue of *The Bucknell Review, The American Renaissance: New Dimensions,* edited by Harry R. Garvin and Peter C. Carafiol (1983). Grateful acknowledgment is made to Alfred A. Knopf, Inc., for permission to reprint lines from "Notes toward a Supreme Fiction" from *The Collected Poems of Wallace Stevens* (1954), and passages from *The Necessary Angel* (1951), and to the Belknap Press of Harvard University Press for permission to quote from *The Journals and Miscellaneous Notebooks of Ralph Waldo Emerson,* edited by William H. Gilman et al., Vols. I–XI, (1960–1975) and *The Collected Works of Ralph Waldo Emerson,* edited by Robert E. Spiller, Alfred R. Ferguson, et al., Vols. I and II (1971 and 1979).

A NOTE ON ABBREVIATIONS
AND EDITIONS CITED

References to Emerson's works, journals, and letters are indicated by abbreviated title, volume number, and page number following the quotation. For material that has not yet appeared in the new Harvard editions of the *Journals* and the *Collected Works*, I have used the Centenary Editions. For ease of reading, in citations from the *Journals and Miscellaneous Notebooks*, I have omitted Emerson's deletions as indicated by the editors.

CEC   *The Correspondence of Emerson and Carlyle*. Edited by Joseph Slater. New York: Columbia University Press, 1964.

CW   *The Collected Works of Ralph Waldo Emerson*. Edited by Robert Spiller, Alfred Ferguson, et al. Cambridge: Belknap Press, Harvard University Press, 1971– .

EL   *The Early Lectures of Ralph Waldo Emerson*. Edited by Stephen Whicher, Robert Spiller, et al. 3 vols. Cambridge: Belknap Press, Harvard University Press, 1960–1972.

Hale   *Ralph Waldo Emerson, together with Two Early Essays of Emerson*. Edward Everett Hale. Boston: Brown & Company, 1899.

IS   *Indian Superstition . . . with A Dissertation on Emerson's Orientalism at Harvard*. Edited by Kenneth Walter Cameron. Hanover, N.H.: Friends of the Dartmouth Library, 1954.

J   *The Journals of Ralph Waldo Emerson*. Edited by Edward Waldo Emerson and Waldo Emerson Forbes. 10 vols. Centenary Edition. Boston and New York: Houghton Mifflin Co., 1910–1914.

JMN   *The Journals and Miscellaneous Notebooks of Ralph Waldo Emerson*. Edited by William Gillman et al. Cambridge: Belknap Press, Harvard University Press, 1960– .

L   *The Letters of Ralph Waldo Emerson*. Edited by Ralph L. Rusk. 6 vols. New York: Columbia University Press, 1964.

W   *The Complete Works of Ralph Waldo Emerson*. Edited by Edward

Waldo Emerson. 12 vols. Centenary Edition. Boston and New York: Houghton Mifflin Co., 1903–1904.

YES   *Young Emerson Speaks: Unpublished Discourses on Many Subjects.* Edited by Arthur Cushman McGiffert, Jr. Boston: Houghton Mifflin Co., 1938.

EMERSON'S
ROMANTIC
STYLE

INTRODUCTION

"THE MIND

GOES ANTAGONIZING ON"

"Literature is now critical. Well analysis may be poetic," Emerson wrote in an 1838 journal entry. "Is not the sublime felt in an analysis as well as in a creation?" (*JMN*.VII.303). The purpose of this book is to trace how Emerson came to answer "yes" to this question. His ambivalent affirmative sounds clearly in his pronouncements on the subject of criticism. A more intriguing and ultimately more persuasive answer, however, is the way Emerson's prose style develops into a poetry of analysis, the way his rhetoric uses criticism in the interests of "the sublime." Like so many of his Romantic predecessors and contemporaries, Emerson's fascination with philosophies of perception, interpretation, and language had formal as well as thematic consequences.

Nevertheless, though theory partly generates style, both aspects of Emerson's prose seem to be the vehicles of more fundamental motives or structures of thought and feeling. "A man's *style* is his intellectual Voice only in part under his countroul [sic]," Emerson observed. "It has its own proper tone & manner which when he is not thinking of it, it will always assume. He can mimic the voices of others, he can modulate it with the occasion & the passion, but it has its own individual nature" (*JMN*.III.26). If style is an "intellectual Voice," its analysis requires a reading of consciousness. Since its "proper tone & manner" persist even when the author "is not thinking of it," it requires us to interpret the significant absence of self-consciousness. Because that voice perpetually "mimics the voices of others," a study of style necessarily involves a writer's response to his tradition. Prose is certainly no less subject to literary influence than poetry, and it is time to develop ways of talking

· 3 ·

about these dynamics concretely, that is, on the level of the sentence and paragraph.[1] And insofar as style modulates "with the occasion," we must take into account generic and historical contexts. For the real importance of understanding the psychological dynamics of Emerson's "intellectual Voice" is that, in them, we discover patterns common to most Romantic philosopher-poets. While a study of his development must to some extent treat Emerson as a unique case, the imaginative configurations eventually produced by that biography are genuinely representative of Romantic nonfiction prose.

Our exploration of the motives of Emerson's development starts with his youthful journals, roughly from 1820 to 1824. These documents exhibit a severe case of literary overinfluence. Emerson would later say, quite accurately, "I have served my apprenticeship of bows & blushes, of fears & references, of excessive admiration" (JMN.IV.278). Awed by the glory of classical and English literature, he expressed his own literary ambitions mimetically. "What we ardently love we learn to imitate," he writes in the well-known "robe of eloquence" passage (JMN.II.239; April 18, 1824). At the same time, he treats his imitations as proof of his inability to match his models. The intensity of his fantasies of identification with great authors of the past is directly proportionate to his contempt for himself as their critic. His gloomy meditations on history and historical awareness express the Romantic sense that self-consciousness is a belated, sentimental condition. His judgments about history, religion, and literature are manifestations of his first vocational crisis, precipitated by the conflict between the dream of an inaccessible eloquence and the habit of criticism. In his late teens and early twenties, he is plagued with uneasiness that leads eventually to the discovery of self-delighting powers.

Stephen Whicher's *Freedom and Fate* was the first coherent account of this transformation, and it remains the most influential. Whicher argues that it was the discovery of "the god within" that decisively turned Emerson from anxious vacillation to exuberant self-confidence. Whicher describes the change in Emerson's stance as tantamount to religious conversion:

The rock on which he thereafter based his life was the knowledge that the soul of man does not merely, as had long been taught, contain a spark or drop or breath or voice of God; it *is* God. . . . Before its revelation of the extent of his own proper nature, of the unfailing reservoir of needed strength that lay unsuspected in his own soul, his previously seemingly crushing disabilities evaporated into insignificance. The astonishing surge of pride and confidence that followed . . . is a genuine rebirth.[2]

Conversion is an appropriate figure for the advent of Emerson's powers. But it is a metaphor that leads Whicher into difficulties. By describing Emerson's change of mind as a radical break with earlier doubts, Whicher is left with the problem of explaining why fate, necessity, and skepticism surface in Emerson's works later on. In fact, these anxieties never leave his consciousness for more than a few pages at a time, even in his earliest literary experiments. If we understand the breakthrough of the 1820s as the consequence of—for Emerson—a new way of *interpreting* threats to his imaginative well-being, we can make better sense of the persistence of negativity and the way it forces him continually to rediscover self-reliance. Close readings of Emerson's prose will, I hope, bear out the hypothesis that, while the tone and arrangement of moods of "freedom" and "fate" change somewhat over the course of Emerson's career, the conflict between them is there from the start.

What is it, then, that enables Emerson to stop berating himself for his critical temper and to begin taking pleasure in it? To answer this question, we have to take Emerson's reading and theories of reading seriously. He moves from early frustrations to a liberating conjunction of imagination and analysis by using tendencies in his intellectual culture that enhance the critic's authority over the text he interprets and the scholar's power to shape myth and history retroactively. Emerson interprets his learning, using hermeneutics that release him from the double bind of idolatry and self-deprecation. It begins to occur to him that there are advantages to being born in "an age so late" (*JMN*.III.20). The models for his "sublime analysis" are the modes of criticism practiced in his day. They include Biblical scholarship, particularly the higher criticism, and the related disciplines of comparative religion and mythology; notions of the sublime; and the aesthetics and psychology of irony. As soon as he deploys Romantic criticisms, in a rhetoric directed against sources, the latter cease to be sources and become analogues of his own strategy and, within his works, analogues of each other.

The higher criticism weakened the past and strengthened the reader. Its practitioners, rejecting revelation, changed a few prophetic authors into many anonymous scribes and editors. As distinguished recent studies have shown, comparative methods revealed discrepancies within the Bible while disclosing analogical relationships between the Bible and other epics, myths, and histories.[3] In conjunction with comparative studies of religions, it enabled scholars to view Christianity as one myth among many. This organized cultural history into a system of analogies that only the modern comparatist was in a position to apprehend. Most studies of the literary manifestations of Romantic mythopoeic thought overlook the fact that it proved to be destructive as well as synthetic.[4] Comparisons that broke down the distinctions between the Bible and other works left the critic master of a vast field of interchangeable mythologies. The import of the Bible ceased to be identified with its depictive accuracy, and began to be located in the experience of mediation among mythologies, that is, in the act of reading. Through complex identifications with and displacements of the Bible's human authors, eighteenth- and nineteenth-century interpreters took apart the Bible in order to repossess it. As a rule, their appropriations depended on the reader recognizing an aspect of himself (though usually of transpersonal origin) in the book he was reading.[5] It is not far from this to Emerson's claim that what draws us in others' works is our own alienated majesty. The higher criticism lent itself to being treated by Emerson as a theory of influence. By depriving the world's most influential text of the unitary meaning that proved God's authorship, it demonstrated the power of interpretation to diminish the intimidating aspect of writers and traditions—a power that, of course, brought with it new anxieties.

The Romantic sublime, like the higher criticism, enacts a scene of reversal, an antithetical conversion that turns the mind from God or nature to the self—a scene found in virtually every Romantic human science. Emerson appropriates elements of the sublime, as he does of the higher criticism, because of this structure or plot.[6] Romantic theories of the sublime convey a great variety of experiences—the wanderer's emotions in nature or before a ruin, the viewer's reactions to a painting, the reader's feeling for a poem. In every case, the subject feels that he is overwhelmed by the literal force or mass or by the imaginative power of the object. This is followed by an excited feeling of being enlarged and inspired by whatever it is he confronts. The sublime, therefore, is not an attribute of the art work but a psychological phenomenon in the witness who recovers from a debilitating percept. When one has been overwhelmed by a book or a literary tradition, this form of sublimity becomes a crisis of literary influence; the "mathematical sublime" becomes the "hermeneutical sublime."[7] The exhilaration associated with the sublime comes about as we convert disorientation and meaninglessness into evidence of our power over the things that cause these sensations. This brings about a sudden pleasure in self-consciousness that further strengthens the perceiving subject. If it is a reader or critic who discovers his ability to create the meanings of the texts that threaten him, criticism becomes the occasion for sublime emotions and for the disjunctive style that accompanies them. In 1826, Emerson described this moment in a letter to Mary Moody Emerson, whom he always associated with the sublime. He begins modestly, referring to life's "little coincidences," but then his heart leaps up. These events "touch all the springs of wonder." Then "the Mind [stands] forth in alarm with all her faculties, suspicious of a Presence which it behoves her deeply to respect" (L.I.170). The movement from wonder to alarm and suspicion betrays the defensive function of the sublime; the confrontation with authority is suggested by the persistent obligation to "respect" it (though Emerson goes on to remark that he is "touched not more with awe than with curiosity"). The structure of the sublime moment and the rhetoric of "sublime analysis" duplicate the less overt anxiety and recuperation we can trace in the work of a century of Biblical criticism.

The Romantic sublime and Romantic irony are not usually treated as related phenomena. I think it can be shown that they are structurally, though not affectively, similar, however, and that they form related sequences in many Romantic works.[8] Irony often involves the overcoming or demystification of cultural and social authority. Like the hermeneutical sublime, on these occasions it marks the pleasure of the ego's victory over influence. The mood of irony is quite different from that of sublimity, however. Friedrich Schlegel's "Socratic irony" rescues the ego from external authority but resists the unidirectional resolution of the Kantian sublime, which rises above confusion toward Reason.[9] Schlegel finds pleasure, not in the mind's ascent, but in its appreciation of the *"indissoluble antagonism* between the absolute and the relative" (emphasis added). In both ironic and sublime configurations, the critical reader is suddenly flooded with a sense of his own power. "The will of the poet can tolerate no law above itself," Schlegel declares. But for the ironist, enforcing this law brings self-enjoyment so great that it overflows in "transcendental buffoonery."[10]

Thus, irony turns not only against overpowering external percepts, but against the temptations of the sublime itself. It challenges the aspirations to unity and closure that are often part of the high seriousness of properly sublime moments and exposes the sublime illusion of originality. Conversely, the sublime can save the ironist from the sterility of excessive self-consciousness. Thus irony is an analogue of the sublime, but irony and sublimity are also criticisms of, or reactions to, each other. Irony diminishes anxieties about tradition and authority through the subject's enjoyment of his power to fragment and play with his culture from within, as it were; the sublime similarly gratifies him by allowing him to behold it from above. At times, in Emerson's prose, irony and sublimity accomplish the same end and appear interchangeable. Frequently, however, irony follows sublimity, deflating its pretensions without relinquishing its pleasures. In Emerson's "poetics of prose,"[11] Schlegel's "Witz" appears as "Whim" and as "the Comic," or that double consciousness which exposes "the radical joke of life, and then of literature" (W.VIII.159–61). Emerson intermittently becomes a transcendental buffoon, recommending "humor, fun, mimicry, anecdotes, jokes, ventriloquism" (*JMN*.VII.265). Just as frequently, though, playful passages intensify into the resonant hyperboles of the sublime. Emerson's irony alternates with his yearning for transcendence and teleology, a tonal emblem of his fluctuation between self-consciousness and surprise.

The long and complex eighteenth-century debate about the origin of language and the related explorations of the properties of poetic language are the basis of Emerson's frequently ironic conceptions of figurative language.[12] From post-Lockean theories of language, he appropriates the fable of an early man who instinctively turned sensible ideas into metaphors for abstract ones. This linguistic primal scene sanctions his own craving for metaphoric proliferation, even though such proliferation invalidates all primal scenes. Words, he writes in "The Poet," are "fossil poetry," preserved pieces of ancient history, and Emerson handles them as irreverently as he does all other forms of history. Words have long since been carried away from their original sites. Our present use of them is quotation out of context—as quotation always is for Emerson. His clusters of metaphor and multiple fables create an image of the past as debris tumbled together in our curricula and in our minds. His figures of speech are motivated by his joy in conversions of meaning rather than by a belief in the intrinsic affinity between a symbol and its referent (despite the almost universal tendency on the part of his commentators to take literally his statements of the latter view). Metaphor, as the trace of the modern mind at play in ancient languages, becomes another version of the anti-authoritarian reader/writer's triumph over the past.

The perspective gained by study of comparative literature and comparative religion begins to organize Emerson's prose. Comparative strategies allow him to perceive the history of civilization as a system of mythologies analogous to each other by virtue of their structural and thematic similarities. When he defines them all as reflections of himself, their equivalence is reinforced. All of Emerson's sources—literature, science, nature, preaching—become similarly interchangeable. Repetition governs the relationship of his essays to each other, as anyone familiar with their predictable way of unfolding knows. One essay may treat history, another love, another America, but these subjects are figurative; they are fables that permit the repeated enactment of a single drama. Subject matters are as interchangeable as the languages of different disciplines and traditions. Within each essay, he composes by restating an idea in the metaphors and diction of many idioms. Because repetitive sentences create parallel rather than linear arrangements, the paragraph strikes us as disjunctive. There is no flow of argument or exposition, but rather a series of discrete acts of substitution. Paradoxically, Emerson's mature prose is closer to the discontinuity of the journals than to his early public performances. His first sermons prove him capable of limpid clarity and smooth progressions. Only when he possesses a justification for fragments and surprise do his published works begin to feel like his miscellaneous notebooks. More important than the justification itself is the fact that Emerson now uses theory and style for aggressive purposes. Disjunction enters his works once they are organized by antagonism. From 1832 on, writing is always resistance.

When this new configuration emerges, however, Emerson does not abandon his old attitudes. He does not renounce or forget his daydreams of glory, his paralysis before excessive knowledge, his sense that he lives in an impoverished age. Instead, he now locates these despairing moods in a sequence of emotions that dramatizes both crisis and resolution. Readers of his journals know that statements of anxiety and self-enjoyment, doubt and pride alternate with each other for decades. His essays come to be organized by the repetition of these movements from deprivation to power. Once the strategy of egocentric interpretation is established, it is Emerson's pleasure to reenter the state of crisis that made it necessary. He celebrates his theory of criticism with narcissistic impudence because it has always just rescued him from a regressive susceptibility to great men.

His progression from weakness to strength turns into a recurring cycle. He reexperiences the power of books and teachers over him, and perpetually turns against them as he again enters their fields of force. Even as he dramatizes the antagonistic relationships among influence, analysis, and invention, he shows, by repeatedly moving through them, that these states are contemporaneous. He takes

more pleasure in the motion that makes them almost simultaneously possible than in the possession of authority:

> [we] renew as oft as we can the pleasure the eternal surprize
> of coming at the last fact as children run up steps to jump
> down or up a hill to coast down on sleds or run far for one
> slide or as we . . . go many miles to a . . . place to catch
> fish and having caught one & learned the whole mystery we
> still repeat the process for the same result though perhaps the
> fish are thrown overboard at the last. The merchant plays
> the same game on Change, the card lover at whist, and what
> else does the scholar? He knows how the poetry he knows
> how the novel or the demonstration will affect him no new
> result but the oldest of all, yet he still craves a new book &
> bathes himself anew with the plunge at the last. (*JMN*.VIII.
> 12–13)

There is an unsolved "mystery" in the most predictable experience.
The mystery is that repetition yields the pleasure of "eternal surprize"; the result is known, but not the reason for it. Why does
the scholar keep reading? It must be to understand his own compulsion. It is precisely because Emerson feels that his "craving"
for books, "the oldest of all" desires, is mysterious that he illuminates for us the cyclical dynamics of criticism. By making our
susceptibility to books and our resentment of them phases of a
repeated series of gestures, Emerson keeps himself as reader—as
well as his readers—in a perpetual state of crisis. This is why "the
sublime" *is* "felt in an analysis as well as in a creation."

Since I have stressed the importance of "antagonism" in the
cycle of attitudes that links criticism and power in Emerson's writing, it is worth looking at the passage where we find his assertion
that "the mind goes antagonizing on." As his phrasing suggests,
aggression is desirable because it keeps the mind "going on." Emerson's will to power takes the form of substitution and repetition,
processes that are his theme in "Experience":

> How easily, if fate would suffer it, we might keep forever these
> beautiful limits, and adjust ourselves, once for all, to the per-

fect calculation of the kingdom of known cause and effect. In the street and in the newspapers, life appears so plain a business that manly resolution and adherence to the multiplication-table through all weathers will insure success. But ah! presently comes a day, or is it only a half-hour, with its angel-whispering,—which discomfits the conclusions of nations and of years! To-morrow again every thing looks real and angular, the habitual standards are reinstated, common sense is as rare as genius,—is the basis of genius, and experience is hands and feet to every enterprise;—and yet, he who should do his business on this understanding would be quickly bankrupt. Power keeps quite another road than the turnpikes of choice and will; namely the subterranean and invisible tunnels and channels of life. It is ridiculous that we are diplomatists, and doctors, and considerate people; there are no dupes like these. Life is a series of surprises, and would not be worth taking or keeping if it were not. God delights to isolate us every day, and hide from us the past and the future. We would look about us, but with grand politeness he draws down before us an impenetrable screen of purest sky, and another behind us of purest sky. "You will not remember," he seems to say, "and you will not expect." All good conversation, manners, and action, come from a spontaneity which forgets usages and makes the moment great. Nature hates calculators; her methods are saltatory and impulsive. Man lives by pulses; our organic movements are such; and the chemical and ethereal agents are undulatory and alternate; and the mind goes antagonizing on, and never prospers but by fits. We thrive by casualties. Our chief experiences have been casual. The most attractive class of people are those who are powerful obliquely and not by the direct stroke; men of genius, but not yet accredited; one gets the cheer of their light without paying too great a tax. Theirs is the beauty of the bird or the morning light, and not of art. In the thought of genius there is always a surprise; and the moral sentiment is well called "the newness," for it is never other; as new to the oldest intelligence as to the young child;— "the kingdom that cometh without observation." In like manner, for practical success, there must not be too much design. A man will not be observed in doing that which he can do best. There is a certain magic about his properest action which stupifies your powers of observation, so that though it is done before you, you wist not of it. The art of life has a pudency, and will not be exposed. Every man is an impossibility until he is born; everything impossible until we see a success. (*W*.III.67–69)

This passage shows us the precise function of "antagonism" in Emerson's prose. He celebrates the forces that sabotage existence contained within the "beautiful limits" of "perfect calculation": "Fate," "Power," "God," "Nature," "Life." This list is an example of the disconcerting metaphoric substitutions that are Emerson's response to the daemonic "angel-whispering . . . which discomfits the conclusions of nations and of years!" The mind liberated from "the kingdom of known cause and effect" can deploy serially and analogically all figures for power. The anti-authoritarian motive of Emerson's prose is heard in that rejection of time and "nations." When he puns on casualties later in the passage, the link between aggression and unconsciousness becomes clearer: "We thrive by casualties. Our chief experiences have been casual." Given the contiguity of "antagonizing," I take him to mean that we thrive by inflicting casualties, though in Emerson's writing, such violence is always a recovery from a prior debility. We can only "thrive by casualties," through a kind of deliberately "casual" forgetting that frees us from the inhibitions imposed by memory and "usage." "Power," he continues, keeps to "the subterranean and invisible tunnels and channels of life." Life can be "a series of surprises"—a significant conjunction of surprise and the phenomenon of serial repetition—only because "God" hides "the past and the future": " 'You will not remember,' he seems to say, 'and you will not expect.' "

Genius is only possible when, without self-knowledge or memory, we face "an impenetrable screen of purest sky." Only in this condition of half-willful forgetting can "spontaneity" transform "the moment." In Emerson's idiom, surprise is always aggressive, a rebellion against continuity, tradition, and authority. When we forget, we are freed into aggression. Experience breaks up into discrete moments of resistance; "the mind goes antagonizing on, and never prospers but by fits." If discontinuity is the weapon of genius, it is also the strategy that preserves the self-respect of the reader. Because the light of genius pulsates, the onlooker is spared "too much design" or "too great a tax." Emerson here wishes for authors who do not embody the temporal consciousness of tradition that "taxes" the patience of the competitive reader. The wish to evade his own self-consciousness and to avoid the "light" of others' leads to a desire to censor the story of his own development: "A man will not be observed in doing that which he can do best. There is a certain magic about his properest action which stupefies your powers of observation, so that though it is done before you, you wist not of it. The art of life has a pudency, and will not be exposed." The artist "stupefies" his reader in order not to be exposed and thus used by him. Fortunately, Emerson left us all the materials we need to "expose" him, including expressions of his desire to be exposed. His celebrations of ignorance, surprise, antagonism, and discontinuity are signs of his self-knowledge. He knowingly elects a style of apparent unconsciousness in order to free himself from his own respect for tradition. Emerson's literary development consists, therefore, of the movement of ongoing antagonism, the movement from memory to surprise, from causality to casualties, from guilt over the exercise of critical powers to delight in them.

· I ·

THE DEVELOPMENTAL NARRATIVE

· 1 ·

INVOCATIONS

As Emerson would later write of other "young and ardent minds,"
he was moved by "a desire, raging, infinite, a hunger, as of space
to be filled with planets; a cry of famine, as of devils for souls"
(*W*.IV.184). This desire to conquer and to be fed, to fill and to
be filled with inspiration, gave rise, during his college and schoolteaching years (1820–1825) to elaborate, ambitious fantasies. The
function of the journals that he began to keep regularly in his
junior year at Harvard was to record daydreams too outrageous to
be uttered publicly in, for example, his two Bowdoin Prize essays,
and too intense to be repressed altogether. In long, passionate
entries, we can trace the dynamics that organize his representations
of creativity, reflection, and piety. By interrogating the style and
structure of these little dramas, we can begin to understand how
his desire for verbal power, his contempt for criticism, and his
religious conscience combined to make him miserable. The journal
selections we are about to examine have a paradoxical structure.
Emerson's desire to be great is expressed through his imitations of
great men. Celebrating the role of inspired reader quickly leads
him to resent the role of critic. His harsh view of religion as the
history of imaginative decline chastizes his naive sentimentalizing
of the literary past. In the passages organized by these ambivalences,
creative power is divorced from reflective self-consciousness; in a
metaphoric analogue of this split between creativity and analysis,
the glorious past recedes from puny moderns. These distances make
genius both more alluring to and more remote from the young
aspirant, who torments himself with scathing critiques of his impossible desires. Close readings of the rhetoric of Emerson's early
journals and college essays—their tone, the plot of their fables,
the point of their allusions, the logic of their transitions—will

provide us with a way to measure his subsequent self-revisions. The anxieties expressed in these writings are significant, not only because they led to Emerson's initial discovery of antagonism, metamorphosis, and surprise, but also because they continued to instigate these reactions throughout his career.

In the first entry of "Wide World I," his first regular journal, Emerson identifies literary greatness with the genre of romance, which thus becomes an emblem of the exercise of the imagination. His vision is a passionate flight into a make-believe realm that mirrors his real desires. This opening flourish takes the form of jocular and clearly embarrassed allusions, almost parodies of the texts to which he refers. Although he utters the invocation in a playful tone, the excessively mannered prose reveals his wish to speak with a conspicuously "literary" voice, to mime authorial gestures, at least. It is obvious from this and similar passages that the precondition for Emerson's resentment of books was an extreme susceptibility to them. He voices an overpowering nostalgia for the golden age of English literature, and populates the domain of fancy with images from *The Faerie Queene, A Midsummer Night's Dream, The Tempest,* "L'Allegro" and "Il Penseroso."

> O ye witches assist me! enliven or horrify some midnight lucubration or dream (whichever may be found most convenient) to supply this reservoir when other resources fail. Pardon me Fairy Land! rich regions of fancy & gnomery, elvery, sylphery, & Queen Mab! pardon me for presenting my first petition to your enemies but there is probably one in the chamber who maliciously influenced me to what is irrevocable; pardon & favor me!—& finally Spirits of Earth, Air, Fire, Water, wherever ye glow, whatsoever you patronize, whoever you inspire, hallow, hallow this devoted paper. (*JMN.*I.4)

The otherwordly subject matter of the works he mimics, witches, fairies, "gnomery, elvery, sylphery," becomes an image of the dream that the works themselves represent for Emerson. His wish to exercise the magical power of poetry takes the form of imitations of stories about magic. For all the confessed silliness of this invocation, the need to begin ceremonially with an invitation to the

"Spirits" created by earlier authors is palpable. Emerson's metaphors suggest an imaginative economy in which he is the needy one. The "rich regions of fancy" must "supply this reservoir"—the journal—when his own "resources fail."

The second entry in Wide World II enacts a more ambitious flight into a spiritual world pervaded by the ardent, somber mood of the sublime. Emerson takes himself more seriously, and hence more anxiously:

> To forget for a season the world & its concerns, & to separate the soul for sublime contemplation till it has lost the sense of circumstances & is decking itself in plumage drawn out from the gay wardrobe of Fancy is a recreation & a rapture of which few men can avail themselves. . . .

He wishes to lose the sense of circumstances in order to forget that he is only engaging in recreation and that his mental wardrobe is secondhand. He takes a long look at his goal, the rapture of original authorship. His fantasy of Fancy, however, immediately triggers his doubts about his own qualifications for greatness. Who can wear the robe of eloquence? Where does genius come from? Is it a matter of nature or culture? He continues:

> this privilege . . . is attainable if not inborn. . . . Ordinary men claim the intermittent exercise of this power of beautiful abstraction; but to the souls only of the mightiest is it given to command the disappearance of land & sea, & mankind. . . .

He momentarily tolerates the "claim" of "ordinary men," those who have learned to be intermittently inspired; that is, he makes room for himself in the event that he lacks genius. But then he negates his leniency by insisting that the true test of power is the ability not just to "forget" the world, but to "command [its] disappearance." This is an early instance of the metaphor for "abstraction" we remember better as the "transparency" brought about by idealism in *Nature*. Its emergence here suggests the painful discrepancy between Emerson's sense of his real status and his dream of power. Here he suspends his doubts and pursues his wish.

In the entry's final scene, he imagines the figure of an "En-chanter," the master he wants to be, admired from afar.

> Then comes the Enchanter illuminating the glorious visions with hues from heaven, granting thoughts of other worlds gilded with lustre of ravishment & delight, till the Hours teeming with loveliness & Joy roll by uncounted. (*JMN*.I. 33–34)

Emerson views the Enchanter from the point of view of the earth-bound individual whose visions are irradiated with heavenly hues. Emerson, the speaker, is not the angelic visitor, but the one who receives "thoughts of other worlds" from him. It is important to notice Emerson's delight in receptivity, in having his "space . . . filled," his "Hours teeming." He often depicts the role of reader or recipient as being intensely pleasurable. Although, as an "ordinary man," his power to annihilate self and world is "inter-mittent," this mediated, vicarious sublimity is almost as good as the real thing. In an example of the instability of roles that makes explaining Emerson's fables so difficult, the contrast between me-diocrity and genius suddenly collapses.

In other entries, fables about magic express the desire for imag-inative power even more clearly. Emerson no sooner thinks about books than he imagines himself imagining them. Often this scenario contains an aggressive impulse:

> Could I seat myself in . . . one of those public libraries which human pride & literary rivalship have made costly, splendid & magnificent it would indeed be an enviable situation. I would plunge into the classic lore of chivalrous story & of the fairy-land bards & unclosing the ponderous volumes of the firmest believers in magic & in the potency of consecrated crosier of elfin ring I would let my soul sail away delighted in to their wildest phantasies. Pendragon is rising before my fancy. . . . (*JMN*.I.10)

Admiration and the thought of competition ("rivalship," "envia-ble") come simultaneously to mind in a way reminiscent of the later journals and the essays. In this fable, the motive behind

Emerson's emotional and stylistic prostration before the splendor of English literature is the desire for "potency." Reading is impelled by the ambition to be envied by his rivals; it is an instinctively conflictual activity. Nevertheless, here, too, Emerson's access to greatness is mediated. His envy of great writers is displaced as the thought of his own "enviable" position as reader; the magnificence of literature and its proud rivalries are transferred to the image of the library. As usual, it takes a litany of allusions to quest romance to incite Emerson's readerly heart to "sail away into . . . phantasies."

Some of Emerson's imitations are comical, such as his attempt at the gothic extremes of "Monk" Lewis:

> Would not Pestilence be a good personage in poetry for description? Wrapt in the long white robes of sickness. entering the town in her awful chariot & her slow approach heard afar off by the anxious fearful listeners—it comes—it rolls over the distant pavement—it draws near—the haggard terrifick form. . . . (JMN.I.15)

But a passage based on the imagery of *Paradise Lost* again shows the depth of Emerson's need to place himself in relation to English classics, as well as his ambiguity about just what that relationship is. The entry is a self-conscious exercise in sublimity; as usual, his protagonist is his own mind. "It enlarges the mind & . . . gratifies it to hold large contemplations regarding the . . . Universe," he begins. In the lines that follow, however, it is hard to tell whether he is the figure who "imagines" the scene described or the one who stars in it as the hero, "Conjecture." His fantasy ambiguously gratifies the writer's wish to describe power and the reader's sense of participation in the figure thus invented:

> We can imagine the shadow of the incomprehensibly large glorious mass blackening the infinity behind it we can send Conjecture forth to ride on the wings that are bearing the worlds forward & sit & explore & discover what is to occur when the wheels shall stop & the wings fall in the immediate presence of the source of light to which for ages past & ages

to come they have been & will be advancing . . . [and so on in the same vein]. (*JMN*.I.5)

The most exciting activity for Emerson, it seems, is the movement from "our" ordinary persepective to "the immediate presence of the source of light." He does not identify himself with that source or even with "the wings that are bearing the world forward," but with "Conjecture"—a hesitant name for a hero—who rides and sits as well as explores and discovers. The moral direction of this motion is also vague, for Emerson seems unable to decide whether the cosmic powers are diabolical or godly. The wings whose shadow blackens infinity suggest Milton's Satan, who soars heroically upward only to "fall in the immediate presence" of the light. But the "wheels" imply that what advances is Christ's chariot. The reasons why Emerson preferred to dramatize the transition between the positions of author or reader and hero will emerge more clearly in later passages, but that tendency is firmly established in these very early journals.

When Emerson's subject is "pulpit eloquence," his ambitions are less likely to be checked by inhibition. In the third entry of Wide World I, for example, he reworks the judgment scene of Henry Hart Milman's *Samor, Lord of the Bright City*.[1] This episode, he writes, is the type of "the eloquence of the senate, bar, or pulpit"—of any occasion, that is, "where one is addressing a multitude on an affair . . . able to produce in the orator an agony of excitement." The climax of the scene is the young minister's public investiture with the robe of eloquence. The depth of Emerson's gratification suggests why he would be slow to abandon his pulpit a few years later:

[L]et us suppose a pulpit Orator to whom the path of his profession is yet untried but whose talents are good & feelings strong & his independence as a man in opinion and action is established let him ascend the pulpit for the first time not to please or displease the multitude but to expound to them the words of the book & to waft their minds & devotions to heaven. Let him come to them in solemnity & strength & when he speaks he will chain attention with an interesting

figure and an interested face. To expand their views of the
sublime doctrines of the religion he may embrace the universe
& bring down the stars from their courses to do homage to
their Creator. Here is a fountain which cannot fail them. Wise
Christian orators have often & profitably magnified the in-
concievable [sic] power of the creator as manifested in his
works & thus elevated & sobered the mind of the people &
gradually drawn them off from the world they have left by the
animating ideas of Majesty, Beauty, Wonder, which these
considerations bestow. Then . . . the spirit is absorbed in
the play of its mightiest energies & their eyes are on him &
their hearts are in heaven then let him discharge his fearful
duty, then let him unfold the stupendous designs of celestial
wisdom, & whilst admiration is speechless let him minister
to their unearthly wants and let the ambassador of the most
high prove himself worthy of his tremendous vocation. Let
him gain the tremendous eloquence which stirs men's souls,
which turns the world upside down, but which loses all its
filth & retains all its grandeur when consecrated to God.
When a congregation are assembled together to hear such an
apostle you may look round & you will see the faces of men,
bent forward in the earnestness of expectation & in this desirable frame of mind the preacher may lead them whither-
soever he will; they have yielded up their prejudices to the
eloquence of the lips which the archangel hath purified &
hallowed with fire & this first sacrifice is the sin offering
which cleanseth them. (*JMN*.I.7–8)

As in the "Conjecture" and "Pendragon" entries, the imagery
of height and depth characteristic of the Romantic sublime here
signifies imaginative power. The orator "ascends the pulpit," wafts
the "minds & devotions" of his listeners "to heaven" with his
"sublime doctrines," and, conversely, "brings down the stars from
their courses" to them. The "speechless" audience is a sign of the
minister's desire for power over others. He wants not only attention, but submission; he imagines bringing about that "desirable
frame of mind" in which "they have yielded . . . to [his] elo-

quence." As in so many cases of the Romantic sublime, the witnesses are both overwhelmed and liberated. The congregation's
attention is "chained"; it is "sobered" and, like the orator,
"drawn . . . off from the world." "Animating ideas" result in a
state of suspended animation. At the moment of apparent paralysis,
however, "the spirit is absorbed in the play of its mightiest energies."
The listeners yield up their collective will in order to admire its
projection in the orator. The ritualistic element in this transaction
is striking. The congregation sacrifices its volition to the preacher
and is cleansed by so doing. He, in turn, is "purified" by the
archangel. In the Biblical paradigm, Abraham's sacrifice requires
Isaac's analogous surrender to him. Authors and orators may usurp
our wills legitimately only when they have first offered up their
own.

The drama of orator and audience is a complex self-portrait. The
figure of the preacher exercises power, but also seems merely to
conduct it, as Emerson suggests that the dynamics of influence take
the form of a cycle of receptivity and conquest. The marvelous
vanity that composed this scene is hardly disguised by the talk of
consecration. The religious motive and themes of the young "pulpit
orator" are transparent sanctions for his pleasure in the admiration
of others. Because his discourse is dedicated to God, it "loses all
the filth & retains all its grandeur." Even this early, Emerson's
morality has a pragmatic edge; he espouses an "aesthetics of *use*"[2]
that does not scruple to "profitably" magnify the power of God,
the institution of preaching, or "the book." As in the other passages
we have examined, however, Emerson pictures himself both as the
source of inspiration and as its recipient. He does homage to the
Creator and submits to the archangel in the same grateful attitude
that his audience assumes in relation to him. His self-characteri-
zations will always be unstable in this way, slipping from the role
of ambassador to that of author, from the vehicle to the source of
power. He is, from the start, both humble and narcissistic. But for
many years he is stricken with guilt when he yields to self-love.

He chastises himself incessantly for indulging in daydreams of
this kind. Under the heading "Greatness," he forces himself to
contemplate how delusions of grandeur portend failure:

Never mistake yourself to be great, or designed for greatness, because you have been visited by an indistinct and shadowy hope that something is reserved for you beyond the common lot. It is easier to aspire than to do the deeds. The very idleness which leaves you leisure to dream of honour is the insurmountable obstacle between you and it. Those who are fitly furnished for the weary passage from mediocrity to greatness seldom find time or appetite to indulge that hungry and boisterous importunity for excitement which weaker intellects are prone to display. That which helps them on to eminence is in itself sufficient to engross the attention of all their powers, and to occupy the aching void. (*JMN.*I.100)

Emerson recognizes in himself an "aching void," an "appetite," a "hungry . . . importunity for excitement" that he satisfies by fantasizing. His discouragement is grounded in quantitative reasoning. If one is thus filled up with unrealities, there is no room for facts; one channels one's quantum of energy either into "indistinct & shadowy hope" or into action. The "dream of honour" is therefore a symptom of passivity and lassitude. Great reputations, he fears, are made by doers, not dreamers ("It is easier to aspire than to do the deeds"). The "passage from mediocrity to greatness" appears to be a practical, colorless affair that does not satisfy the desire for excitement. This conforms to a strictly Protestant ethic; the hero is too busy to "find time" to "indulge" an illicit "appetite."

This tone and argument, characteristically, do not last long. The passage continues, "Greatness never comes upon a man by surprise, and without his exertions or consent"—just the opposite of Emerson's later psychology of creative surprise. But despite this denial and perhaps because of it, certain "Genii" do surprise him: Poverty, Contempt, and Anger, antagonists that frequently appear at his moments of weakness, enabling him to gain strength from opposition. They are threatening, aggressive personages who must be combatted on the road to greatness. Poverty "travels like an armed man," Contempt "meets you in the corners and highways with a hiss," Anger "treads you down as with the lightening."

Imagining success as the defeat of enemies rather than as the filling of an interior void rouses Emerson to optimism, one of the primary functions of antagonism in his works. Now the presence of desire foretells triumph, not failure:

> This very *hope*, and panting after it . . . is . . . an earnest of the possibility of success. . . . [T]he extraordinary effects of education attest a capacity of improvement to an indefinite degree. And this is certain that every man may be higher & better than he is. It is then not only safe but salutory to make sacrifices and efforts for greatness, while it were madness and perdition to become stationary or retrograde. (*JMN*.I.100)

But he remains uneasy, worried that a determinism of temperament dooms him to second-class citizenship in the domains of art. At this stage, he still thinks of critics as inferior beings, accepting Coleridge's self-punishing conviction that excessive introspection makes a man unfit for poetry:[3]

> [T]here are two sorts of people in society; one . . . capable of making those generalizations and signal master-pieces of power which flow from and ascertain greatness, and the other . . . sometimes with more pride and jealous self-respect, confines itself to the task of watching and analyzing those efforts. . . . [T]he second class is . . . distinguished by an acuteness, which should seem destined for the first but fallen upon the second, to measure and compare, with lilliputian accuracy, the progress, conduct or defects of first minds. (*JMN*.I.101)

His "jealous" interest in "first minds," the obsession with greatness that he has been confessing, relegates him to the ranks of petty book reviewers. This embarrassed self-consciousness is the attitude that must change for his mature poetics to develop. Only when he reimagines the figure of the critic is he freed from his inferiority complex.

In the passage now before us, however, the distinction between the first and second classes continues to condemn him. He attributes the obscurity of the great to their own "self-willed unconcern to the rewards and prosperity which their fellow men have it in their power to bestow." Because it is precisely those rewards and recognitions that Emerson craves, he consigns himself to mediocrity:

> [T]he highest order of greatness, that which abandons earthly consanguinity, and allies itself to immortal minds, is that which exists in obscurity and is least known among mankind. . . . If . . . there are any who are above the solicitation of wealth, honour, and influence, and who can laugh even at the love of Fame . . . there will be nothing left worth offering them, to attract them from their solitudes. (*JMN*.I.102)

Great men are solitary because their vertical relationship to the transcendent or ideal precludes horizontal relationships with their fellow men. Emerson's lack of "earthly consanguinity" (fame?) may mean that he is allied to "immortal minds"; his very obscurity may be evidence of greatness. In this journal entry, ambition first prevents the development of genius by draining off energy, then becomes a sympton of greatness, and subsequently turns into the obsessive criticism of others that makes the "second order" incapable of "signal master-pieces of power." Ambition comes to designate the consuming egotism that, like most forms of acute self-consciousness, is alternately paralyzing and enabling. The second of Emerson's great discoveries, therefore, along with learning to equate sublimity and criticism will be learning to surprise himself out of reflection.

Given the ambivalence that gives rise to the mood changes of Emerson's college journals, the remarkable thing about his public performances during these years is the degree to which they do not reflect his private thoughts. His two Bowdoin prize essays, "The Character of Socrates" (1820) and "The Present State of Ethical Philosophy" (1821) display a temperate—indeed, an ostentatiously judicious—persona. They show Emerson in the process of mastering the conventions of lucid argument and rational exposition that he will later disavow.

In the first essay, he questions the superiority of the moderns; in the second, he seeks to demonstrate it. But in both, he respect-

fully presents the current state of informed discussion, then modestly corrects it. Particularly in "Socrates," he conveys his sympathy
with prevailing opinions through constant references to them. He
begins:

> The philosophy of the human mind has of late years com-
> manded an unusual degree of attention from the curious and
> the learned. The increasing notice which it obtains is owing
> much to the genius of those men who have raised themselves
> with the science to general regard, but chiefly, as its patrons
> contend, to the uncontrolled progress of human improvement.

He invokes the aristocrats of culture, the "curious and the learned,"
"men of genius," the "patrons" of a certain view. In his mature
essays, any representative of taste and sensibility in the opening
paragraphs, however well-meaning, invariably appears as an enemy.
But in "Socrates," Emerson almost literally begs to differ from
these figures:

> The zeal of its [progress'] advocates, however, in other respects
> commendable, has sinned in one particular,—they have laid
> a little too much self-complacent stress on the merit and suc-
> cess of their own unselfish exertions, and in their first con-
> tempt of the absurd and trifling speculations of former
> metaphysicians, appear to have confounded sophists and true
> philosophers, and to have been disdainful of some who have
> enlightened the world and marked out a path for future ad-
> vancement.

Emerson manages gently to parody his elders' disdain without
sounding disdainful himself. His tact is elaborate: "in other respects
commendable," "in one particular," "a little too much . . . stress,"
"their unselfish exertions." He merely wishes to suggest that "the
giant strength of modern improvements is more indebted to the
early wisdom than is generally allowed, or perhaps than modern
philosophers have been aware" (Hale, 57–58). His gentle criticism
is more than atoned for by the conservatism of his project, which
is, after all, to honor the "plain good sense" of one of humanity's
teachers. Socrates ends up sounding rather like a Yankee merchant,

endowed as he is with "a shrewdness which would not suffer itself to be duped . . . concealed under a semblance of the frankest simplicity" (Hale, 66). Emerson's style is as decorous as his argument. Always using the editorial "we," he tells his readers exactly what he is going to do, then does it. The essay is sharply, even somewhat nervously, delimited:

We shall proceed to examine the character of the philosopher, after premising that we do not intend to give the detail of his life. . . .

We must now hasten to our great task of developing the moral superiority of the great philosopher. . . .

We must now proceed to say something of his ambiguous genius. . . .

We must hasten to take our leave of the illustrious Grecian. (Hale, 66,73,83,93)

Emerson is less ostentatious about his literary manners in "The Present State of Ethical Philosophy" and is somewhat more aggressive as a defender of progress than as its critic. Still, although the essay culminates in a celebration of liberal democracy, the conservatism of the speaker's fundamental stance has not altered much. He condemns "the system of fanatic philosophy" spawned by Hobbes, "the accursed fruits of whose prevalence were abundantly reaped in France." He opposes revolution, which "sweeps away all the duties which we owe to others," and deplores values that "elevate the ostrich to a higher rank in the scale of merit and wisdom than the man, old and honorable, whose parental affection dictates actions of wise and profound calculation" (Hale, 111). Such untroubled filiopiety is found nowhere else in Emerson's public or private writings, and is responsible for the patent inauthenticity of the Harvard essays when read in conjunction with contemporaneous journals and later published works. The inauthenticity is felt only by the reader who knows where Emerson is headed, however. The urge to succeed in established ways is sincere. From the invocation to Wide World I on, Emerson has defined literary achievement as, among other things, fancy's reenactment of respected models. What is missing in these essays is the "raging, infinite" hunger for greatness that cannot be uttered in polite rhetoric.

When Emerson graduates from Harvard and begins to teach, he is harder on himself than ever. His ambition is as intense as before, its fulfillment more remote. In a journal entry of May 1822, he compares his present state of mind to that of the preceding spring, when he had been "delighted with . . . recent honours" (the relative success of his Bowdoin Prize essays), "proud of a poet's fancies," and "pleased with ambitious prospects." "But now," he laments, "I'm a hopeless Schoolmaster just entering upon years of trade to which no distinct limit is placed." Greatness seems to be passing him by, preferring his more fortunate classmates. He winces at an encounter with a college friend who, he thinks, "is advancing his footing in good company & fashionable friends." Even more trying than the success of his Harvard contemporaries must have been watching his brothers' careers moving ahead, literally at the cost of his own. Partly financed by Waldo, the "droning schoolmaster," William went to Germany in 1824, and Charles took his turn at Harvard. Waldo's competitiveness took the form of constantly measuring himself against others, to his disadvantage.[4] Typically, he concludes this entry by criticizing it: "[T]hese are the suggestions only of a disappointed spirit brooding over the fall of castles in the air" (JMN.I.129–30). In this difficult period of balked progress, his fantasies continue, but are punished much more harshly than before, as Emerson tries to force himself to be practical.

In the same month, May 1822, he sets down one of the most self-wounding analyses of his seemingly hopeless aspirations:

In twelve days I shall be nineteen years old; which I count a miserable thing. Has any other educated person lived so many years and lost so many days? I do not say acquired so little for by an ease of thought & certain looseness of mind I have perhaps been the subject of as many ideas as many of mine age. But mine approaching maturity is attended with a goading

sense of emptiness & wasted capacity; with the conviction
that vanity has been content to admire the little circle of
natural accomplishments, and has travelled again & again the
narrow round, instead of adding sedulously the gems of knowledge to their number. Too tired and too indolent to travel up
the mountain path which leads to good learning, to wisdom
& to fame, I must be satisfied with beholding with an envious
eye the laborious journey & final success of my fellows, remaining stationary myself, until my inferiors & juniors have
reached & outgone me. And how long is this to last? How
long shall I hold the little acclivity which four or six years
ago I flattered myself was enviable, but which has become
contemptible now? It is a child's place & if I hold it longer I
may quite as well resume the bauble & rattle, grow old with
a baby's red jocky on my grey head & a picturebook in my
hand, instead of Plato and Newton. Well, and I am he who
nourished brilliant visions of future grandeur which may well
appear presumptuous & foolish now. My infant imagination
was idolatrous of glory, & thought itself no mean pretender
to the honours of those who stood highest in the community,
and dared even to contend for fame with those who are hallowed by time & the approbation of ages.—It was a little merit
to concieve [sic] such animating hopes, and afforded some poor
prospect of the possibility of their fulfillment. This hope was
fed & fanned by the occasional lofty communications which
were vouchsafed to me with the Muses' Heaven and which
have at intervals made me the organ of remarkable sentiments
& feelings which were far above my ordinary train. And with
this lingering earnest of better hope (I refer to this fine exhilaration which now & then quickens my clay) shall I resign
every aspiration to belong to that family of giant minds which
live on earth many ages & rule the world when their bones
are slumbering, no matter, whether under a pyramid or a
primrose? No I will yet a little while entertain the Angel.
(JMN.I.133–34)

Again he judges his daydreams by the standards of the work ethic.
He has failed to collect knowledge "sedulously" and has been "too

tired and too indolent to travel up the mountain path" (an appropriate adaptation of *Pilgrim's Progress*). He has been a bad steward, wasting time and talent: "Has any other educated person lived so many years and lost so many days?" His disciplined "fellows," by contrast, have "reached & outgone" him by pursuing the "laborious journey." His self-loathing is expressed in the image of himself as an old man with a baby's playthings and in the savage precision with which he summarizes the motives of his "brilliant visions of future grandeur": "My infant imagination was idolatrous of glory."

But criticism of "presumptuous & foolish" ambition ceases as he remembers "lofty communications" from the muse, "remarkable sentiments & feelings" and moments of "fine exhilaration" which offer "better hope." And so, in the end, he opts for the imagination. In doing so, he chooses solitude over brotherhood, electing to cultivate his relationship with the father, God, or the past, "that family of giant minds which . . . rule the world when their bones are slumbering." As in the earlier passage about the young pulpit orator, greatness abandons "earthly consanguinity" for immortality. Thus he removes himself from competition with his contemporaries and from susceptibility to their opinions. At the same time, he connects himself to a power that channels energy through him, the "Angel" who will reward him with the success he has not sought. Again, one cannot help but wonder whether this distaste for consanguinity arises from his experiences in a family of brothers. In his childhood romance, he recalls "the warm sympathy" among several "eager blushing boys" who, their chores completed, "kindle each other . . . with scraps of poetry or song" (W.VII.118–21). His exaggerated idea of their talents and memory of the competitive kindling of ambition possibly exacerbate his later feeling of being surpassed by his own generation. The fact that he prefers solitude to fraternity, an absent father to living brothers, suggests that he was not entirely comfortable with his siblings in spite of the genuine affection among them. It may be that his reiterated praise of their gifts and deprecation of his own are ways of suppressing aggressive urges toward them. The early death of his father perhaps explains why he associates solitude with a godlike source of power who stands above and behind him. The orphaned child imagines a father who will recognize his gifts and prefer him to his brothers.

After 1820, a dark view of man's miserable nature enters Emerson's journals as if in judgment of his escapist fantasies of literary splendor. There is clearly a division of emotional labor between poetic fancy, on the one hand, and history, particularly Christian history, on the other. The former is the faculty of optimism and desire, the latter, of pessimism and the reality principle. For Emerson, imaginative redemption occurs outside of the scheme of history. When he contemplates literature, he senses miraculous possibility in the present and hopes for personal salvation in the future. He is divided between a backward-looking religion that is really no more than moral history and the literary imagination that aspires to greatness and looks only forward. In 1822, for example, we find him arguing that fiction originates in man's need to escape from despair at "life and truth."

> [T]he source of fable is *human misery*. . . . [T]o relieve one hour of life, by exciting the sympathies to a tale even of imaginary joy, was accounted a praiseworthy accomplishment; and honour & gold were due to him, whose rare talent took away, for the moment, the memory of care and grief. (*JMN*.I. 109)

If art evades orthodoxy, the imagination that makes secular salvation possible is heretical. Emerson perhaps assuages a bad conscience on this score by attacking remoter forms of irreligion. In the early 1820s, he damns as "superstition" what he will later dignify as "myth." The topic of his Harvard exhibition poem, "Indian Superstition," was assigned, and the attitudes expressed in it, as Cameron shows, are entirely derivative (*IS*.17–35). His assiduous reading in oriental subjects throughout his college years indicates, however, that he relished the color and exoticism of the Indians' "immense 'goddery' " (*JMN*.II.195). Like fairyland, it offers a sensuous contrast to the New England quotidian. The poem opens with a reprise of the early Wide World invocations and contains romantic material borrowed from Spenser, Shakespeare, Milton, and Southey. But Indian superstition, however glamorous, was the antithesis of Unitarianism, for which even three persons in one god were too many. So we find Emerson denouncing the pagan East, the very image of his romantic fancies. "In quantity & absurdity their superstition has nothing to match it" (*JMN*.II.195), he remarks complacently. The thought is rendered more violently in the poem itself:

> . . . Superstition crowds his haggard court.
> The bloated monster gluts his hellish brood,
> Gorging his banquet with the people's blood.
>
> (*IS*, 11.15–17)

This and other passages of Gothic gore, which blend horror and delight, exceed any of Emerson's possible sources. In order to achieve his easy victory over superstition, he exaggerates its depravity, avoids altogether the question of what differentiates superstition from faith, and sides with the angels—the figures of Fate and Freedom who weave "the laurelled lightenings round Columbia's brow" (*IS*, 1.102). In his later thinking, Hinduism, Christianity, and fairy tales become equally figurative analogues of each other. Paganism rises in his estimation, and orthodoxy loses its power to intimidate. Then, when he can regard all faiths as fictions, he no longer needs to escape into fairyland to let loose his imagination or to scorn superstition as the illegitimate sister of romance. At that point, the emotional structure of his writing changes.

In the early 1820s, however, his faith centers on the consequences of the Fall. His religious musings in the journals take the form of observations on history. These meditations on the decline of civilization are not so much devotional acts as oblique commentaries on what Emerson fears is his own place in history. The nineteen-year-old who worries in a prematurely old voice that history is passing him by finds his apparent failure confirmed in humanity's decline. His vision of civilization translates the divorce between criticism and power into diachronic forms. The opening paragraph of what would become his first published work, "Thoughts on the Religion of the Middle Ages"[5]—the subject is no accident—concludes:

> There seems to be a direct ordination of Providence that man and states shall grow old & decay; that the purposes of mutability & frailty shall be answered in nations & events as well as individual histories and some imposed necessity of infancy and decay to greatness. (*JMN*.I.305)

The tones of the jeremiad are pronounced in an even earlier entry:

> In all ages self-complacent people prate much about the dignity of human nature. . . .
>
> Look over the whole history & then name the vice, however odious, what degrading enormity, the degenerate perverseness of man has not crouched unto & adored. (*JMN*.I.173)

Scattered throughout the first journals are briefer meditations on "The Day of Judgement," the sufferings of Martyrs, Sin and Death, and "whether the fall of Adam affects the moral estate of his children" (*JMN*.I.43,120,292,312). Emerson is present at such moments as "a melancholy voice which . . . makes itself heard, teaching the vanity of joy, the neighborhood of remorse." He intones,

> Nature acts the part of a deceiver. . . . Man shall find as he lifteth up his eyes to enjoy his wide dominion that there lurks amidst this abundant Paradise an infant pestilence growing up to be a Minister of Vengeance and the enemy of the nations. (*JMN*.I.122–23)

It is hard to take these passages seriously as expressions of religious belief. They remind us of Emerson's attraction to the Calvinism of Mary Moody Emerson, but that attraction, too, is not religious; it reflects a desire for human intensity, not divine judgment. Here, a religious idiom yields parables of personal anxieties. Nature is a deceiver because it inspires thoughts of "wide dominion"; the "Minister of Vengeance" is the self-doubting and self-tormenting conscience, which acts on behalf of the moral economy in punishing

Emerson's dream of Paradise. This dark view of man's nature and the vanity of all human creations both encourages the escape into the fantasies of artistic splendor and at the same time punishes them. Emerson is divided between a depressing moral history and literary aspirations. The imagined future appears to redeem him from the fallen past. However, because fantasy is another manifestation of the imaginative impotence he associates with historical decline, the two end up being versions of each other; the melancholy of the modern indicates that he lives in a lesser age than that enjoyed by prophets and patriarchs. Emerson's historical and religious broodings leave him with the same sense of inferiority as his bookish daydreams.

In the privacy of the journals, the suppressed resentment of contemporaries and predecessors becomes explicit, and he begins to rage against the past. An entry of February 1824 is one of the first times that dissatisfaction finds an outlet in aggression; it is a paradigm for all such conversions in his prose. His subject is no longer his own dreams and fears but the mass of knowledge that prevents him from choosing a vocation. His anxiety, focused on an external object, turns to impatience. His sentences are short, declarative, demanding; if he still has unanswered questions, he is at least confident in his polemic:

> Noah was not dinned to death with Aristotle & Bacon & Greece & Rome. The patriarchs were never puzzled with libraries of names & dates, with First ages & dark ages; & Revivals & upper empires & lower empires; with the balance of power & the balance of trade; with fighting chronologies & dagger-drawing creeds.

The catalogue conveys his frustration with an excess of information, which results in an excess of choices. Remembering everything he has learned at home and at Harvard makes him miserable. He envies the patriarchs who, by coming at the beginning of time, did not have to remember history. Writing increases geometrically with each new age. Modern men not only uncover ever-increasing quantities of ancient texts; their commentaries help to augment the number at a rate frightening to the conscientious reader. Emerson's view of history clearly stems from his demand for a vocation. Characteristically, he feels that only education, which he defines as reading, can prepare him to make vocational choices. If there is too much to read, action is indefinitely postponed. The journal entry continues:

> Life is wasted in the necessary preparation of finding which is the true way. . . . An antedeluvian had the advantage . . . of forming his own opinion & indulging his own hope without danger of contradiction from Time that never had elapsed or observation that never had been made. Unknown troubles perplex the lot of the scholar whose inexpressible unhappiness it is to be born at this day. He is born in a time of *war*. A thousand religions are in arms. Systems of Education are contesting. Literature, Politics, Morals, & Physics, are each engaged in loud civil broil. A chaos of doubts besets him from his outset. Shall he read or shall he think? . . . Shall he nourish his faculties in solitude or in active life? No man can answer. He turns to books—the vast amount of recorded wisdom but it is useless from its amount. He cannot read all . . . but how to choose. . . . Must he read History & neglect Morals; or learn what *ought* to be, in ignorance of what *has been*? Or must he slight both in the pursuit of science, or all, for practical knowledge & a profession? Must he . . . abandon all the rest to be profoundly skilled in a single branch of art, or . . . smatter superficially in all? . . .
>
> [S]hall I subdue my mind by discipline, or obey its native inclination? govern my imagination with rules or cherish its originality? . . .
>
> These & similar questions . . . are a real & recurring calamity. . . . [H]alf of the time of most scholars is dissipated in fruitless & vexatious attempts to solve one or another of them in succession. . . . It is an evil that demands a remedy. (*JMN*.II.218–20)

He frets about the accumulated products of civilization until the "vast amount of recorded wisdom" overwhelms him. The catalogues are our first clue to the imminence of what is truly the reader's sublime: "libraries of names & dates . . . First ages & dark ages," and so on. The fact that the sensation of excess is produced by contemplating history suggests that the sublime and the problematics of modernity are part of a single process.[6] Quantity brings about crisis. Unable to learn everything, he must make a forced choice among professions. This pressure leads him to regard culture as an arena of warring specialties: "He [the scholar] is born in a time of *war*"; "religions are in arms"; "Systems . . . are contesting"; disciplines clash in "loud civil broil." Cultural warfare is a projection of the "chaos of doubts [that] besets" the student who must choose a vocation. He cannot begin without selecting a usable past, and, possessing no firm sense of himself, he has no criteria by which to select one from the histories of morality, art, and science which are simultaneously and massively present to him. Demanding answers, he spins his wheels over the relative morality of action and contemplation, society and solitude, and ends up completely stalled. These propaedeutic questions are, indeed, his "calamity." I do not think that vocational choice is the issue here. At twenty-one, Emerson already knows that he wants to be a minister, and dreams of the pulpit as the platform for eloquence. Indeed, it is because his fantasies have found a concrete focus that his anger at the necessary delay in realizing them breaks out at this time. What passages like this one show is an altered, more aggressive stance toward the accumulated wisdom of the ages and the need for a mastering analysis of it.

Later in the spring of 1824, a few days after the "robe of eloquence" entry written in anticipation of his twenty-first birthday (*JMN*.II.237), we catch him in the process of discovering what to do with all those books. Again, he muses irritably about his prospects, fuming about the "limited choice" of professions and the inadequacies of existing systems of belief. "Men's creeds can never, at least in youth, set the heart . . . at ease," he declares. They are "fine spun textures through which rebellious doubt is impatient, sometimes desperate, to plunge." His antagonistic gesture here indicates that what he really dislikes is limitation itself, not a dearth of professional options. He takes this plunge and discovers that he may not have all the answers but "the profoundest scholar" doesn't, either. In all those books, he announces, there is nothing that he does not already know:

> There is no such thing . . . as satisfactory knowledge. Metaphysics teach me admirably well what I knew before; setting out in order particular after particular, bone after bone, the anatomy of the mind. My knowledge is thus arranged not augmented. Morals, too . . . are chiefly occupied in discriminating between what is general & what is partial, or in tying rules together by a thread which is called a system or a principle. But neither metaphysics nor ethics are more than outside sciences. They give me no insight into the nature & design of my being.

The boast that he carries civilization within himself corresponds to the decision that "my being" will henceforth be the test of knowledge. Here he is no longer the student but a critic, an interpreter whose standard of evaluation is wholly personal. Morals and metaphysics have no power to intimidate once he has become convinced that, despite their internal coherence as intellectual structures, they have no necessary connection with the design of "being." As the possessor of "being," he effects a crucial shift in the balance of power. The human sciences now must serve him, not he them (JMN.II.244–45).

Emerson becomes increasingly resentful of the accumulated productions of "Time," the "real & recurring calamity" that perplexes "the scholar whose inexpressible unhappiness it is to be born in this day" (JMN.II.219), but it occurs to him that there are advantages to being born "in this late age." In an 1822 draft of "Thoughts on the Religion of the Middle Ages," he had written, "Not percieving [sic] ourselves the connection which binds events, we are unable to discover how far a sublime uniformity may prevail, or whether the seeming disorder may not be like the series of a drama a harmonious succession of events" (JMN.I.306). A year later, his vision of progress has sharpened into a vision of control;

Emerson has grasped the power of a comparative approach. Now he asserts confidently that when mind "looks . . . with the experienced eye of Centuries into the bosom of nature, it is able to unite things severed by long intervals, to compare mean beginnings with remote & mighty results, & thus to restore order to a Chaos of mighty things . . ." (*JMN*.II.140–41). He now defines belatedness as superior knowledge instead of as imitation. His "eye" bestows coherence on history which, to those in its midst, is "Chaos." Causes ("mean beginnings") and effects ("remote & mighty results") appear severed. Only later—only now—is their order perceptible. The modern who brings this order out of chaos effects a second Genesis; retrospection becomes origination.

We can trace in these journal entries Emerson's movement from the negative or "blocked" phase of the sublime to its outcome in sensations of power and release. Neil Hertz defines blockage as a critical phenomenon, the reaction of a reader overwhelmed by the "scary proliferation" of books. The task of the critic or historian is "the reduction to narrative order of a large, sometimes seemingly infinite mass of detail." Hertz shows that the "mathematical sublime" (the "intellectual's" or "hermeneutic" sublime) occurs when the imagination is inadequate to the chaos it perceives. The reader is nevertheless gratified. While he cannot bring the "infinite or indefinitely plural" into a perceptual unity, he can think unity by leaping to the higher level of generality, by inventing the thought of, for example, "infinity." Reason rescues cognition with the rush of exhilaration always associated with the sublime. The subject's paralysis is succeeded by "a compensatory positive movement" in which the mind exults in "its ability to think a totality that cannot be taken in through the senses." When we have been overwhelmed from without by perceived quantities, the part of our minds that is capable of organizing them surges into our awareness. Through "the play of apprehension and comprehension," we prove to ourselves that we possess self-subsistent reason.[7] The pleasure of the sublime comes about as we convert disorientation and meaninglessness into evidence of our power over the objects that cause these sensations. If it is a critic or reader who discovers his ability to create the meanings of the texts that threaten him, we have a truly "hermeneutical" sublime, for the act of interpretation effects the crucial conversion. The antagonism between the scholar and the blocking agent allows the former to discover, through conflict, his own integrity.

The Kantean sublime, as Hertz suggests, sums up the psychology and aesthetics of the many eighteenth-century variants of the sublime. It is not surprising, then, to find in it part of the plot of Emerson's journals. Nor is it remarkable that Emerson's case allows us to suggest further refinements in the theory of the sublime. Emerson's use of the word "sublime" indicates that his associations with it are representative of the tradition formulated by Kant and now by Monk, Weiskel, and Hertz. For him, the term designates an upward movement: a "sublime spirit" will "[m]ount on [its] own path to Fame" (*JMN*.I.7); "in the heavenly bodies" man has "the perpetual presence of the sublime" (*CW*.I.8). It also connotes solitude ("sublime incomprehensible solitude" [*JMN*.I.46]), and divinity, for in this solitude, one might find "the immediate presence of God . . . [to be] a fine topic for sublimity" (*JMN*.I.9), or, even better, one might say with Jesus in a "jubilee of sublime emotion, 'I am divine' " (*CW*.I.81). This condition consequently "transfer[s] nature into the mind" (*CW*.I.34). In Emerson's earliest journal entries, all the meanings attached to the Romantic sublime are present. The word designates the leap of noble aspiration toward the solitary exercise of power.

In these youthful journals, we remember, fantasies of power (like that featuring the young pulpit orator's "tremendous eloquence" or like Emerson's identification with English literary genius) alternated with passages of self-revilement that punish the "dream of honour." He interpreted history as the record of human failure and proof of the futility of such visions. Subsequently he begins to move away from this set of attitudes into the "blocked" or confrontational phase of the sublime. It is at this stage that we find him complaining of being "dinned to death" with "the vast amount of recorded wisdom." He resents information because he is unable to organize it; his tone is panic-stricken and angry. The "chaos of doubts" that besets him is an image of the "loud civil broil" of the surrounding civilization. When he announces that he is "desperate to plunge" through the "cobwebs of existing beliefs," the sublime motion is antagonistic. The discovery of a perspective that bestows "sublime uniformity" on "a chaos of mighty things" is certainly an overcoming, a mastering gesture. But insofar as Emerson has simply reversed the earlier scenario of being mastered by civilization, it is also imitative, a moment of identification in which history's domination of Emerson turns into his domination of it.

Trying to force himself to accept the role of critic, he tries to be a conscientious one and ends up paralyzed by quantities of knowledge. The crucial freedom comes when he changes his mind about criticism. For it is by the transvaluation of reading that Emerson makes possible the gratifications of the sublime. The (secondary) interpretation of (primary) inherited texts becomes a way of controlling, even of creating them. For if the modern reader, with his overview of history, endows the past with meaning, he is virtually inventing it. Psychological redactions of Kant's analytic of the sublime allow us to see why aggression, self-enjoyment, and a theory of reading emerge simultaneously in Emerson's journals. He matures by convincing himself, not that he is a great writer, but that it is better to be a great reader. His leap from cognition to Reason is a leap up to an effective theory. The movement to the level of what, in *Nature,* he calls "Idealism" is always, for him, a rebellion and a seizure of power. The higher criticism becomes important at this stage of his development. For it offered, in a subdued and repressed form, the reversal inherent in the hermeneutic sublime and offered it in a way that would permanently associate sublimity and reading in Emerson's mind.

He received multiple exposures to the works in which the principles of the higher criticism were set forth and applied. His contacts with the pastoral and academic leaders of Unitarianism put him in touch with the most active adapters of the higher criticism in America. His close acquaintances included Theodore Parker, who published a journal called *The Scriptural Interpreter,* devoted to propagating the higher criticism, and who translated De Wette's *Introduction to the New Testament;* and Elizabeth Palmer Peabody, who translated Herder's *The Spirit of Hebrew Poetry.* He read a good deal of German Biblical criticism (a rather surprising amount of which was translated) and many of the proliferating studies of mythology. He absorbed more in an impressionistic way through his reading of German literature, book reviews, De Stael's *De L'Allemagne*, Carlyle's essays, and Coleridge's prose works, all of which gave him a good sense of the cultural atmosphere in which Biblical criticism was carried on.[8] Indeed, Elinor Shaffer's brilliant reading of "Kubla Kahn" suggests that Emerson's exposure to English Romantic poetry alone would have sufficed to convey the radical implications of subjecting Christianity to the techniques of comparative study. It is clear that the influence of the higher criticism on Emerson is a case of overdetermination.

More importantly, the power of hermeneutics to change men's lives was proved in Emerson's own family during this unsettled period. His older brother, William, studied theology in Göttingen in 1824–1825. Just as he returned to America, he abandoned his plans for the ministry.[9] While abroad, he was passionately interested in Biblical criticism, especially that of Eichorn and Herder, and was enamored of German methodological rigor. He wrote his brother, Waldo, another minister-in-training, "You must prepare yourself to come too." "A theologian of the present day cannot dispense with the results of German diligence and ingenuity." Again, "Learn German as fast as you can, for you must come here, even if I take to schoolkeeping again." "Study German—Greek— Hebrew for all of them you *must* know." Waldo replied in playful tones, interested but skeptical. "I have made some embryo motions in my divinity studies," he wrote. "I shall be glad of any useful hints from the Paradise of Dictionaries & Critics." "Say particularly if German & Hebrew be worth reading for tho I hate to study them cordially I yet will the moment I can count my gains." His serious, professional older brother responds, "I fear you do not value the languages quite highly enough." He was right; Emerson never had much taste for Biblical scholarship, which he regarded as "a work of weighing of phrases & hunting in dictionaries." It was clearly William's critical education that led him to drop his plans for the ministry; ultimately, he could see no way to reconcile criticism with popular belief. "In this connexion," he wrote Waldo, "the remark occurs, that every candid theologian after careful study will find himself wide from the traditionary opinion of the bulk of his parishioners. Have *you* yet settled the question whether he shall sacrifice his influence or his conscience?"[10] Emerson's resignation from the ministry seven years later repeats his brother's precedent and settles the question. The higher criticism largely enabled that decision.

What distinguished the higher criticism from other approaches to the Bible was its concern with the total history of the Biblical text: historical milieu, generic conventions, authorial intent, interpretive tradition. It was defined methodologically by the premise that all texts are the productions of ordinary mortals written without divine inspiration. This could be proved by comparison. Scholars compared conflicting accounts (the Synoptic Gospels) with each other, compared Biblical narratives with other mythologies (*any* mythology—Greek, Roman, Hindu, Germanic, Egyptian, Icelandic), and finally, compared Christian versions of history with other surviving historical evidence, physical or written. The effect, though rarely the intent, of the higher critics' enterprise was to deprive the Bible of its traditional status by calling into question its historical validity and by challenging the unitary canon. Biblical scholars "deconstructed" the revelations of prophets. That is, by close rhetorical analysis of selected passages, they did away with the illusion of univocity and showed these writings to be miscellaneous compositions by unglamorous, often nameless, redactors. Their comparative methods turned up *discrepancies within* the Bible between the Synoptic Gospels or other parallel accounts. The import of the Scriptures ceased to be identified with their depictive accuracy and began to be located in the experience of reading. The loss of the Bible's authority was thus a gain for the living critic, whose mind became one possible source of unity for a fragmented canon. The same methods used in the closely related field of comparative religion disclosed *relationships between* the Bible and other epics, myths, and histories. The history of civilization was transformed into a system of multiple sacred books which, by virtue of their similarities, were equally figurative—and whose validity, again, could only be defined by the modern who alone apprehended them.

Emerson vigorously exploits the discovery that his accumulated knowledge about the past gives him the opportunity to determine its meaning. He utilizes the tactics of Biblical critics but gleefully abandons their conscientious focus on a single hermeneutical undertaking. "What can we see, read, acquire but ourselves?" he demands (*JMN*.III.327, 1832). "The soul has a divine power of assimilating all its acquisitions to its own nature. . . . If it be great it converts them with instantaneous magic to its own predominant character" (*JMN*.III.98–99, 1827). His egocentric reader resembles the intuitive Biblical critic:

> Thou art the *law;*
> The *gospel* has no revelation
> . . . until there is response
> From the deep chambers of thy mind thereto.
> (*JMN*.III.290–93, 1831)

The same interpretive trick works wonders with his chronic inferiority complex about his literary forefathers: "In the wisdom, or fancy . . . of Bacon & Shakspear we do not admire an arbitrary alien creation," as he had for so long, "but we have surprize"—the emotional correlative of the Emersonian sublime—"at finding ourselves, at recognizing our own truth in that wild, unacquainted field" (*JMN*.III.240, 1831). Making external reality into a mirror image converts its threatening otherness into supportive presence, at least for the moment. The specular structure of the sublime is nowhere clearer.

In the late 1820s, hope alternates with Emerson's more habitual gloom. Sublime conversions of blockage into strength in his journals are not enough to resolve his anxieties. Brooding and duty-bound, he fluctuates between protest and resignation until he leaves the ministry in 1832. Mood swings characterize Emerson's journals all his life, of course. Nevertheless, the sense of being the conscientious, willing victim of history is never again so pronounced as during these years. He continues to feel oppressed by sheer quantities of culture and, more often than not, cannot rise into the mastering phase of the sublime.

In the spring of 1826, for example, he ruminates on the Bible's history of our forefathers' hopes and disappointments. However gloomy the past looks, he grudgingly admits, "there is no doubt we are the better that they have lived." The "no doubt" construction conveys a tone of depressed resignation. He presents a rather terrifying vision of "venerable tradition," history bound together only by the consciousness of influencing and being influenced:

> it behoved us to know what had been done, that we might acknowledge & exercise the moral affinities which time & place do not affect. . . . This is the only unity . . . [a] human principle in which our hearts are constrained to find a consanguinity & so to make the registers of history a rule of life. . . . [T]he fortunes of Assyria, of Athens, & of Rome have not become a dead letter—have not fulfilled their effect . . . till they have taught me & you and all men to whose ears these names may come.

The past requires careful stewardship. The passage continues, "[O]ur duties [are] proportioned to our opportunities. . . . I am answerable for whatever wisdom I can glean from the wisdom of Rome" (*JMN*.III.20–22). The inherited civilization is felt as a superego that assigns duties and evaluates performance and to whom we are "answerable." "Consanguinity" defines an eternal present in which our fathers live on by virtue of our continued obedience to them. It is not a happy relationship but one we are "constrained" to acknowledge. The elders do not offer love but "a rule of life." The obligation of stewardship is a burdensome debt that can never be paid off: "There is no man . . . who is not more a debtor . . . to others than to himself" (*JMN*.III.34).

Emerson has, by this time, discovered how indebtedness can be redefined as "use" and inherited wisdom as a field for conquest. But this cognitive breakthrough is isolated in momentary expressions. To some extent, of course, this is true of Emerson's entire life work. He contemplates the night sky and announces, "[A] career of thought & action . . . is expanding before me into a distant & dazzling infinity." Two weeks later he writes, "My days . . . have no honour among men . . . no grandeur in the view of the invisible world." Regardless of the justifications for self-reliance which he is beginning to record in the journals, Emerson's sense of his place in history is consistently gloomy. Just before announcing his engagement to Ellen Tucker in 1828, he despairs of "a great progressive destiny in as much as regards literature. . . . Well," he sighs, "I am afraid the season of this rare fruit is irrecoverably past; that the earth has made such a mutation of its nodes, that the heat will never reach again that Hesperian garden in which alone these apricots & pomegranates grew" (*JMN*.III.78–81, 148). As always, it is the past that foils his progress toward the infinite. Grandeur and honor are possible either in the golden age, or now, but not in both. Past and present glory are mutually exclusive. In a competitive system, one is always sacrificed to the other.

In a poem of 1827, he dramatizes the struggle between these conflicting emotions and, with remarkable accuracy and self-consciousness, predicts its outcome. The poem opens by confessing the respect for "Place" in society that Emerson felt so strongly. He characterizes himself as an "idler,"

> A little liable to ridicule
> Because he cares a particle too much
> For the opinion of the fickle world.
> And notes how Merit does not swim to Place.

The self-deprecating irony which chooses to present a stock type from Restoration drama quickly modulates into an admission of his "scorn" for the "uncivil fate that made his fortunes vile." The idle malcontent is transformed rapidly into a poet who, lamenting the vanishing gleam of Wordsworth's "Intimations Ode,"

> Mourned in the hour of manhood, while he saw
> The rich imagination that had tinged
> Each earthly thing with hues from paradise
> Abandoning . . . forever his instructed eye.

Bewailed its loss, & felt how dearly bought
Was wisdom at the price of happiness.

Wordsworth remembers; Emerson rebels. As it turns out, the poem is not a comedy of manners or a Romantic ode, but a parable of freedom from "the opinion of the fickle world." The charms of nature that surround his poet

Enticed him oft in heady wantonness
To scoff at knowledge, mock the forms of life
Cast off his years & be a boy again.

Being a boy again does not mean a return to vision, but the freedom to "mock" authority. He leaves "his books, & vulgar cares" (a significant equation) and sallies forth "across the freshened fields" like the poet of "Lycidas," who knows he is off to become a great writer. Emerson already enjoys a foretaste of the "heady wanton-ness" of his resignation from the ministry, but he asks for time before he actually makes the break:

Leave the heart
Alone to find its language. . . .
It hath a sovereign instinct that doth teach
An eloquence which rules can never give.
In the high hour when Destiny ordains
That thou bear testimony to its dooms
That hour a guiding spirit shall impart
The fervid utterance art could never find
Wait then, stern friend, wait in majestic peace.
(*JMN*.III.84–86)

He states his task correctly. He will, in fact, need to discover a "sovereign" eloquence that can openly defy the world's "rules." The issue for Emerson is precisely that of deciding when and in what "language" publicly to "bear testimony" to his ambitions. The question for us, given his extraordinarily clear vision of the eventual necessity of abandoning ministerial "books and cares," is, what has to happen in the meantime? Once he is capable of insights like this, there is no immediately apparent reason why he should not be ready to sit down and compose *Nature*. Part of the reason for the delay is his image of the church as the setting for eloquence. It had seemed like the only possible equivalent in Boston of the grandeur he loved in literature. He had chosen preaching as his forum, and his desires had crystallized around its image. But a more fundamental reason for his long wait is the need to come to terms with certain "guiding spirit[s]."

· 2 ·

EXPEDIENTS

The years of Emerson's first marriage (1829–1832) and clerical career (1826–1832) were a time of compromise and ambivalence, during which he increasingly adjusted both his marriage and the ministry to unorthodox ends. The patriarchs and his sanctioning muse need to be absorbed into the fables about tradition that Emerson invents to free himself from it. In the journals, we can trace how, using a conventional religious vocabulary, he makes God and Ellen into the patron saints of his rebellious critique. By the time he does "cut & run" (JMN.III.324–25), he possesses a coherent set of beliefs developed under the protective cover of his ministry, and, more importantly, he has transformed potentially censorious figures into benevolent ones. Using a religious idiom and working through institutional forms such as sermons and instructional lectures, he works out the arguments in favor of a new god—the self. He composes parables of his rebellious but ambivalent ego, which, like the poem just examined, are a way of preparing for and of predicting his resignation from the ministry. The peculiar contradictions between his ideas and the vocabulary in which they are stated arise from his need to interpret apostasy—even to himself—as the logical conclusion of orthodoxy. For years, he goes to extraordinary lengths even in the journals to translate his private speculations into religious language. His prose never entirely loses the parodic quality which comes from habitually concealing radical ideas in conventional terms.

As his theology of the self is articulated in the journals, the sermons become vehicles for its themes. His voice is far stronger, his subjects more self-serving, his form tighter than in the Harvard essays. Forceful and clear, the sermons make good reading. But in the difference between them and the later essays we find a clue to the time lag between the development of Emerson's ideas and of his rhetoric. The sermons are not compulsively organized— Emerson is relaxed enough to be genial, associative, anecdotal. Nevertheless, they are cogently argued and logically constructed. The first sentences of each paragraph of a typical performance, "Trust Yourself," demonstrate this:

> All the instructions which religion addresses to man imply a supposition of the utmost importance, which is, that every human mind is capable of receiving and acting upon these sublime principles. (Matthew XVI:26: "For what is a man profited, if he gain the whole world and lose his own soul?")

> It is the effect of religion to produce a higher self-respect, a greater confidence in what God has done for each of our minds than is commonly felt among men.

> I wish to enforce the doctrine that a man should trust himself; should have a perfect confidence that there is no defect or inferiority in his nature. . . .

> It is not uncommon to hear a man express with great interest his regret that he possesses some particular manner of intellectual superiority or some quickness of feeling which, though reckoned advantages, he thinks rather stand in the way of greatness.

> One measure of a man's character is his effect upon his fellowmen.

> Now what is it to speak from one's own conviction, to trust yourself . . . but to keep one's mind ever awake, to use the senses and the reason, to rely on your birthright of powers which God bestowed?

> It is important to observe that this self-reliance which grows out of the Scripture doctrine of the value of the soul is not inconsistent either with our duties to our fellow men or to God.

> Nor on the other hand let it be thought that there is in this

self-reliance anything of presumption, anything inconsistent with a spirit of dependence and piety toward God.

A good man, says Solomon, is satisfied from himself.

My friends, the deep religious interest of this question is apparent to you. (YES.105–11)

McGiffert quite rightly points out that this sermon on "self-reliance" indicates how much of Emerson's later thinking "is an amplification rather than addition or revision of his earlier thought" (YES.236). The theme and the problematics to which it gives rise are self-referential. The ambivalence generated by the wish to be greater than one's fellow men without being guilty of harming them, the sense of anxious inferiority that alternates with the desire for greatness, are central to the later essays.

Despite their thematic affinities, however, nothing could sound less like "Self-Reliance." These sentences indicate, above all, Emerson's interest in consistency, the conscientious setting forth of premises and conclusions. His respect for the sermon's formal consistency is inseparable from his public willingness to make self-trust agree with Christian doctrine. It is important that "this self-reliance . . . is not inconsistent with our duties"; that there is in it nothing "inconsistent with a spirit of . . . piety toward God." Consistency, here, is the intellectual and stylistic correlative of piety. It is a willingness to conform—to form—one's self to authority. When Emerson's public discourse ceases to be reverent, it becomes inconsistent. Retrospectively, in the light of "Self-Reliance," one can see the contradiction in this sermon between the preacher's decorous manner and the subversive implications of his idea. One sees that he must frame the discussion of self-trust with religious professions, must keep a tight hold of his argument. For his ideas are so close to blasphemy that only by precise and careful reasoning can they be made to derive from orthodoxy. This formal piety is symptomatic of the thing that keeps Emerson from making his private language public. Because the most powerful prose of the journals is organized by aggression and narcissism, he has to censor his rhetoric when speaking to others. Using notions like "self-reliance" in a sermon that blandly discovers them in the Gospels is far less dangerous than indulging in an antithetical tone and a whimsical construction. The problem for Emerson was first to discover and then to tolerate a discourse of open antagonism.

The same kind of semi-conscious repression occurs in the journals, so Emerson's long wait is not simply a matter of bringing his public rhetoric into congruence with his private idiom. He celebrates egotism in religious terms and praises God while showing Him to be man's emanation. In an entry of September 1830, a devout resolve to "study the scriptures in a part of every day" is followed by a passage on self-trust: "Every man has his own voice, manner, eloquence. . . . Let him scorn to imitate any being, let him scorn to be a secondary man." Then he interposes an orthodox correction: this "scorn" is possible because Everyman trusts "his own share of God's goodness," which is to say, he *is* secondary to God. Emerson still finds God in religious observances—prayer, sermons, scriptural study—even as he tries to make these practices the vehicles of ideas that expose their obsolescence. He goes so far as to turn atheism itself to the glory of God: "Every influx of atheism of skepticism is . . . made useful as a mercury pill assaulting & removing a diseased religion & making way for truth, & itself is presently purged into the draught." And then, how conventionally, "The only way to stand is to cling to the Rock. Keep the soul always turned to God" (*JMN*.III.198–99,239).

Emerson's God is not a stable entity. We can trace the steps by which He becomes a specular image of Emerson's ambition. Spurning the pious, Emerson claims an unmediated relation to God:

> Suicidal is . . . this doctrine that 'tis pious to believe on others' words impious to trust entirely to yourself. . . . Is a man afraid that the faculties which God made can outsee God—can find more than he made or different—can bring any report hostile to himself? To reflect is to receive truth immediately from God without any medium. . . . A trust in yourself is the height not of pride but of piety, an unwillingness to learn of any but God himself. (*JMN*.III.279)

He avoids heresy by making God the creator of the self-reliant soul, but insists on an exclusive relationship to the deity that allows him to reject public opinion. Refusing to respect any authority but God makes him God's equal. He does not address Him as servant to master, son to father, but speaks to Him directly. In this passage, he is God's reflection, the secondary image of a primary truth ("To reflect is to receive truth"). Still, this is an advantage over belief based on the multiple refractions of "others' words."

A short time later, Emerson tells himself,

> Be as great as doth beseem
> The ambassador who bears
> The royal presence where he goes.
>
> . . . .
>
> Look straight before thee as befits
> The simplicity of Power.
> And in thy closet carry state
> Filled with light walk therein
> And as a King
> Would do no treason to his own empire
> So do not thou to thine.
>
> (*JMN*.III.291–92)

"It is by yourself without ambassador that God speaks to you," he writes in a prose rendition of the same thought, in which the role of ambassador is similarly eschewed for that of king. One speaks to God as "a sovereign with a sovereign" (*JMN*.III.279,268). Again, the energy of the statement is directed against human intermediaries (ambassadors). When man becomes God's peer and a king in his own right, he discovers that he is truly made in God's image.

One senses that Emerson finds it easy to love God as *his* reflection. Resemblance becomes the basis for a love that is not quite openly narcissistic: "Nobody will ever be loved by compulsion. . . . Tell me not to love my saviour. No do him not that injustice. But fill me with his goodness & I shall love him of course" (*JMN*.III.279). What Emerson is really saying is that "compulsion" does him, Emerson, an injustice. His love of God is a consequence of self-love, the reverse of orthodox Christianity in which one loves his neighbor and himself because he loves God. When religion consists of equality between a single God and a self-reliant man, the true believer is superior even to Jesus. "Smother no dictate of your soul, but indulge it," he counsels:

> There are passages in the history of Jesus which to some minds seem defects in his character. . . . [C]ount them defects & do not stifle your moral faculty & force it to call what it thinks evil, good. For there is no being in the Universe [even God] whose integrity is so precious to you as that of your soul. (JMN.III.212)

In all these passages, God retains chronological, generative priority. But Emerson moves from imagining himself as God's creature or reflection to characterizing himself as His twin. Soon, seeing himself everywhere ("What can we see, read, acquire but ourselves?" [JMN.III.327]), he infers that he is the center of the universe and displaces God from that position. Emerson treats God as a superior only in order to carry out, through an alliance with divine forces, his aggressive strategies toward men and institutions. When he confronts God directly, he becomes the original of which God is the copy, loved because only in Him can Emerson see and know himself.

His desire is to feel like God in relation to the world. In a journal passage of 1827, he states in its entirety his mythology of the "divine" self who, in a moment of sublime "conversion," turns nature and culture into its mirrors:

> The soul has a divine power of assimilating all its acquisitions to its own nature. If it is weak & little, events over bear it, and give it their own hue & complexion. If it be great it converts them with instantaneous magic to its own predominant character. It converts calamity to knowledge; knowledge to power; hope to happiness. As you have seen by night the clouds that threaten to blot the moon are turned by her light to silver drapery and relieve her glory with exquisite orna-

ments, whatsoever vexations or dangers or difficulties befall the soul it turns them to felicities to stimulants, by its omnipotent virtue. Like the messengers sent to arrest the person of our Saviour they are touched with awe & prostrate themselves. "Like a drop of water," says Jeremy Taylor, "falling into a tun of wine it is ascribed into a new family, losing its own nature by a conversion into the more noble." (*JMN*.III. 98–99)

The aggressive verbs that describe the soul's triumph—assimilate, acquire, convert, and predominate—are a reaction against having been assimilated. Emerson knows what it is to be the mirror image of the world, to take on the "hue & complexion" of events, by which he means authors. Typically, he imagines an "instantaneous" reversal. (Speed is always associated with the Emersonian sublime, surprise.) The magical consequence is to turn the world to glass—a looking glass, as he will write in "The Poet." He is the substantial body; "events" are now reflections of his "predominant"—that is, dominating—character. The "omnipotent virtue" of his soul has turned competitors, potential "vexations or dangers," into "exquisite ornaments." The metaphor is a remarkably fierce one. One of the two entities will be effectively annihilated. Emerson's pleasure in living at the center of multiple self-images— and it is enormously pleasurable for him—derives largely from the fact that those images are the corpses of his opponents.

In the passage cited above, Emerson's will to power is brilliantly figured in three allegories of assimilation—the simile of the moon, the reference to the New Testament, and the quotation from Taylor. The most audacious example is the use of "our Saviour" as a figure for the "divine power" of Emerson's soul. The ability to draw casually on the New Testament to "ornament" the ego goes hand in hand with the claim to be one's own savior. After the paraphrase of Scripture, the direct quotation of Taylor reinforces the impression that citations are the textual consequence of absorbing the Not Me into the soul. Other writers are reduced to Emerson's figurative language; the colors of rhetoric are the soul's own "hue."

As Emerson turns God into a source of energy that makes him

independent of other men, he transforms the spirit of Ellen into the comforter of his solitude.[1] In both cases, orthodox divinities are made to bestow approval on a heretic. The figure of Ellen is closely bound up with the tensions between Emerson's ambitions and his religious attitudes, particularly after her death in February 1831. As he writes about her in the language of the subversive orthodoxy we have been tracing, he "converts" another potentially censorious figure into a permissive one. She elicits from him a rather sentimental piety but at the same time becomes the muse of his rebellion—not least, as Porte points out, because of the liberating possibilities of her estate, which came to Emerson in 1834.[2]

On her death bed Ellen told him, " 'she should do me more good by going than by staying; she should go first & explore the way, & comfort me.' " He accepted her rationale. Five days after her death he is writing, "Ellen went to heaven to see, to know, to worship, to love, to intercede." Already she is his envoy to the deity, not a humble petitioner but rather the ambassador who establishes contact between two "sovereigns." Clearly she is meant to "intercede" for his earthly success as much as for his eternal soul: "Pray for me Ellen," he implores, "& raise the friend you so truly loved, to be what you thought him." In poetic fragments composed two days later, he fears that "I am forgotten by the dead / And that the dead is by herself forgot." If this is the case, he threatens, "I no longer would keep terms with me." His breach of self-trust would not "break the peace of towns." He would simply "bury my ambition / The hope & action of my sovereign soul / In miserable ruin." This, he repeats, would not "harm my fellow men / . . . 'twould harm myself" (JMN.III.226–29).

Ellen's image coincides with the thought of ambition and the idea of self-regard. If she is not immortal, he vows to harm himself; if she is, to improve himself. The link is obvious in a long journal entry of July 1831. It begins with verses on Ellen's death repeating the *topos* of "the good die young":

> Let me not fear to die
> But let me live so well

As to win this mark of death from on high
That I With God, & thee dear heart may dwell.

After this conventional prayer, there is a break followed by a more self-assertive stanza:

I write the things that are
Not what appears;
Of things as they are in the eye of God
Not in the eye of Man.

Another space, then, in Greek, "Know thyself," which introduces an antinomian poem on the implications of "this fact"—"God dwells in thee." The assured first person voice that resounds in the preceding stanza ("I write the things that are") urges the reader ("a happy youth") to throw over the religious mythology that informs the lines on Ellen:

since the Soul of things is in thee
Thou needest nothing out of thee.
The law, the gospel, & the Providence,
Heaven, Hell, the Judgment, & the stores
Immeasurable of Truth & Good
All these thou must find
Within thy single mind.

(JMN.III.290–93)

Ellen and her self-reliant lover call forth opposing doctrines, religious attitudes, and tones of voice. Ellen seems to require penitence, vows of moral improvement, and a subordinate stance before divinity. Were she in life as Emerson imagines her in death, she would have had to disapprove of the ferocity she inspired. The ambitious soul she is made to sponsor, for all his orthodox protestations, strikes aggressively at the state of mind that needs a god, a heaven, and a guardian angel outside itself. It could have been some such conflict that impelled Emerson to open Ellen's grave on March 29, 1832 (JMN.IV.7), during one of his frequent walks to the Roxbury cemetery.[3] It has been plausibly suggested that he dreamed this episode, but my point about what Ellen stands for still holds.[4] Acute anxiety about his imminent decision to leave the ministry may have forced him to confront Ellen face to face, as it were. She represented his aspirations, but also the orthodoxy he was just a few months away from rejecting. A torment of ambivalence could well have provoked him to throw open her coffin, or to dream of doing so, not in order to commune with her spirit, but to exorcise it.

Throughout this period (1828–1832) the problem of language gradually becomes more acute. As Emerson converts the inhibiting figures of his own imagination into enabling ones, he becomes more resentful of the rhetorical compromises required of him in the pulpit. The discrepancy between his thoughts and his sermons is closely bound up with the issue of Scriptural interpretation. His growing feeling that the Scriptures, like all texts, are to be used, not obeyed, puts him at odds with popular belief and clerical decorum. Even before his ordination at the Second Church (March 1829), he is chastized by one of the founders of Harvard Divinity School. In December 1828, and again in July 1829, he responds to criticisms by Henry Ware of his treatment of Scripture in sermons. Apparently Ware had warned him against using "irreverent or profane illustrations" at the expense of Scriptural examples. Emerson concedes that he has "affected . . . a mode of illustration rather bolder than the usage of our preaching warrants" and reluctantly apologizes; "I can readily suppose I have erred in . . . failing to add to my positions the authority of scripture quotation." Emerson is courteous and humble, thanking Ware for his criticisms "as it is an object of serious ambition with me to make preaching as effectual an engine as I can" (*L.*I.257n.,257). The following summer, he seems to have been compelled by further objections to offer Ware an explicit confession of orthodox belief: "I consider [the Scriptures] as the true record of the Revelation which established . . . the Immortality of the Soul . . . the being & character of God." It would give him "great uneasiness," he writes, if "the idea sh'd be given to my audience that I did not look to the Scriptures with the same respect as others" (*L.*I.273).

There is little doubt that Emerson was saying the politic thing to Ware and that these letters do not reflect his opinions about either Scripture or preaching. Ware's impression that Emerson is verging on infidelity is accurate. As we saw in the excerpts from "Trust Yourself," Scripture provides Emerson with pious opening and closing flourishes; in between, the sermon is given over to wholly secular concerns. The fact that Emerson refers to his own aspirations in the letters to Ware no doubt confirmed the older man's suspicions. In a journal entry written a few months after the second letter, Emerson reflects on Swedenborgian interpretations of Scripture. The analogy between his own sermons and the way Swedenborgians cloak the truth with error is clear: "if the fool-part of man must have the lie, if truth is a pill that can't go down till 'tis sugared with superstition, why then I will forgive the last" (*JMN*.III.166). Some part of the statement to Ware about Scriptural revelation, some part of his Scriptural quotations in the pulpit, were concessions to "superstition," the false sugar coating of Emerson's truth.

His sense of hypocrisy increases with time. After Ellen's death, he initiated a series of Tuesday night lectures on the Scriptures for young people. When reviewing Biblical criticism for these meetings, he wrote his brother William, of the Göttingen education, asking for arguments *against* divine inspiration.[5] The split between his private skepticism and his public role as teacher of the faith exacerbates his discontent. He knows that he will soon have to answer the question William had posed in 1825, "whether [the minister] shall sacrifice his influence or his conscience" when he finds himself "wide from the traditional opinion of the bulk of his parishioners." Early in 1832, he states unequivocally that his efforts at compromise have failed:

> Every man hath his use no doubt and every one makes ever the effort according to the energy of his character to suit his external condition to his inward constitution. If his external condition does not admit of such accommodation he breaks the form of his life, & enters a new one which does. If it will admit of such accommodation he gradually bends it to his mind.

He refers to various clergymen who have successfully "bent" their profession to their inclination—or vice versa—and continues, "But what shall poor I do who can neither visit nor pray nor preach to my mind?" Significantly, his frustrations are all verbal ones; he cannot converse, pray, or preach freely. He knows that in order to "break the form" of his constricted language, he must change his life. Even this entry concludes with an upsurge of doubt as he averts his eyes from the decision before him: "Can you not be virtuous . . . temperate . . . charitable?" he says to himself. "[P]ossibly when you have learned these things you may find the others" (*JMN*.III.324). But within a few days, he carries the thought to its logical conclusion: "Settle everything anew for yourself. . . . I believe a hundred dollars a year would support me in the enjoyment of what I love best. Why toil I then for 20 times as much? Might I cut & run?" (*JMN*.III.325).

"The Lord's Supper"

It is not surprising that "The Lord's Supper," Emerson's resignation sermon, should be his declaration of hermeneutic and stylistic independence. In the last sermon he ever has to preach (though not the last one he does preach), the inhibiting coherence of previous sermons disappears. The second part of the sermon cancels out the first; the speaker shifts unpredictably from logical to emotional modes of persuasion. The mannerly treatment of Scripture also comes to an end. Emerson's use of Scriptural and scholarly materials is casual, at times cavalier. The sermon shows how, once he has made God into his mirror image, he can dispense with arguments about the meaning of Scripture. The resignation sermon reenacts Emerson's discovery of the higher critical perspective that led him, indirectly, to compose it. He conscientiously uses higher critical techniques to expose the past's perpetual lack of knowledge about itself, then rejects critical interpretations of the Bible altogether—even those that uphold his position. Part I of the sermon is a critique of the sources of religious authority which deauthorizes them. In Part II, the issue becomes "expediency" in a celebration of the will and pleasure of the newly liberated individual.

In a gesture that would become habitual, he starts by placing himself in an arena of conflict. Emerson's strength does not precipitate his aggressive gestures, but flows from them. Attack is his way of escaping a condition of vulnerability or receptiveness. When a work opens, as it almost always does, with an invocation of conflict, one must posit, I think, a prior moment of weakness. It is a sign of considerable anxiety that the sermon opens with an account of liturgical and exegetical battles that puts him at the end of a long line of quibblers. "In the history of the Church," he begins, "no subject has been more fruitful of controversy than the Lord's Supper. There never has been any unanimity in the understanding of its nature, nor any uniformity in the mode of celebrating it." After surveying these more or less "frivolous" controversies from the Fourth Lateran Council down to the Quakers, he calls attention to his procedure, speaking in the first person for the first time: "I allude to these facts only to show that . . . there has always been the widest room for difference of opinion." He identifies himself as the happy heir to a tradition of unstable, competing points of view. He is less interested in the substance of the disagreements he has described than in the textual ambiguity that caused them. Ambiguity frees him to venture his personal reading of Scripture, he implies. At this stage, he is still careful to point out that he has "recently given particular attention to this subject"; his personal feelings can be verified by academic experts. Still, the declarations of independence hold firm: "I was led to the conclusion that Jesus did not intend to establish an institution for perpetual observance . . . and . . . to the opinion that it is not expedient to celebrate it as we do" (W.XI.3–5).

Once he has established a strong personal presence, Emerson takes up the question of Jesus' intentions in Part I of the sermon, on the "authority of the rite." He arrives at the conclusions of the higher criticism, using its methods. However, he draws on this material eclectically, making no effort to reconcile different strategies. The casualness of his methodological borrowing is one clue to the fact that Biblical criticism is being used to undo the authority, not merely of "the rite," but of all previous interpreters. First, in classic Germanic fashion, he undertakes a comparison of the Synoptic Gospels, assuming the persona of the historical critic more earnestly than he would ever do again. "Now observe the facts," he begins. He considers which of the disciples were present at the Last Supper, which are trustworthy writers, and whether the accounts indicate "the slightest intimation of any intention on the part of Jesus to set up anything permanent." His tone quickly verges on sarcasm, which betrays the aggressive motives behind the academic mannerisms:

> I have only brought these accounts together, that you may judge whether it is likely that a solemn institution, to be continued to the end of time by all mankind . . . would have been established . . . in a manner so slight, that the intention of commemorating it should not appear . . . to have caught the ear or dwelt in the mind of the only two among the twelve who wrote down what happened. (W.XI.11–12)

Having clarified the status of the relevant Scriptural texts, he proceeds to consider the meaning of the anomalous dictum in Luke 22:19, "This do in remembrance of me." His focus shifts from text to context as he pursues another tendency of the higher criticism, the linking of verbal meaning to the writer's historical situation. "Jesus is a Jew, sitting with his countrymen, celebrating their national feast," he reminds his auditors. Proper consideration of the speaker's milieu, furthermore, requires projecting oneself into it. Emerson "can readily imagine" the whole scene. "He [Jesus] thinks of his own impending death, and wishes the minds of his disciples to be prepared for it." The interpreter goes on to put words in Jesus' mouth: " 'In years to come . . . the connection which has subsisted between us will give a new meaning . . . to the national festival, as the anniversary of my death.' " Emerson approves of the "natural feeling and beauty" of his script. After justifying his active intuitions by pointing to the ambiguity of the text, he seizes upon the higher critic's designation of the reader as the source of coherence. He concedes that his account of the Last Supper is one of many possible interpretations: "many opinions may be entertained of [Jesus'] intention." The contemporary self-reliant soul is the beneficiary of a fantasy that relieves Jesus of "an authority which he never claimed." The presumptuousness of telling us what Jesus intended further strengthens Emerson's self-regard. "You say, every time you celebrate the rite, that Jesus enjoined it," he concludes: "But if you read the New Testament as I do, you do not believe that he did." His resentment of any liturgical authority betrays the fact that religious history is, for him, a drama of influence. Rites must be rejected because they are both the symbols of prescriptive authority and its actual means of enforcement. "I appeal brethren, to your individual experience," he urges, as he appeals to his own: "I will love [Jesus] as a glorified friend, after the free way of friendship, and not pay him a stiff sign of respect, as men do those whom they fear" (W.XI.7–8,20).

Historicism, by making each context unique, undoes the New Testament's claims to universality. Emerson demonstrates that the Gospels provide simply "a faithful account" of the Jewish Passover. The similarity between the Judaic and Christian ceremonies provides grounds for rejecting the Eucharist. To the ethnic argument, he joins a rhetorical one. The "extraordinary and emphatic" expressions of Jesus are merely examples of his figurative style, another Semitic convention: "He always taught by parables and symbols. It was the national way of teaching." Emerson manages to reject the Eucharist both because, as a type, its meaning is universal and because "it was a local custom . . . unsuitable in western countries" (W.XI.9–10,12). Characteristically, he does not explain the relationships among his historical and stylistic analyses or imaginative projections. This habit of exploiting every available method without taking them seriously enough to acknowledge their incompatibilities is precisely the kind of discontinuity that appears in his work once anti-authoritarianism becomes its theme.

At this point in the sermon, history ceases to matter. It seems to have been dissolved by analysis. In Part II, Emerson takes up the issue of "expediency," obviously more pleasurable for the individual created out of the critical encounters of the first section. He imagines a challenge from the congregation: "Admit that the rite was not designed to be perpetual. What harm doth it?" It becomes clear, I think, that Emerson finally does not care about what Biblical criticism can demonstrate. Whether Jesus intended a perpetual rite or not becomes irrelevant as Emerson becomes more willing to say aloud that only his own intentions matter. The second part of the sermon thus radically undercuts the first. In this section, he pursues the implications of his earlier statements that Jesus' discourse and actions were figurative languages. He speaks more confidently as the intuitive reader whose perceptions impart meaning to the text. What do Jesus' media figure forth? Emerson himself. "What I revere and obey" in Christianity, he writes, is "the echo it returns to my thoughts, the perfect accord it makes with my reason." The text becomes a figure for the reader. By calling the New Testament "allegorical" and "typical," he means that the Scriptures are open to as many different meanings as there are readers. He contrasts the authoritarian book which is assigned a single literal meaning to the liberating allegorical work which permits multiple individualistic responses: institutions, he declares, "should be as flexible as the wants of men" (W.XI.16,21). Figurative interpretation is "expedient," indeed.

This explicit celebration of the self is one of the sublime moments that solve his youthful complaints about the divorce between critical self-consciousness and the imagination. It is one form of the intensifications, shifts into higher gear, that occur somewhere in virtually all of Emerson's mature works. At such moments, the speaker's analysis of the past and his discovery of an aggressive stance toward it take place together. At the end of the sermon, he claims disingenuously that it is only "for the satisfaction of others" that

I have labored to show *by the history* that this rite was not intended to be perpetual. . . . I cannot help feeling that it is time misspent to argue to or from [Paul's]convictions, or those of Luke and John, respecting any form. I seem to lose the substance in seeking the shadow. (Emphasis added.)

But it was not time misspent. The historical criticism he repudiates had yielded the autonomy from history he desired. "That is the end of my opposition" to the Eucharist, he declares: "I am not interested in it" (W.XI.22,24). For Emerson, to be interested in something is to be opposed to it; to be uninterested is to be victorious.

As we look back over the process of development traced in this section, we find, I think, that it turns on the discovery and implementation of a theory of interpretation, a defensive hermeneutic directed against literary and religious tradition. By implementation, I mean the gradual absorption of people, experiences, and ideas into a theoretical structure. Another way of describing this is as the internalization of theory, the matching of its terms with the needs of a particular mind and set of circumstances. Emerson had to plot the relationships among father, brothers, wife, and God; among books, preaching, and his journals, before he found an adequate language. He had to discover pleasure in antagonism and decide to show that pleasure in his public utterances. Theory thus makes Emerson's style possible. When he possesses—is possessed by—an aggressive interpretive strategy, then he abandons rhetorical order for randomness and prefers substitution to linearity. It would be untrue to say that his development stops here. Yet the essays we are about to examine do not reveal new crises and solutions. Rather, they recapitulate the movement from imitation to frustration to a sublime reading and back again which forms the history of Emerson's young adulthood. Since the essays all reenact, in nonteleological fashion, the same narrative, they stand in analogous, not evolutionary, relationships to one another. Our interpretive problem becomes repetition, not change.

ENGLAND

But before the major phase of Emerson's work comes his trip to Europe in 1832–1833. This journey is a dramatization of the disestablished soul, a rigged test of his theory of influence. The trip is, in fact, a parody of the usual nineteenth-century intellectual pilgrimage of the kind Channing (whose footsteps Emerson retraces to Coleridge and Wordsworth) took in 1822 (W.V.11,21). Emerson visits all the right places and all the right people in order to find himself more interesting. The crucial encounters—those with Coleridge, Wordsworth, and Carlyle—constitute a premeditated rite of passage. Years later, in *English Traits* (1856), he could acknowledge this:

> I suppose if I had sifted the reasons that led me to Europe, when I was ill and advised to travel, it was mainly the attraction of these persons. . . . Besides those I have named . . . [Coleridge, Wordsworth, Landor, De Quincey, Carlyle] there was not in Britain the man living whom I cared to behold. (W.V.4)

The calls were made in order that on September 1, 1833, he might say, "I shall judge more justly, less timidly, of wise men forevermore." When he thanks "the great God" who brought him to "this last schoolroom" and showed him "the men I wished to see," he observes with satisfaction that "he has thereby comforted & confirmed me in my convictions" (JMN.IV.78–79). His disillusion is calculated; he offers up his admiration for great men in order to be disappointed.

Before he left for Europe, he had noted Carlyle's definition of imitation as "a leaning on something foreign; incompleteness of individual development, defect of free utterance" (JMN.IV.28).[6] A journal entry written a little later indicates that "imitation" is his name for the kind of admiration that blocks "individual development" and suppresses "free utterance":

> much is lost by imitation. Our best friends may be our worst enemies. A man should learn to detect & foster that gleam of light which flashes across his mind from within far more than the lustre of whole firmaments without. (JMN.IV.50)

For young Americans, imitation involves leaning on something quite literally "foreign." When Emerson arrives in Europe he applies the imitation/self-reliance dichotomy to the whole Continental experience. He has to deny that he stands in an imitative relation to European culture, for he is the self-reliant individual. As part of this denial, he finds that Europe stands in an imitative, or false, relation to the soul, of which he is the representative. Europe treacherously tries to get him to imitate its imitation, drawing him ever further away from reality. Pretending to be his "best friend," it is his "worst enemy." In order to protect his autonomy, he diminishes the Old World's power through criticism. The tactics that worked in his reimagining of God work now in his negotiations with human authors:

> what the intercourse with each of these suggests is true of intercourse with better men, that they never *fill the ear*—fill the mind—no, it is an *idealized* portrait which always we draw of them. Upon an intelligent man, wholly a stranger to their names, they would make . . . no deep impression—none of a world-filling fame. . . . (*JMN*.IV.78–79)

This is the desire for sublimity that Emerson attributed to youth, the "raging, infinite . . . hunger, as of space to be filled with planets" (*W*.IV.184), the desire to have the ear, mind, and world filled and thus to be overpowered. But what sounds like a wish for a more impressive effect shades easily into a celebration of the traveler's critical independence. Emerson's response to European architecture illuminates the nature of the impossible demands he tacitly presents to Coleridge, Wordsworth, and Carlyle: "nothing is truly great, nothing impresses us, nothing overawes, nothing crowds upon us, & kills calculation[.] We always call in the effect of imagination." Only the "imagination" of the spectator can create a sublime "effect," the impression that "kills calculation"—that is, one's critical distance. American and European buildings look like "imitations" of a sublime original because "It is in the soul that architecture exists & Santa Croce & this Duomo are poor far-behind imitations" of the spiritual power they inevitably remind us of (*JMN*.IV.75). "Imitation" is clearly Emerson's term for the absence of expected sublimity. But the failure of his masters to "overawe" him redounds to his benefit; as usual, he finds that they are the imitations and he the original.

His defiance of great men in these journal passages, written a month or so after the visits, contrasts markedly with the accounts entered immediately after each conversation (Coleridge on August

5, 1833, Carlyle on the 16th, Wordsworth on the 28th). His tone in first recording the encounters with Coleridge and Wordsworth conveys neither awe nor irritation. Thus, while his conversation with Coleridge is intellectual comedy of the first order, he betrays not the slightest consciousness of it. At Highgate, the former "rising Star of Unitarianism" confronts the American. Coleridge begins to attack Unitarianism and, Emerson records, "I remarked to him that it would be cowardly in me . . . not to inform him that I was an Unitarian, though much interested in his explanations. Yes, he said, I supposed so & continued as before." The spectacle of Coleridge saying to Emerson at this juncture in the latter's career that "he had once been an Unitarian & knew what quackery it was" strikes me as one of history's great moments of dramatic irony. "So," Emerson might have replied, "do I." Less amusing, however, is the querulousness with which Coleridge wonders why "after so many ages of unquestioning acquiescence . . . this handful of Priestleians should take upon themselves to deny [the doctrine of the Trinity]." For the patron saint of "the first philosophy" to advocate "unquestioning acquiescence" gives substance to Emerson's disillusion. The Coleridge he had admired had been his own invention, he concludes; the actual man was "any thing but what I had imagined." Even though "the visit was rather a spectacle than a conversation," his hero was hardly overwhelming (*JMN*.IV.408–11, *W*.V.14).

Wordsworth is just as self-centered as Coleridge, though more willing to engage in dialogue. He is happy to discuss America, "the more that it gave occasion for his favorite topic," remarks the by now somewhat suspicious Emerson. Like Coleridge, Wordsworth is obsessed with one or two subjects on which he speaks as a defender of conservative values. Whereas the gap between Emerson and Coleridge arose from divergent religious ideologies, the distance between him and Wordsworth is more literary, and becomes apparent when he inquires about Wordsworth's reading. Emerson finds his teacher intellectually out of date. Wordsworth mouths conventional censures of *Wilhelm Meister*, doesn't know Cousin, and finds Carlyle "sometimes insane." ("I stoutly defended Carlyle" and Goethe, Emerson comments in his journal [*JMN*.IV.223].)

Like Coleridge, Wordsworth volunteers to recite his poetry and does so "with great animation." One of the choice passages of *English Traits*, which does not appear in the journal, describes Emerson's reaction:

> This recitation was so unlooked for and surprising,—he, the old Wordsworth, standing apart, and reciting to me in a garden-walk, like a school-boy declaiming,—that I at first was near to laugh; but recollecting myself, that I had come thus far to see a poet and he was chanting poems to me, I saw that he was right and I was wrong, and gladly gave myself up to hear. (*W.V.*22–23)

This gives us a clue as to what the rather toneless prose of the journal account suppresses—laughter. Throughout the interviews, the contrast between the actual man and the figure he had imagined results in the desire to laugh—at his own naïveté and at the shrunken god before him. However, by invoking ("recollecting") the sublime name of "poet," Emerson is able to "give himself up" to the proper emotion. This is a clear example of the way irony ("The Comic," in Emerson's terms) and sublimity compete with and slip into each other. Irony and sublimity are called forth simultaneously by the confrontation with authority. In this instance, the impulse to laugh is the more rebellious response; the willingness to be moved by—and to—sublimity preserves the young writer's original awe for the elder man. It is significant that this admission can only be made long after the event. Emerson's later condescension when writing about Wordsworth and Coleridge compensates for his real acquiescence in the role of respectful provincial. "His [Wordsworth's] egotism was not at all displeasing—obtrusive—as I had heard," he comments. "To be sure it met no rock. I spoke as I felt with great respect of his genius" (*JMN.*IV.225). Characteristically, he is rather passive and yielding in person, venting (and probably only realizing) his impatience later. The final irony is that his criticism takes the form of a complaint about his hosts' insufficient presence. But in Chapter One of *English Traits*, a curious mixture of insight and distortion when tested against the original record of his first journey to England, he still partly censures his disillusionment. Against the evidence of the anecdotes he is about to relate, he insists, "I have . . . found writers superior to their books. . . . [They] give one the satisfaction of reality, the sense of having been met, and a larger horizon" (W.V. 8–9).

Emerson's encounter with Carlyle, "[a] white day in my years," is, of course, quite different. Though not exempt from the deficiencies of "wise men," Carlyle is distinguished by his extreme "amiableness." Emerson's special feeling for the Scot is due less to the latter's temperament—Wordsworth had been amiable, after all—than to his relative youth (eight years older than Emerson, who refers to him as "the youth I sought"), his aggressive prose style, and his unpopularity among figures of the English literary establishment, including Coleridge and Wordsworth (JMN.IV.219–20). His utter solitude becomes for Emerson an emblem of all these attributes:

> I found the house amid desolate heathery hills, where the lonely scholar nourished his mighty heart. Carlyle was a man from his youth . . . and as absolute a man of the world, unknown and exiled on that hill-farm, as if holding on his own terms what is best in London. (W.V.15)

The bond between the two men, which neither can ever bear to let lapse completely, has more to do with the image of one coming upon the solitary dwelling of the other and being greeted as an "apparition" of "an undoubtedly *supernal* character," than with common intellectual concerns (CEC.101). Each confirms the other's mythology of self-reliance.

This is not to suggest that shared ideas are unimportant. Carlyle is, as Coleridge had been, Emerson's bibliography of the moment. As translator of Goethe and student of contemporary German literature, he could be immediately useful, as Coleridge and Wordsworth could not (although "Plato he does not read, and he disparaged Socrates; and, when pressed, persisted in making Mirabeau a hero" [W.V.16]). Furthermore, because Carlyle is not surrounded by the aura of fame, they can treat as equals. The irreverent tone captured in Emerson's fragmentary notes on Carlyle's conversation reflects a very different kind of speaker from Wordsworth and Coleridge; the Scot was "full of . . . a streaming humor which floated everything he looked upon. His talk playfully exalting the familiar objects, put the companion at once into an acquaintance with his Lars and Lemurs" (W.V.15). But the American visitor is largely responsible for the altered tone. Emerson's own humor clearly invited the irony that makes them comrades-in-arms against convention. The discovery of an ally is as intentional on Emerson's part as his disillusion with Coleridge and Wordsworth. Craigenputtock would not have been on his itinerary had he not already perceived Carlyle as a proponent of "the first philosophy." This new fraternal bond compensates for whatever sense of loss Emerson might feel after demythologizing his elderly idols.

The rejection of Coleridge and Wordsworth and the acceptance of Carlyle have their intended effect. They send Emerson home with an immensely heightened self-esteem and an appetite for work. Having made his reader's pilgrimage, he is now ready to become a theorist of reading. Having confronted literature impersonated, he is ready to make a career of showing how its influence may be overcome. In the course of the next decade, he repeatedly maps the progress from necessary submission in the act of reading to the compensatory dominance of the reader.

· II ·

THE STRUCTURE OF
THE ESSAYS

INTRODUCTION

When we turn to Emerson's essays, we have no trouble recognizing the themes of earlier journals. His preoccupation with the modern scholar's reading of religious and literary history takes more aggressive, individualistic forms, but is easily related to previous writings. The stylistic qualities of the essays raise more complex questions about Emerson's development, however, focusing on the nature of the connection between his rhetorical and intellectual strategies. If the subject of the essays is the drama of transfiguration that makes possible "sublime analysis"—a drama of interpretation, of theorizing—then what are the stylistic consequences of this "plot"? If Emerson's subject is reading, how does this affect his writing? How are his shifts among the roles of student, critic, and author formally registered? If, as he announced, criticism is creative, can we demonstrate this through close reading of his works?

Emerson's prose appears to resist efforts at such demonstrations. It is at once discontinuous and repetitive. Celebrations of vision, influx, power, and freedom alternate with complaints of opacity, constriction, and fatigue. Moods "do not believe in"—or even, it seems, remember—"each other" (CW.II.182). It is almost impossible to determine the extent to which he is ironic, the precise degree of his tonal control. He invents fables of transcendence, transparency, fluidity; he also values concrete detail, palpable fact, the resistance of matter. Concepts like "correspondence," "analogy," "metamorphosis," and "metaphor" sometimes describe the bond between spirit and matter, at other times their separation. Closure, imposed on such oscillations, is inevitably problematic.

Readers in every generation have nevertheless devoted themselves to resolving these alternations into patterns they find more satisfying. Their metaphors for the unity they discover are almost comically varied.[1] At one point, a critical consensus seemed to have been reached that Emerson intentionally endowed his works with "dialectical unity." A number of writers converted antitheses into dialectic by seeking in his reading for models he might have followed. They mustered passages in which he expresses his methodological indebtedness to Plato, Coleridge, and other dialecticians. In addition to these specific attributions, most other commentators referred loosely to his works as "dialectical," again taking him at his occasional word (JMN.IX.214; W.IV.62–63).[2] However, Emerson's habit of explaining away his difficulties by invoking the concept of dialectic is part of our difficulty with him, not proof of its solution. His expressions of an optimistic faith in dialectical synthesis should not be honored over his periodic recognitions of irreconcilable polarities. He alternates between the hope for transcendent resolutions and skepticism toward them. When antitheses do issue in synthesis, it rarely endures for more than a paragraph; contradiction is no sooner resolved than it is repeated. Dialectic, by definition, cannot mean mere alternation, and so necessarily misdescribes prose that accumulates but does not progress. Emerson's writing can just as well be called anti-dialectical, for its possible unities continually break apart into antagonistic opposites. Attempts to organize his life and works according to dichotomies like Whicher's "freedom and fate" or Porter's progression from conventional poetry to "the spaciousness of prose" also reflect our desire to impose coherence.[3] These approaches, too, evade the central interpretative problem, namely, the constant tension between freedom and fate, convention and rebellion *within* each essay. Eric Cheyfitz's recent book represents an encouraging shift of emphasis away from critical descriptions of fixed polarities toward the problem of why Emerson's antitheses are so unstable.[4]

Emerson's essays are not, I think, really "about" their ostensible subject matter. The essays I have chosen to discuss—*Nature*, "The American Scholar," the Divinity School "Address," "The Poet," and "Quotation and Originality"—appear to have different subjects: the uses of nature, America's cultural destiny, the disestablishment of the moral sentiment, the Orphic imagination, the status of citations. However, they are structurally identical. Despite the apparently occasional character of orations like "The American Scholar" and the "Address," every "occasion" brings forth a variation of a recurring pattern. Subject matter does not determine structure. Not surprisingly, the irrelevance of subject matter to argumentative form has created difficulties for Emerson scholars. Because he utilizes the idioms of any and all ideologies, doctrines, disciplines, and professions, the essays can be interpreted by applying any one of these idioms to them. Emerson becomes explicable in sociological, religious, or nationalistic terms. His eclectic writing is like the Tar Baby; any interpretation will find surface enough to stick. Such readings take the subject matter of Emerson's non-referential, nonmimetic prose too literally. Whatever his topic, he represents some form of interpretation as an anti-authoritarian, metamorphic act which makes possible a freedom so absolute that, though it can be described as natural, or political, or religious, or literary, or all of these simultaneously, it will always (Emerson hopes) exceed its representations.

By way of introduction to the following chapters on individual works, I offer a plot summary of a paradigmatic essay. The plot is that of Emerson's own development—not his personal biography, but the emergence of a critical voice and a heterogeneous style that typifies the history of Romantic writers of nonfictional prose. In the "earliest" phase (not necessarily corresponding to the beginning of the essay), the imagination of the figure I will call the "reader" projects its powers onto the "writer" in order to recognize in that figure its own alienated authority. Overwhelmed by what appears to be an external source of inspiration, the reader reacts with defensive aggression. He draws on the higher criticism, comparative mythology, or some other hermeneutic process to disintegrate the individual author, replacing him with less threatening collectivities. Like Emerson during his post-graduate education, he learns to dissolve texts into their sources. He writes by reassembling the fragments of tradition—that is, by quoting.

Throughout this cycle, in the essays as in the journals, Emerson oscillates between self-awareness and apparent forgetfulness, a motion that makes possible all the other changes of stance. As he humbly and beautifully explains,

That which is done, & that which does, is somehow, I know not how, part of me. The Unconscious works with the Conscious,—tells somewhat which I consciously learn to have been told. What I am has been conveyed secretly from me to another whilst I was vainly endeavoring to tell him it. He has heard from me what I never spoke. (*JMN*.VIII.10)

Whatever necessary forgetfulness they record, Emerson's essays are made possible by the fact that he remembers what it was like to be overwhelmed by other writers, or, rather, he never ceases to be overwhelmed. Every essay contains moments when a book or an author "invades me displaces me; the law of it is that it should be first, that I should give way to it" (*JMN*.VIII.254). The need for aggressive recoveries is not surprising, considering the extent of his surrenders. In the act of reading, he abandons his will to that of the author:

> I go to Shakspear, Goethe, Swift, even to Tennyson, submit myself to them, become merely an organ of hearing, & yield to the law of their being. . . . Each new mind we approach seems to require an abdication of all our past & present empire. A new doctrine seems at first a subversion of all our opinions, tastes, & manner of living. (*JMN*.V.178)

He never yields without reasserting himself, however: "I . . . have no right to give way and, if I would be tranquil & divine again, I must dismiss the book" (*JMN*.VIII.254). This is precisely the sequence of events in the essays. The book is an aggressive, militant entity seemingly possessed by an internal "law" or intention; it invades the reader's territory and evicts him from it. Political and military metaphors represent reading as a state of war between unequal powers. This exile is temporary, for the reader recovers his lands and appropriates the mind that has occupied them. Emerson is "paid for *thus being nothing* by an entire new mind . . . a Proteus I enjoy the Universe through the powers & organs of a hundred different men" (*JMN*.V.178; emphasis added). Hence his incessant "Protean" quoting of a hundred different writers.

A fable composed in 1836, surrounded in the journal by future paragraphs from *Nature*, recapitulates the essays' essential narrative, the movement from imitation to quotation:

Each new mind we approach seems to require an abdication of all our past & present empire. A new doctrine seems at first a subversion of all our opinions, tastes, & manner of living. So did Jesus . . . Kant . . . Swedenborg . . . Cousin . . . Alcott seem. Take thankfully & heartily all they can give, exhaust them, leave father & mother & goods, wrestle with them, let them not go until their blessing be won, & after a short season the dismay will be overpast, the excess of influence will be withdrawn, & they will be no longer an alarming meteor but one more bright star shining serenely in your heaven & blending its light with all your day. (*JMN*.V.178-79)

This statement of the law of compensation ends by echoing the "Intimations Ode." In that poem, however, the threat to the poet is that the gleam will fade, not that it will appear as an "alarming meteor." Emerson's gratification does not come through the workings of Wordsworthian memory. Rather, his serenity is achieved through the conscious struggle of the will, the contest between reader and writer, Jacob and the angel. In the conflation of Christ's call to "leave father & mother & goods" and Jacob's wrestling, we have one of Emerson's brilliant offhand blasphemies. He cannot conceive of the blessing without the struggle. "We read either for antagonism or for confirmation," he observes elsewhere. "It matters not which way the book works on us, whether to contradict & enrage, or to edify & inspire" (*JMN*.VIII.134). His whether/or construction is inaccurate; it is the distinction of his theory of reading that it shows how the same book inspires *by enraging* us.

Interpretation is a conflict between the reader and the angelic author. The reader throws himself "into the object [the book] so that its history shall naturally evolve itself before me." When it does, he discovers an infinite regress into sources:

Shakspeare how inconceivable until we have heard what Italian Novels & Plutarch's Lives & old English Dramas he had. . . . A Webster's Speech is a marvel until we have learned that a part of it he has carried in his head for years, & a part . . . was collected for him by young lawyers & that Mr

Appleton furnished the facts & a letter from Mr Swain turned the paragraph. St. Peter's did not leap fullgrown out of the head of the Architect. The part that was builded instructed the eye of the next generation. . . . The poem, the oration, the book are superhuman, but the wonder is out when you see the manuscript. Homer how wonderful until the German erudition discovered a cyclus of homeric poems. It is all one; a trick of cards, a juggler's sleight, an astronomical result, an algebraic formula, amazing when we see only the result, cheap when we are shown the means. (JMN.IV.284-85)

This kind of interpretation empowers Emerson at crucial moments in the essays. Its provenance is clear. "German erudition" gave rise to the close textual ("manuscript") studies that simultaneously disintegrated the Bible and the classics. Homer "separates before the German telescope into two, ten, or twenty stars" (JMN.IV.312). Emerson expresses a sense of loss at the critical destruction of art's mystique and allows himself to feel this loss fully, despite the fact that, when used against other writers, criticism works to his advantage. What used to seem "superhuman," "wonderful," "amazing" stands exposed as a cheap trick. Anyone who has encountered the resistance of undergraduates to textual analysis or who remembers his or her own sense of desecration when first asked to perform such readings will find this reaction familiar. But the possibilities of doing away with the illusion of originality outweigh the disappointments. It is, Emerson writes, "As if modern society was composed of the *debris* of the foregone structures of religion & politics a mixed composite bronze just as the soil we till is made up of the degraded mountains of the elder world" (JMN.VII.304). Or, as Thoreau wrote in a letter to Emerson,

> Is it not singular that, while the religious world is gradually picking to pieces its old testaments, here are some coming slowly after, on the seashore, picking up the durable relics of perhaps older books, and putting them together again.[5]

The style of belated moderns is a recovery from and exploitation

of the criticism that has taken all testaments "to pieces." For when
integral works are fragmented, we perceive the value of fragments.
As modern texts are found to be collections of old "debris," discontinuity becomes desirable. If the greatest writers "have questions of identity & of genuineness raised respecting their writings"
(*JMN*.IX.164), then no one and everyone is original: "Make your
own Bible. Select & Collect all those words & sentences that in
all your reading have been to you like the blast of trumpet out of
Shakespear, Seneca, Moses, John, & Paul" (*JMN*.V.186). When
authors melt into a generalized, anonymous past, their works are
public property: "as soon as [a writer] acknowledges that all is
suggestion, then he may be indebted without shame to all"
(*JMN*.V.59). Emerson's theory of inter-textuality does away with
the aggressive daemon that haunts a great book. "[I]t is pleasant
to have a book come down to us of which the author has . . . lost
his individual distinctness," he remarks disingenuously, "the book
seems . . . rather . . . to have the sanction of human nature
than to totter on the two legs of any poor Ego" (*JMN*.V.78). We
must, he says, "strip [the book] of this accurate individuality"
(*JMN*.VII.275). Unlike someone else's "poor Ego," a diffuse tradition has no designs on him.

Once a work has been disintegrated into its sources, it can be
absorbed into the self, as Emerson had remade God, Ellen, and
other writers into narcissistic reflections. Interpretation is taking
possession; the reader is "a principle of selection & gathers only
what is like him as unerringly as a sparrow builds her nest"
(*JMN*.VI.222). Emerson repeats this claim so often that he eventually must insist that his response to others is not wholly narcissistic:

> I am not such a fool but that I taste the joy which comes from
> a new & prodigious person . . . flinging wide to me the doors
> of new modes of existence, and even if I should intimate by
> a premature nod my too economical perception of the old
> thrum that the basis of this joy is at last the instinct that I

am only let into my own estate, that the poet & his
book . . . are only fictions & semblances in which my thought
is pleased to dress itself, I do not the less yield myself to the
keen delight of difference & newness. (*JMN*.VIII.97-98)

Emerson's desire for newness is ultimately a desire for self-
aggrandizement. His power over literature, based on "semblance"
(Me), follows from its power over him as "difference" (Not Me).
Poetry, he suggests in the same entry, should "descend like a
foreign conquerer from an unexpected quarter of the horizon upon
us, carry us away with our flocks & herds into a strange & appalling
captivity, to make us, at a later period, adopted children of the
Great King, &, in the end, to disclose to us that he was our real
parent, & this realm & palace is really our native country"
(*JMN*.VIII.97). This fable elucidates the necessary fiction of what
Emerson, with facetious ponderousness, termed "Otherism" or
"Alienation" (*JMN*.V.254). Most significantly, it shows that the
power, actually our own, which is incorrectly seen at first as "a
foreign conquerer," is associated in Emerson's mind with "our real
parent," the "Great King" whose "adopted children" we are. What
we perceive as our alienated majesty is tradition, the past seen
alternately as tyrant and father. So he is alarmed to catch himself
slipping too easily into the "old thrum" about resemblance. Since
his authority is a reaction to (or at least, is justified by) his previous
inferiority, he must voluntarily become subordinate in order to
feel strong again. He is well aware that his equation of reading and
writing is a fiction:

> We seem to be capable of all thought. We are on a
> level . . . with all Intelligences. . . . And yet familiar as
> that state of mind is . . . books . . . still retain their value
> from age to age. So impassable is at last that thin imperceptible
> boundary between perfect understanding of the author, perfect
> fellowship with him, *quasi* consciousness of the same gifts,—
> & the faculty of subordinating that rapture to the Will in
> such degree as to be able ourselves to conjoin & record our
> states of mind. . . . [T]he glory of the name of Shakspear,

Bacon, Milton, an index of the exceeding difficulty with which
the reader who perfectly understands what they say & sees
no reason why he should not continue the sentence—over-
leaps that invisible barrier & continues the sentence. Whilst
he reads, the draw bridge is down. Nothing hinders that he
should pass with the author. When he assays to write,—lo
suddenly! the draw is up, & will not down. (*JMN.*VII.
160-61)

Reading is not writing, he concedes; the act of recognition is not,
after all, creative. The reader's equality with the author proves to
be illusory. But his failure is necessary and even desirable, for it
is the source of the "glory" of the art work. The restoration of
literature's aura completes a cycle of attitudes and, more importantly, permits the repetition of the cycle. First, the reader is overcome by a book. He defends himself by affirming "the ultimate
identity of the artist & the spectator" (*JMN.*VII.275), a strategy
that appropriates the work and diminishes its author. After this
presumptuous gesture, he discovers that he cannot write an equal
masterpiece, and the book regains its original power. Through the
"invisible barrier" between reader and writer, he sees the work in
all its initial glory, and the cycle begins again. Since this repetition
permits Emerson to go on writing, it makes good his admitted lies
about the reader's power.

In the readings of Emerson's essays which follow, I identify these
roles and trace his shifts among them. As the preceding sketch of
the essays' structuring motives indicates, this involves more than
a simple oscillation between the roles of reader and writer. The
reader appears both as an aggressive, narcissistic critic who creates
meaning and as a desirous admirer, yearning to be original but
resigned to his secondary status. Likewise, the figure of the author
speaks as a youth struggling against inhibition and obscurity; he
also dons the "robe of eloquence" and utters the prophecies of the
Orphic poet. It is difficult to make assured distinctions between
the self-confidence of the critic and of the writer, or between the
doubts of the reader and of the poet. The extraordinary instability

of a limited number of positions may be the definitive attribute of Emerson's style. The slight motions that turn readers into authors and back again enable him to keep writing prose that hovers between sublimity (authorship) and analysis (criticism), that is, to keep writing.

3

NATURE

N_{ature} is structurally different enough from Emerson's essays to justify omitting it from this section. The ways in which it is atypical, however, illuminate the development of his essays' dynamics. Furthermore, the way theoretical criticism emerges as one of the central activities of *Nature* makes the book indispensable to a discussion of Emerson's interpretive dramas. For *Nature* is an investigation of theory. Its partial genesis in Emerson's excited visits to the Musée Nationale d'Histoire Naturelle and the Jardin des Plantes during his 1833 visit to Paris suggests that he was inspired by a sudden vision of the coherence of nature. An organized interpretation of natural history, visibly demonstrated in the arrangement of zoological and botanical miscellanies, was, to him, proof of the modern mind's interpretive power. When he exclaimed, before the cabinet of natural history at the Jardin des Plantes, "Not a form . . . but is an expression of some property inherent in man the observer," he was enjoying man's position as observer. The "strange sympathies" that moved him to declare, "I will be a naturalist," are effects that he recognized as consequences of the naturalist's organizing perception (*JMN*.IV.199-200). In *Nature*, he tries to produce a similar ordering of natural history apprehended by the cultured mind. The differences between the naturalist and the philosopher are subsumed in the figure of Emerson's theorist, who is the hero of both realms by virtue of his critique of origins, analogies, causes, and effects.

The subject of criticism arises immediately in *Nature*, only to be scorned. Emerson begins the "Introduction" with a typically conflictual strategy. He contrasts undesirable sources of knowledge, "biographies, histories, and criticism," to true ones, "insight," "revelation," and originality (*CW*.I.7). The essence of his dichotomy here is the opposition between the past and himself, a conflict represented by the shabby inheritance of "dry bones" and a "faded wardrobe," and "the powers" that he attributes to nature. No sooner does he reject criticism as the means by which our dead fathers bequeath to us their sepulchral knowledge, however, than he sets out to invent a form of criticism that will serve his own "revelation." He devotes the rest of the introduction to showing that experience and theory are "hieroglyphic" versions of each other and, therefore, that they are not necessarily opposed; man "acts . . . as life" what "he apprehends . . . as truth." Emerson describes his own project in *Nature* as a scientific one, taking the term in its broadest sense to mean the kind of analytical or systematic thought which reveals the true structure of experience. "All science has one aim," he announces, "namely, to find a theory of nature." He still acknowledges the pettiness of critics, manifested in the disputes of "religious teachers" and in the fact that "speculative men are esteemed unsound and frivolous." But he does not, accordingly, dismiss speculation. Rather, he calls for a speculative hero whose "sound judgment" will invent "a true theory," and thus displace the oppressive past by critical means. Abstract thought becomes a metaphor for power, a figurative equation that characterizes all of Emerson's mature works. "[T]he most abstract truth is the most practical" because "it will explain all phenomena." The present generation must gain its freedom from "biographies, histories, and criticism," therefore, by being more speculative, more theoretical, more critical than its predecessors, not less. Emerson's binary opposition ends up being the difference between two meanings of the word "criticism," one connoting an undesirable mediation between our experience and our thoughts about it, the other referring to the potential energy of those thoughts. He casually acknowledges that "Philosophy distinguishes" between nature and soul, Not Me and Me, nature and art, then breezily claims that in "inquiries so general as our present one . . . inaccuracy is not material." He is right. These distinctions are not material because his real interest is not in the object of study, be it man, nature, soul, or art, but in the interpreting mind that brings them all under its control (CW.I.7-8).

The formal structure of *Nature*, which purports to depict the hierarchy of our "uses" of nature, somewhat inhibits its dramatic or tonal form, which reflects the growing confidence felt by an increasingly abstract thinker. This is why, in my discussion of Emerson's essay structures, *Nature* is treated only briefly. In it, he fusses with logical sequences as though abstract thought had to be literalized in argumentative systems. His chapter headings mark an ascent up the moral and metaphysical axis from "Commodity" to "Spirit." Then we have the "threefold distribution" of "Beauty" into 1. the sensual, 2. the spiritual, and 3. the intellectual. Likewise, "Language" contains three numbered propositions that proceed in ascending and expanding order from the relationship of words to things to the relationship between nature and spirit. The functions of "Discipline" are divided into the education of 1. the inferior Understanding and 2. the superior Reason. "Idealism" becomes a list of five "effects of culture," which proceed vertically from changes in physical perspective to the results of poetry, philosophy, and religion. The logical numerical sequences of *Nature* are an awkward version of the later essays' sudden metamorphoses from a tone of realistic humility to one of aggressive self-reliance. *Nature* should therefore be read and taught not as Emerson's quintessential utterance but as a rather unrepresentative work in which he imitates "scientific" method. If it is so read, his essays can be seen developmentally as texts in which the constraints of a more naive phase have relaxed and Emerson's paradigmatic structure has come into its own. In them, he collapses step-by-step demonstrations into large, rapid transitions from one level to another.

Nature does contain that later essayistic structure. The essay within the book progresses not by the demonstration of logical relationships but by the repetition of key gestures and metaphoric associations. Instead of proceeding from the level of commodity, matter, and literal meaning to the plane of ideas, Reason, and truth, as the chapter titles promise, Emerson evades his own logical framework in *Nature* by leaping from commodity to spirit on every page. These transitions build to a kind of hyperbole or crescendo; their power is produced by accumulation, not progress. The chapter sequence—"Beauty," "Language," "Discipline"—does not trace an ascent to the ideal because each of these chapters effects that ascent. The chapters of *Nature* are almost interchangeable by virtue of their identical actions. Emerson begins section 1 of "Beauty," for example, by announcing that here he will demonstrate that "the simple perception of natural forms is a delight." The first paragraph applauds the "medicinal" effect of nature on tired minds and bodies. The next paragraph asserts that "in other hours, Nature satisfies the soul purely by its loveliness, without any mixture of corporeal benefit." In a reprise of Emerson's dilation into a transparent eyeball on the bare common, the central event of Chapter One, "Nature," he admits to feeling, at sunrise, "emotions which an angel might share": "I seem to partake its rapid transformations; the active enchantment reaches my dust, and I dilate and conspire with the morning wind. How does Nature deify us with a few and cheap elements!" In section 2, he tells us, "The presence of a higher, namely, of the spiritual element is essential to [Beauty's] perfection. . . . Beauty is the mark God sets upon virtue" (CW.I.15). The reader receives this as repetition, a summary of what has preceded it in section 1 and in earlier chapters. We do not, I think, feel it as a step from the level of mere perception up to the "higher" plane of moral significance. This kind of redundancy is important because it reveals that the jump from literal to figurative meaning, from perception to idea, is the governing structural principle of Emerson's prose. Even in *Nature*, where the chapter plan seems designed to restrict him to one long, slow ascent toward visionary order, the need for repeated, rapid oscillations between viewpoints prevails. Emerson does not value repetition for its own sake, but craves the repetition of certain pleasures, chiefly, the discovery of "theory."

One of the most frequent evidences of his delight in the power of thought is the repeated fusion of nature and culture. He describes nature through cultural allusions. The mind's conquest of fact by such means serves the desire to make criticism the mode of revelation, for the speaker who constructs these allusive series does so from the point of view of the Romantic comparative scholar. This thinker plays with the analogical parallels between mental faculties, intellectual disciplines, and symbolic geography. "The dawn is my Assyria; the sun-set and moon-rise my Paphos, and unimaginable realms of faerie; broad noon shall be my England of the senses and the understanding; the night shall be my Germany of mystic philosophy and dreams," he declares in section 1 of "Beauty," purportedly on the "simple perception of natural forms." Nature is incorporated into a cultural system which comprehends all of Western and Eastern civilization. As such, it gratifies all the mind's faculties—faith, imagination, understanding, dream, Reason. Emerson looks at the world and thinks, not of "the integrity of impression made by manifold natural objects," but of the eclectic impression of multiple cultural inheritances. Although he refers to nature's meaning as that which "Homer or Shakespeare could not re-form for me in words," the text of *Nature* repeatedly breaks down the distinction between nature and culture; the book is really about the appropriation of the former by the latter. In section 2 of "Beauty," on "the spiritual element," Emerson represents the relationships between beauty and virtue through the metaphors of historical paintings, tableaux, theater. He describes heroic deeds as "scenes"—the defense of Thermopylae, Columbus' landing, the execution of Sir Harry Vane. "[C]an we separate the man from the *living picture?*" he asks. "Does not the New World clothe his form with her palm-groves and savannahs as *fit drapery?*" Nature's "frame" will suit the human "picture," not so much in the mind of the participants, as in the mind of the later spectator. It is the retrospective glance that appreciates the suitable natural setting: "Homer, Pindar, Socrates, Phocion, associate themselves fitly *in our memory* with the geography and climate of Greece" (CW.I.13, 9, 14; emphasis added). Nature and culture are conflated in *Nature* because they are both the contents of history. The author who would resist the past theoretically puts them both into the category to be resisted.

By the time we get to the next chapter on "Language," which I will take up in a later chapter, we are so used to having nature defined as a cultural artifact that the treatment of nature as a language comes as a variation on established themes. Then "Discipline" shifts to the model of formal pedagogy to represent nature's value in another, but analogous, way. Mechanical forces "give us the sincerest lessons. . . . They educate both the Understanding and the Reason. Every property of matter is a school for the understanding. . . . The exercise of the Will, or the lesson of power, is taught in every event" (CW.I.23, 25). The move from reading ("Language") to teaching ("Discipline") substitutes one metaphor of cultural transmission for another. Nature is an object known by Emerson as commodity, as language, as spirit, and so on. The book becomes a demonstration of the speaker's transformations, not those of nature. His apparent movement toward higher uses of nature is undermined by our sense that the basic tactic of describing nature as a cultural phenomenon has been repeated in order continually to gratify his appetite for transformational abstraction. It would be inaccurate to say, however, that Emerson's repetitions do away with feelings of intensification and climax. The movement from "Commodity" to "Spirit" corresponds to the speaker's drive toward the most abstract theory. The chapters on "Idealism" and "Spirit" and the transition between them best illustrate the relationship between theory and aggression.

Emerson begins "Idealism" by announcing that "all parts of nature conspire" to discipline man; they convey the "meaning of the world." Then he introduces his famous qualification: "A noble doubt perpetually suggests itself, whether this end be not the Final Cause of the Universe; and whether nature outwardly exists." This is a contrived crisis. He brings up the "noble doubt" only to dismiss doubt as irrelevant to his aggressive ends. He shifts into the first person to reply to his rhetorical question: "In my utter impotence to test the authenticity of the report of my senses . . . what difference does it make . . . ?" He has introduced the idea of doubt in order to create an occasion for his cavalier refusal to engage in philosophical debate. The breezy tone of this refusal indicates that his real goal is the exercise of power and that "Idealism" is its trope. "Idealism," while clearly a term derived from philosophy and validated by that origin, is transformed into a metaphor for the speaker. Whether the world is substance or "apparition," he is clearly at the center of it; "it is alike useful and alike venerable *to me*" (CW.I.29; emphasis added). Dismissing the "noble doubt" of idealism leads to the noble confidence of Emerson.

His topic in subsequent paragraphs is the usefulness of idealism, the kind of power it makes possible. Allegory is the rhetorical equivalent of theory here, as in most of Emerson's prose. Idealism and the Idealist are allegorical entities, but these terms also refer to the allegorical reduction itself. For what does Emerson say idealism accomplishes? It relaxes the "despotism of the senses, which binds us to nature . . . and shows us nature aloof, and, as it were, afloat." Reason (a synonym for idealism) makes "outlines and surfaces become transparent . . . causes and spirits are seen through them." Finally: "Idealism . . . beholds the whole circle of persons and things, of actions and events, of country and religion . . . as *one vast picture, which God paints on the instant eternity, for the contemplation of the soul*" (emphasis added). Idealism, then, reveals or creates a coherent pattern of lawful relationships. Its point of view is above the earth, a point from which nature is spread out below as "one vast picture." Emerson expresses the power of abstraction through the image of visual mastery. His idealistic method forces us to subordinate real objects to pure meaning, to "causes and spirits." This perceptual conversion turns the world into figurative language, allowing the poet to make "dust and stones" into "the words of the Reason." As Emerson concludes, "the use which the Reason makes of the material world" is "subordinating nature for the purposes of expression" (CW.I.30, 36, 31). We usually think of allegory as a technique which fixes ideas in the form of objects, rather than one which dissolves objects or makes them "float" or become "transparent." Emerson does hypostasize consciousness by calling it "Idealism," but then, revealing the aggressive motives of allegory and of theory, proposes that the consequence of this is the dissolution of the allegorical entity itself.

The power of the idealist's theory in Chapter Six of *Nature* is appalling. Emerson demonstrates that the "irrefragable analysis" of poet, philosopher, astronomer, geometer "transfer[s] nature into the mind, and [leaves] matter like an outcast corpse." "The material is ever degraded before the spiritual," he announces. The purpose of reducing nature to an allegory of spirit is to make the author-idealist feel powerful by treating the world as an element of his own mind: "Possessed himself by a heroic passion, he uses matter as symbols of it." The use of matter as symbol expresses and further inflames the heroic passion: "Whilst we behold unveiled the nature of Justice and Truth . . . [w]e apprehend the absolute. As it were, for the first time, *we exist*. We become immortal." This is allegory as wish-fulfillment. Emerson frankly admits that the "advantage of the ideal theory is . . . that it presents the world in precisely that view which is most desirable to the mind" (CW.I.34, 31, 35, 36). The desired view is that which offers alienated figurative evidence of the poet-philosopher's power.

It is no accident that, as Emerson celebrates the theorizing mind in "Idealism," he reflects on the role of culture. He has described nature from a cultured point of view throughout. Now he argues explicitly that culture is the vehicle of idealism, the means by which theory masters nature. "[A]ll culture tends to imbue us with idealism," he concludes, and idealism "put[s] nature under foot." Culture is generated by the will to power, that is, the will to theory. As Emerson proceeds through the catalogue of "the effects of culture," which makes up the bulk of "Idealism," it is clear that his idea of power is inseparable from the momentary pleasures of interpretive conversions. What really attracts him are the forms of gratification available to individual men through intellectual aggression. When he discusses Shakespeare as his representative poet, therefore, he focuses not so much on the metaphoric techniques that spiritualize nature (though he quotes examples of these at some length), as on "the passion of the poet" of which metaphor is the result. Shakespeare's "imperial muse tosses the creation like a bauble from hand to hand, and uses it to embody any capricious shade of thought that is uppermost in his mind." Will is manifested in theory and results in metaphoric play: "The perception of . . . *ideal* affinities . . . enables the poet thus to make free with the . . . forms and phenomena of the world, and to assert the predominance of the soul." If there is less emphasis on the thinker's pleasure in the sections of "Idealism" devoted to philosophy, science, religion, and ethics, there is a greater stress on the association between interpretation and violence. All theories, all systems of natural or moral law, forcefully explain nature: they pervade, dissolve, seize, degrade, put an affront upon nature, to use some of Emerson's verbs (*CW*.I.35, 30, 32–33). "Criticism" has become "revelation" by being redefined as aggression. At the beginning of *Nature*, culture was the burdensome past which intervened between man and world. Now, as a synonym for abstract thought, it makes possible man's independence from a world he no longer wants to be close to.

At the end of "Idealism," Emerson becomes aware that his gestures are likely to appall conventional sensibilities and that they misrepresent his own intuitions. He apologizes: "I have no hostility to nature, but a child's love to it. . . . I do not wish to fling stones at my beautiful mother, nor soil my gentle nest." The short-lived efficacy of aggression, but its repeated dramatization, is a consistent feature of his prose. Theory functions as a source of power for a few sentences, or, in this case, chapters, but then yields to self-doubt and self-correction. These pauses, however, frequently carry us forward once again to another notion that will temporarily serve as the figurative vehicle for Emerson's desire. Thus, characteristically, in Chapter Seven of *Nature* he partly repeats and partly regrets the aggressive sequence of Chapter Six. Idealism gives way to "Spirit" in what looks like the culmination of the ascending subjects of the book, but is, in fact, a repetition of or substitution for the preceding idea. In order to substitute "Spirit" for "Idealism," Emerson conveniently forgets that he has not been treating idealism philosophically but metaphorically. Now he turns against it because it is mere philosophy: "Idealism is a hypothesis to account for nature by other principles than those of carpentry and chemistry. Yet," says Emerson's imaginative appetite, "if it only deny the existence of matter, it does not satisfy the demands of the spirit. It leaves God out of me." Of course, idealism *has* satisfied the demands of the spirit, which are for both denial and godliness, but these demands are too strong to be gratified by any one term. Spirit repeats the Idealist's accomplishment by interpreting nature as a mental phenomenon, "a projection of God in the unconscious" (*CW*.I.35–38).

"Spirit" is particularly interesting for the tension it displays between love and aggression. At the end of "Idealism," Emerson acknowledged his "hostility" to nature, and in the following chapters, he tries to compensate for it. He defines Spirit as the feeling of communion or identity with nature, as opposed to Idealism, which depends on our conscious difference from the "Not Me." Idealism, he now asserts, "makes nature foreign to me, and does not account for that consanguinity which we acknowledge to it." The terms "Spirit" and "Idealism" refer to Emerson's moods rather than to mental faculties or operations. The chapter on Spirit is tender and conciliatory, a correction of the eager roughness of the one on Idealism. His images and language are religious, as well as intellectual, and convey an attitude of humble devotion. Nature stands like "the figure of Jesus . . . with bended head and hands folded upon the breast," a "lesson of worship" Emerson urges upon humanity. He speaks less of the mind's power over nature and more of finding God in "the course [sic], and, as it were, distant phenomena of matter." These pious chastisements of the fierce intellect that has emerged throughout the first six chapters as the true protagonist of *Nature* are signs of the ambivalence felt by Romantic philosopher-critics about interpretation. Emerson now writes that nature "is not . . . subjected to the human will," that its "serene order is inviolable by us." Nevertheless, Nature does vanish in the meeting of human and divine minds. Man's power decreases and God's increases in the chapter on "Spirit," but Emerson's real interest is still in the power of mind, wherever that mind be located. Man draws from God "inexhaustible power," "has access to the entire mind of the Creator," and reads nature, therefore, as an allegory of transcendent order. Emerson's considerable misgivings about reducing nature to theory persist, however. "Spirit" closes with a lament over humankind's falling away from nature. Difference, earlier celebrated as evidence of a superior relationship to phenomena, is now treated as proof of "discord." Nature "is a fixed point whereby we may measure our departure. As we degenerate, the contrast between us and our house is more evident. We are as much strangers in nature, as we are aliens from God" (CW.I.38, 37, 38–39). *Nature's* coda begins with a mournful reprise of its opening complaint, in the "Introduction," about our lack of an original relation to the universe. Only through another meditation on the right kind of theory does Emerson partially recuperate.

The closing chapter of *Nature*, "Prospects," is largely given over to quotations of George Herbert and the "Orphic poet." Their utterances assume that man should resemble, "fit," coincide with nature, and so they have the elegiac, conciliatory tone of "Spirit." Emerson no longer praises the abstract thought that frees us by consciously alienating us from nature. Nevertheless, he does again take up his opening question: what is an appropriate "theory of nature"? Where is it to be located among contemporary arts and sciences? He is primarily concerned with distinguishing what he had called Idealism and now calls "the highest reason" from "[e]mpirical science" which gets bogged down in "functions and processes," "preciseness and infallibility." Although his tone is less ferocious than before, he still identifies the true theory of nature with the powerful "self-recovery" of the thinker, whose proper object finally becomes the "tyrannizing unity" in his own "constitution." Emerson never abandons the position that the role of thought is "to reduce the most diverse to one form"—to one's own form. Though his tone in claiming this becomes more temperate, he still itemizes "examples of the action of man upon nature with his entire force," the "resumptions of power" before which nature is "obedient" (CW.I.42,39–40, 43).

I confess that I am always disappointed to find Emerson backing away from his courageous acceptance of the necessary aggressiveness of thought and lapsing—I cannot help seeing it as that—into the desire for "consanguinity" with nature. My disappointment is less than my feeling of recognition, however, for his fluctuations in this regard are representative of the Romantic ambivalence about analysis which still pervades our critical debates. When Emerson is confident that theory legitimately alienates us from nature, he composes scenes of conflict in which pleasure flows from aggression. But when he doubts the critic's claim to heroism, he feels himself to be once again the reader who yearns for inspiration instead of the one who demands mastery. His fables reflect this, and so we have the Orphic poet's sorrow over our lost "sympathy with nature," our unconsummated "marriage" with it. Though *Nature* closes with a prophecy of the "kingdom of man over nature," this conquest is described in metaphors of natural change that hold in check Emerson's proclivity for instantaneous transformation. Swine, spiders, snakes, pests, mad-houses and the like may "vanish" in a moment, but the spirit advances "as when the summer comes from the south, the snow-banks melt, and the face of the earth becomes green before it" (*CW*.I.42, 45). The last two chapters of *Nature* are a palinode in which Emerson seeks to atone for his divisive theorizing earlier. Such alternations between fables of visionary aggression and those of pastoral union are the vehicles—one is tempted to say, the symptoms—of Emerson's critical philosophy in virtually all of the writings that follow *Nature*.

4

"THE AMERICAN SCHOLAR" AND
THE DIVINITY SCHOOL
"ADDRESS"

The theorist who determines the meaning of nature also organizes literary tradition. "The American Scholar" instructs young
American intellectuals in the "creative reading" of European literature; the Divinity School "Address" speaks to one segment of
that "scholarly" class in offering future ministers a revolutionary
variant of the higher criticism. These orations draw heavily on
Emerson's own experience in the ministry and abroad. They show
how he turned his resignation from the pulpit and his purposeful
disillusion with English writers into dramas of reading as resistance.
Just as those acts of defiance were made possible by self-centered,
anti-authoritarian interpretations, so the action of these manifes-
toes is also hermeneutic.

"THE AMERICAN SCHOLAR"

What most of us remember about "The American Scholar" is the
exhortation to ignore the siren song of "the courtly muses of Europe" (CW.I.69), and to pursue America's manifest poetic destiny.
But America is not the essay's subject. Rather, Emerson speaks
about "the discontent of the literary class." Our "intellectual Declaration of Independence" is, in fact, a treatise on "creative reading."[1]
The American Revolution provides Emerson with a paradigm for
the liberation of "the booklearned class" (CW.I.67, 58, 56) and

with a tradition of anti-British rhetoric that serves interpretive aggression in the guise of nationalism.

The opening ploy is one that will reappear at the beginning of many other works. Emerson sets "us" against "them," in this case, Americans against Europeans. He intensifies the mood of conflict by defining the occasion negatively, and, despite the negative, competitively: "We do not meet for games of strength or skill, . . . nor for the advancement of science," but to honor "the love of letters," which Emerson immediately wishes could be transformed into "something else." He identifies two antagonists: "our cotemporaries in the British and European capitals" and the "sluggard intellect" of merely "mechanical skill" at home. The spokesman for the American scholar stands beleaguered between his sources, "the learning of other lands," and his countrymen, the "millions . . . rushing into life" demanding to be "fed" (CW.I.52). Emerson's stance between two opponents is typical of the early paragraphs of the essays. He sets up the antagonistic relationships that later in the essay will be gratifying to him in other ways, but that now allow him to describe his own condition as one of need or desire. The possibility of feeding either the American millions or himself seems remote indeed. The fable of "One Man" is a grotesque parody of the Eucharist that links Emerson's feeling of diminution to his obsession with origins:

> this original unit, this fountain of power, has been so distributed to multitudes, has been so minutely subdivided and peddled out, that it is spilled into drops, and cannot be gathered. . . . [T]he members have suffered amputation from the trunk and strut about so many walking monsters—a good finger, a neck, a stomach, an elbow, but never a man.

Communion celebrates the belief that the broken body of Christ gives rise to union in the church. Emerson's inversion of the Eucharist suggests that the myths that feed his generation cannot make men or society whole. Images of dehumanizing reduction describe the consequence: "The priest becomes a form; the attorney, a statute-book; the mechanic, a machine; the sailor, a rope of the ship," and the scholar "the parrot of other men's thinking"

(CW.I.53). Emerson replicates his own youthful predicament. Dependent on foreign sources of inspiration, he had imitated them only to feel himself turn into a parroting voice empty of consciousness or meaning. The violence of his allegorical figures—a dismembered body, tools, mere objects—reminds us of the punishment he inflicted on his fantasies of power in the early journals.

When Emerson turns to the subject of "influences" on the scholar, he takes a step toward recovery. Nature sets the standard by which all subsequent influences will be evaluated. She is not source or teacher or the "Not Me," but a projection of the self. "This world,— this shadow of the soul, this *other me,* lies wide around," he writes later in the oration (CW.I.59). Since nature reflects him, he is origin, not "parrot." Nature "resembles [the scholar's] own spirit, whose beginning, whose ending he never can find—so entire, so boundless." When viewed as the reflection of "the ambitious soul," nature gives rise to a "thought too bold—a dream too wild" which anticipates "an ever expanding knowledge . . . a becoming creator" (CW.I.54–55). What we have here is a brief reprise of *Nature*: displaced from culture to nature, the protagonist changes from a reflection to that which is reflected. Nature's inferior relationship to him is the same as his imitative relationship to culture. Emerson's rereading of his cultural predicament makes manifest an excess of ambition.

This ambition first appears as a regressive admiration for the past. The second influence on the scholar, the "best type of the influence of the past," is books, the tradition against which nature is a defense. The violent language of this oration's opening paragraphs begins to return, as Emerson's resentment confronts its object. He celebrates the books of the world's "first age," which transformed "Life" into "truth," "short-lived actions" into "immortal thoughts," "business" into "poetry," "dead fact" into "quick thought." The books of his own day, however, undo these metamorphoses and poetry disintegrates once again into "the conventional, the local, the perishable." The closer the speaker moves to his own time, the less he likes books. At a remote distance, they are benign and inspirational; viewed in uncomfortable proximity, the majesty of alienation fades and their ordinary materials are revealed. "Instantly," says Emerson, "the book becomes noxious. The guide is a tyrant." His attack on modern literature initiates another outpouring of contempt for those who admire it, "[m]eek young men . . . in libraries," "the restorers of readings, the emendators, the bibliomaniacs of all degrees" (CW.I.55–56). These caricatures of Emerson as collegian, schoolteacher, youthful journal-keeper echo the tirades against criticism he had once addressed to himself. The speaker of the essay, like the young Emerson, is trapped in excessive admiration of the past and disgust for contemporary readers (Americans) and writers (Englishmen).

A moment later, however, the meek secretary to the past, the victim of the emasculating power of influence, rises up against the tradition he has praised. Books

> are for nothing but to inspire. I had better never see a book than to be warped by its attraction. . . . The one thing . . . of value, is the active soul . . . free, sovereign. . . . This every man is entitled to. . . . [I]t is . . . not the privilege of . . . a favorite but the sound estate of every man.

Books are negated by their inspirational effect. The rhetoric of American democracy serves Emerson well here. Its outraged denunciations of privilege and tyranny provide a vocabulary strong enough for his resistance to bookish influences. Nevertheless, he confesses here that this combative stance originates in an earlier phase when he was "warped" by a book's "attraction." We witness the oscillation between influence and antagonism that structures so much of Emerson's prose. His tirade against literature grows hyperbolic as he equates books, the past, and all institutions: "[the soul] is progressive. The book, the college, the school of art, the institution of any kind, stop with some past utterance of genius. . . . They pin me down. They look backward, not forward." Yet he still acknowledges the essential ambivalence of the writer-as-reader. "Genius," he states, "is always sufficiently the enemy of genius by over-influence." His warlike metaphors reverse that "over-influence," the voluntary surrender to books that occurred prior to, but which is the true occasion of, "The American Scholar." The oration corrects a hermeneutical error. The "right way of reading," he insists, is to "read God directly," not to waste time on "other men's transcripts of their readings" (CW.I.56–58). This does not mean that we should run out of the library into the fields. Rather, it means that we must interpret books as we have always interpreted nature, as images of our own creativity and freedom.

He continues his attack on books by conceding that they have a certain usefulness. Returning to the "millions demanding to be fed," he elaborates on the metaphor of eating in a condescending tone that treats literature as a commodity. "I would not be hurried by any love of system, by any exaggeration of instincts, to underrate the Book," he begins, with a pompous double negative. Then, underrating books almost farcically, he grants them the nutritive value of "boiled grass and the broth of shoes"; after all, "the human mind can be fed by any knowledge." The discussion of books finally brings into being a reader strong enough to free himself from them. "[I]t needs a strong head" to bear a steady "diet" of "the printed page," Emerson warns. Only those capable of "creative reading" will thrive on it. Here an unabashed "I" materializes, capable of surviving the encounter with his own alienated majesty, "that which lies close to my own soul, that which I also had . . . thought and said" (CW.I.57–58). Aggression virtually always precipitates a recuperative moment in Emerson's essays. The speaker who initially possesses no authority of his own engages in conflict that makes possible a tonal change and a fierce first-person voice.

Section III of the essay repeats this pattern of revilement that generates revival. Again Emerson mocks the "mincing and diluted speech" of effeminate scholars, repeating the commonplaces of pub-lic opinion: "Men . . . are called 'the mass' and 'the herd.' " "The spirit of the American freeman is already suspected to be timid, imitative, tame." Throughout these paragraphs, he mimics the voices both of the "so-called 'practical men' of America" and of English reviewers (CW.I.59, 65, 69). The impersonal passive constructions in which he phrases these unpleasant banalities allow him to parody and to concur with both groups of Philistines. As in the journals of the mid-1820s, he hates scholars like himself as well as those who ignore them. Once again, aggression leads to egotism. He defines action as the thoughts of "the heroic mind" and defines heroism as reflection, "the transition through which [thought] passes from the unconscious to the conscious." Through reflection, a secondary or critical form of knowledge, the "disfranchised" establish "dominion." As in section I, the proliferation of first person pronouns signals the advent of a confident reader: "Only so much do I know, as I have lived. Instantly we know whose words are loaded with life, and whose not." Dominion restores community, though the sociable "ring" or "circuit" he enters becomes, in the passage that follows, the measure of the self. The world's attractions, he writes,

> make me acquainted with myself. I run eagerly into this resounding tumult. I grasp the hands of those next me, and take my place in the ring to suffer and to work, taught by an instinct that so shall the dumb abyss be vocal with speech. I pierce its order; I dissipate its fear; I dispose of it within the circuit of my expanding life. (CW.I.59)

In his next variation on the movement from deprivation to possession, the speaker initially presents himself as an author who is devoured by his readers. Economic metaphors convey his fear of the fate of writers "who have written out their vein." "I will not . . . trust the revenue of some single faculty, and exhaust one vein of thought," he vows (CW.I.60). But as a consumer of literature, he works authors to exhaustion. The omnivorous reader is responsible for the writer's depletion: "we drain all cisterns, and waxing greater by all these supplies, we crave a better and more abundant food. The man has never lived that can feed us ever" (CW.I.66). But Emerson knows that the roles of reader and writer give rise to each other, that "each fit reproduces the other" (CW.I.61). His biography of a poet, a vision of a career that proceeds from dumb withdrawal to articulate emergence, sums up the dynamics that organize "The American Scholar." The apprentice must accept "poverty and solitude," endure "the disdain of the able," and "stammer in his speech" (phrases echoed at the end of "The Poet"). The scorn heaped upon the young scholar is a necessary trial. His reward is to "receive and impart" the heart's "oracles," to "hear and promulgate" the verdicts of "Reason," in other words, to possess power over others: "he is master . . . of all men whose language he speaks, and of all into whose language his own can be translated" (CW.I.62–63). In the course of this fable, Emerson has traced his own progress from stammering self-contempt to self-determining eloquence. In the pages that follow, he reveals the extent to which this transformation or "translation" depends on acts of reading.

Like all good Romantics, Emerson knows that he lives in "the Reflective or Philosophical age," "the age of Introversion": "We are embarrassed with second thoughts. We cannot enjoy any thing for hankering to know whereof the pleasure consists. We are lined with eyes." After mimicking conventional Romantic laments about the sentimental condition, he interrogates them energetically, an equally Romantic gesture: "Must that needs be evil? . . . Is it so bad then? . . . Would we be blind?" The "discontent of the literary class" is a healthy sign of its ability to criticize past and present. Emerson identifies anti-authoritarianism with comparative criticism; the "age of Revolution" occurs "when the old and new stand side by side, and admit of being compared." Possessing this perspective, he echoes Wordsworth's glorification of "the near, the low, the common" and breezily dispenses with "the great, the remote, the romantic; what is doing in Italy or Arabia; what is Greek art, or Provencal Minstrelsy" (CW.I.66–67). He has reversed his youthful position, which consisted of admiring the exotic past and despising the ordinary present. In the course of this reversal, he has discovered the "new importance" of the individual. Criticism, philosophy, and "second thoughts" have made it possible for "each man" to "feel the world is his," something Emerson never feels except as a second thought. The ability to treat with others "as a sovereign state" and the feeling of confident originality are products of reading, not writing. In his final summary of the oration's central drama, Emerson once again draws on the confrontational possibilities of the historical enmity between Europe and America. America's young men, tired of imitating English culture, "turn drudges, or die of disgust,—some of them suicides." A reversal of their point of view would correct the balance of power, for "if the single man plant himself indomitably on his instincts, and there abide, the huge world will come round to him" (*CW*.I.68–69). A strong America is a metaphor for the scholar who has interpreted his sources and found them defective. Reading is the act of aggression necessary for his restored self-regard.

THE DIVINITY SCHOOL "ADDRESS"

The breakthrough from imitation to criticism is reenacted in most of Emerson's essays. In the Divinity School "Address" (1838), it occurs in the form of a more specialized demonstration of "creative reading." He undertakes to persuade professional students of the Bible that interpretation can make them free, "now," as he says in a journal entry, "that the SS [Sacred Scriptures] are read with purged eyes" (*JMN*.IV.93). Because of the prominence of its higher critical strategies, the "Address" bears careful comparison with "The Lord's Supper." We can evaluate just how Emerson's style has changed since the resignation sermon delivered six years earlier. In some ways the "Address" is more coherent than the sermon. It is wholly organized by the imperatives of Emerson's need to represent his own development and is not interrupted by efforts to conform to sermon conventions. On the other hand, Emerson's mature style is far more discontinuous than his earlier one. In the "Address," he again draws on the methods and subject matter of Biblical scholarship, but applies them even less systematically. The critical material is more fragmented, like all his "sources" by this time. He displays his learning, not in examinations of specific texts, but in the form of offhand remarks and casual illustrations. References are not seriously mustered as learned support for his arguments. Rather, they constitute a code. Emerson's irreverent citations let his academic audience know that the critical idioms in which they are expert can be turned against them. The language that he shares with his listeners is the means by which he differentiates himself from them. Allusion is no longer a way for him to pay homage to traditional authority, but to combat it. The "Address" is unique among Emerson's post-clerical works for its explicit reference to the higher criticism. Nevertheless, its structure is typical of his essays on any subject. Indeed, the difference between the Divinity School "Address" and "The Lord's Supper" can be accounted for largely by the more complete absorption in the "Address" of comparative criticism into the dynamics of the reader's sublime.

As in "The Lord's Supper," the speaker establishes himself before he introduces his arguments, showing that he cares more for self-dramatization than for his program. He makes himself present, above all, as an interpreter—of nature, of the Bible, of men. He has no need now to acknowledge the quarrels of institutional religion. Instead, he asserts himself with a demonstration of the power of figurative interpretation. The beautiful celebration of "refulgent summer" in the first paragraph "shrinks" in the second to "a mere illustration and fable" as "the mind . . . reveals the laws which traverse the universe" (CW.I.76). Nature becomes "merely" a figure for that mind. The discovery of unity turns all surface variety to "fable." The shocking reductiveness of this tactic, dramatized by the shift from luxurious, incantatory evocation to imageless statement, indicates that criticism will prove destructive as well as creative. As though sensing the violence of his opening move, Emerson quickly modulates into a more reverent tone. It is the desirous young reader of his early journals who says now, "I would study, I would know, I would admire forever" the "works of thought" of all ages. Admiring submission is a dangerous stage for the scholar, who always has to repudiate it. But in Emerson's essays, it is the earliest phase of the hero's biography. The fact that this phase is largely missing from "The Lord's Supper" suggests that it took Emerson longer to find a place in the essays for weakness than for strength. The Divinity School "Address" depicts the next phase as one in which he is led, through his perceptions of God, to self-consciousness, a typical movement of recovery. When he becomes aware of his "moral sentiment" as a spiritual law, man "is made the Providence to himself." This moral sentiment is an internalization of universal law; at this point in the "Address," self-consciousness still derives from the Not Me. As Emerson's praise of the moral sentiment waxes enthusiastic, however, this faculty sounds increasingly egotistical, or even, when he declares it to be "divine and deifying," blasphemous (CW.I. 76–79).

Emerson proceeds to treat psychological development and cultural education as episodes in a single process. He defines the religious or moral sentiment as man's knowledge that he is "illimitable." This is the onset of all self-consciousness: "Through [the religious sentiment] the soul first knows itself." Self-knowledge, in turn, marks the end of imitation and the beginning of originality; it "corrects the capital mistake of the infant man, who seeks to be great by following the great, and hopes to derive advantages *from another.*" Reflection shows the scholar that "the fountain of all good" is "in himself" and so he rejects external influence (CW.I.79). Self-knowledge is self-reliance, and self-reliance requires a turning against or away from cultural authorities. The radical criticism that turns nature into a figure for mind initiates a series of equations that lead to a theory of influence: moral sentiment = perception of universal law = self-consciousness = belief in self = divinity = end of imitation.

Having set forth the history of the self, Emerson begins his anti-authoritarian critique of the history of religion. His discourse on historical Christianity starts in paragraph 10, where for the first time in the "Address" he deploys the techniques of the higher criticism and of comparative religion. He does not dwell on the details of the Scriptural record. As relaxed as his use of critical learning had been in "The Lord's Supper," in the "Address" this material is even more malleable to the speaker's intentions. The moral sentiment, he declares, "successively creates all forms of worship." This sentiment "dwelled always deepest in the minds of men in the devout and contemplative East, not alone in Palestine, where it reached its purest expression, but in Egypt, in Persia, in India, in China." Simply by locating Christianity in a catalogue of the world's major religions—a characteristically offhand use of his reading—he espouses the conclusions of comparative scholars who treated them as analogous mythologies. Although Jesus made a "unique impression," he was only one of many "holy bards" who articulated "oriental genius." Emerson no sooner adduces history, however, than he devalues its historicity. Without "inspiration," spiritual experience—"[m]iracles, prophecy, poetry"—exists "as ancient history merely" and appears "ridiculous." It was not just Emerson's views on miracles or Jesus that proved offensive to his Unitarian audience, I believe, but also this assertion, in an academic setting, that truth cannot be taught, that knowledge about the past is incommunicable. "[I]t is not instruction, but provocation, that I can receive from another soul" (CW.I.80).

Because we have "forgotten" ourselves, religion is "ancient history merely"; the conviction that revelation occurred only in the past keeps us from exercising our power to experience it now. Mankind is trapped in a vicious circle. Emerson depicts, on the one hand, the maturation of the spiritual hero who knows that he is the meaning of the universe and tests all beliefs against his own "religious sentiment": "What another soul announces, I must find true in me, or wholly reject." Religion originates at any moment in the responses of such individuals. On the other hand, he treats this personality as the type of an earlier age from which we have fallen: "Once man was all; now he is an appendage, a nuisance." Emerson joins in a single narrative the man of moral sentiment and a culture so immoral that it relegates that sentiment to the past. This results in a curious oscillation between arrogance and despair. His tone shifts between the proud intransigence of the "I" ("on his word . . . I can accept nothing") and harsh pronouncements on the "comic or pitiful" life of his own time (CW.I.80). Significantly, the first use of a strong first person voice occurs when Emerson begins to excoriate the contemporary mind. As in virtually all of his essays, the ego requires an antagonist, or an antagonistic condition, in order to develop out of its imitative, submissive phase. The self-reliant soul can only appear in a civilization that oppresses him. The speaker of the "Address" defines himself by way of a cultural critique.

Emerson invites the graduating class to regard its religion critically as "the Cultus, or established worship of the civilized world." It is, he says, of "great historical interest for us." This is an example of Emerson's irony. We know by now what he thinks of "mere" history. He draws on the idiom of comparative religion to dispense with Christianity's special status in history. The single word "Cultus" applied to Boston Unitarianism annihilates its claims to exclusive possession of doctrinal truth simply by classing it with the religious practices of other tribes. At this point, Emerson's announcement that he merely intends to point out "two errors in . . . [the] administration" of Christianity blandly overlooks the fact that, according to his own reasoning, there is nothing worth administering (CW.I.81). Even when he is drawing continuously on Biblical scholarship, then, we often find that sequential statements do not relate logically. His ad hoc arguments and the references that support them rarely hold for more than a paragraph. The critique is overdetermined and indiscriminate. Nevertheless, these multiple deconstructions and reconstructions do not inhibit him. Emerson's borrowings derive their coherence from the dynamics of his voice, not from his ratiocination.

In the "Address," Emerson focuses less on the Bible's historical context and more on the crucial relationship between text and reader than in "The Lord's Supper." The first "error" he takes up is hermeneutical. Speaking figuratively in a "jubilee of sublime emotion," Christ said, "I am divine." But he was the victim of a disastrously literal misinterpretation: "The understanding caught this high chant from the poet's lips, and said, in the next age, 'This was Jehovah come down out of heaven. I will kill you, if you say he was a man.' " This error is specifically literary in nature. "The idioms of [Jesus'] language, and the figures of his rhetoric, have usurped the place of his truth" because we have failed to recognize that they are merely figures, Emerson contends. "[C]hurches are not built on his principles, but," mistakenly, "on his tropes." Institutionalization is the consequence of misinterpretation. Readers who take the Gospels literally develop an authoritarian style. "Historical Christianity"—like "eastern monarchy" (the very archetype of oppression)—"describes Christ to Europe and America" in language that is "appropriated and formal." It "paints a demigod, as the Orientals or the Greeks would describe Osirus or Apollo" (CW.I.81–82).

Read properly, however, the New Testament becomes a "Mythus," like "the poetic teaching of Greece and of Egypt." The same traditions that a few lines before represented oriental despotism now stand for the power of the imagination. Christian texts are joined with the other figurative modes Emerson celebrates, which he calls fable, poetry, metaphor, trope. His reading of the Gospels illustrates that what he values in figurative language is the fact that the reader, free to invent idiosyncratic or multiple interpretations, determines meaning. Jesus is Emerson's model reader because he "felt respect for Moses and the prophets; but no unfit tenderness at postponing their initial revelations." He "would not . . . be commanded" (CW.I.81). This is a useful precedent for Emerson, whose "respect" for Unitarians does not stop him from "postponing" their doctrine in favor of *his* personal law.

Figurative interpretation quickly becomes the basis for aggression. Emerson quotes Wordsworth's 1807 sonnet to express his revulsion from dogma:

One would rather be "A pagan suckled in a creed outworn,"
than to be defrauded of his manly right in coming into nature,
and finding not names and places, not land and professions,
but even virtues and truth foreclosed and monopolized.

Whereas Wordsworth blames himself ("We have given our hearts away . . . "), Emerson assumes that the offense of the fathers is deliberate. The denunciation of the elders' tyranny leads to an egotistical outburst in which he shows that he reads as Jesus did: "The divine bards are the friends of my virtue, of my intellect, of my strength. . . . Noble provocations go out from them, inviting me also . . . to resist evil; to subdue the world; and to Be. And thus . . . Jesus serves us, and thus only." He responds to the Scriptures no differently than to "Empaminondas, or Washington . . . a true orator, an upright judge, a dear friend" (CW.I.82–83). Statements like these carry to an impudent extreme the higher critics' dictum that sacred texts must be read like secular ones.

"The second defect of the traditional and limited way of using the mind of Christ" follows from the interpretive errors explored in the first part of the "Address." In Part Two Emerson attacks contemporary preachers and educators (well-represented in his audience) for failing to make "the Moral Nature, that Law of laws . . . the fountain of the established teaching in society." As he urges that Christianity be taught as art, his theme continues to be "creative reading." He offers his younger auditors the skills with which to displace their elders. Instead of treating revelations as poetry, which Herder and others had done, he defines poetry as revelation. The man "enamored of . . . excellency, becomes its priest or poet"—a subversive equation. If every man is potentially a poet, then there is potentially an infinite number of inspired texts—which, as he points out, contradicts "the assumption that the Bible is closed." The received text of the Bible itself becomes the symbol of a constricting past. The critical yet still desirous reader is as powerful as the poet. He demands to know "[w]here . . . sounds the persuasion, that by its very melody imparadises my heart, and so affirms its own origin in heaven? Where shall I hear words such as in elder ages drew men to leave all and follow?" (CW.I.83–85,89). At the very moment Emerson declares his autonomy from teachers, he calls for a Christ; he is enamored of the romance of alienated majesty. This evaluative speaker, with his half-nostalgic, half-parodic echoes of the Gospels, now determines the validity of religion. This characteristic Emersonian shift from imagining himself as creator to expressing a reader's wishes indicates that, despite the intensity of each voice, they are perpetually collapsing into each other. Neither suppresses the other for very long. As the ending of the "Address" will show more clearly, these two fantasies, of origination and receptivity, seem to precipitate each other.

The exercise of critical power by this reader/poet can be frightening. The splendid scene of a preacher competing with a snowstorm for the churchgoers' attention shows what happens when the auditor's subjective response is the measure of revelation. Emerson treats the failure to inspire as an act of aggression against the parishioner: "Whenever the pulpit is usurped by a formalist, then is the worshipper defrauded and disconsolate. We shrink as soon as the prayers begin, which do not uplift, but smite and offend us." But the bored listener "need not smite the negligent servant" in return, for "the swift retribution of his sloth" will be automatic.

Any encounter with "a man of wit and energy" will strike "terror" into the heart of "the hollow, dry, creaking" formalist. To the Divinity School senior, this must have sounded more like a threat than a promise. The prospect of having to thrill one's congregation every Sunday or else face the charge that one has "travestied and depreciated . . . behooted and behowled" (*CW*.I.85–88) the law is daunting, to say the least. The new authority granted to the reader or auditor imposes a new burden on the poet or preacher.

Emerson has come full circle. Criticism frees the young scholar (the speaker of the essay) from excessive humility, only to make him so potent that other young scholars (his listeners) are threatened with paralysis in turn. The escape from influence that he proposes is, in fact, a substitution, not a structural change. The original relation of source to student persists transposed in his image of demanding congregations bullying inadequate speakers. The pressure to be great comes from the present audience instead of past masters. As always, however, Emerson relieves the potential oppressiveness of his system by rapidly moving individuals through it; no one occupies any stance for more than an instant, which is why, of course, "transition" is one of his favorite words. He addresses the uneasiness he has aroused by urging the students to join the reader's rebellion. They must ignore "secondary knowledge" of "Saints and Prophets" such as St. Paul, George Fox, and Swedenborg. As imitators, they are doomed to "hopeless mediocrity," but if they "slight" these influences and hold to "high and universal aims," they "instantly . . . must shine" (*CW*.I.89–91). The way to cope with the discomfort of being interpreted is to reinterpret one's sources, which enables one to be an original preacher, which satisfies those intimidating parishioners.

Emerson invites the Divinity School graduates to follow him into the open air, the "refulgent summer," of free speech: "Yourself a newborn bard of the Holy Ghost,—cast behind you all conformity, and acquaint men at first hand with Deity. . . . [L]ive with the privilege of the immeasurable mind." He proposes that the future preachers behave aggressively toward the parishioners who, in Emerson's quasi narrative, have just threatened them. The graduates should not be "too anxious to visit periodically all families" in their "parish connection." The preacher should play hard-to-get and thus seduce his flock. Solitude is power because others are drawn to it. By "trusting your own heart," "present or absent you shall be followed by their love as by an angel." Emerson thus advises young men to treat their congregations as they would their teachers. "Slight . . . by preoccupation of mind," he urges, "orators . . . poets . . . commanders" until they "feel your right" (CW.I.90–91). As always, his model of social relations corresponds to his theory of how to cope with cultural influence. Both turn on an aggressive reaction to felt inferiority. The "robe of eloquence" that represented to Emerson the glamor of literary tradition and mastery of that tradition (JMN.II.237–42) becomes, in the following passage, the emblem of resistance:

> There are men who rise refreshed on hearing a threat; men to whom a crisis which intimidates and paralyzes the majority . . . comes graceful and beloved as a bride. Napoleon said of Massena, that he was not himself until the battle began to go against him; then, when the dead began to fall in ranks around him, awoke his powers of combination, and he put on terror and victory as a robe. (CW.I.91)

In his peroration, Emerson revives the vocabulary of his earlier discussion of "historical Christianity." "What shall we do?" he asks. Clearly, "all attempts to . . . establish a Cultus with new rites and forms" are "vain." Through preaching, "the speech of man to men," however, "new life [can] be breathed . . . through the forms already existing." The essay ends with a call for "the new Teacher, that shall follow so far those shining laws, that he shall see them come full circle; shall see their rounding complete grace; shall see the world to be the mirror of the soul." The image of the circle is an artful form of closure, for we are carried back to the discovery of law with which the "Address" began. The consciousness of universal laws within and without ourselves, we recall, is the origin of power; the critical acts which reveal "the world to be the mirror of the soul" generate the "newborn bard" (CW.I.93,90). Emerson's artfulness should not blind us to the fact that he is returning to dependency. This is a move that did not occur at the end of "The Lord's Supper," but which is crucial in the later essays. He ends by desiring a teacher who will show us that the world is his mirror. Once again, we will be reduced to accepting secondhand revelations. The yearning tone of this concluding expression of desire seems wholly unnecessary, since the "new Teacher" came into being in the first two pages of the "Address," when Emerson found himself at the center of the universe. We have encountered similar gestures of surrender before in the "Address"; they occur within and at the end of many of the essays. Why does Emerson abandon self-reliance and elect dispossession? It can only be in order to move again through the roles I have traced: the figure of the "youthful" reader who feels himself invaded by authors; the aggressive critic who speaks in ironic disjunctions; the creative ego that finds itself in others. I have treated this as a developmental sequence, which it is, as we meet it in the journals and in "The Lord's Supper." In the Divinity School "Address" and other essays, however, the linear progression becomes a recurring cycle. Emerson does not rest at the point of his greatest power. Instead, he reexperiences the power of books and teachers over him and perpetually turns on them as he again enters their fields of force. Even as he dramatizes the antagonistic relationships among influence, analysis, and invention, he shows, by repeatedly moving through them, that these states are contemporaneous. He finally takes more pleasure in the motion that makes them almost simultaneously possible than in the exercise of authority.

· 5 ·

"THE POET"

I turn now to "The Poet" (1844) in order to trace in greater detail the motions that have become apparent in *Nature,* "The American Scholar," and the Divinity School "Address." "The Poet" has the advantage of being typical; it is not generically one of a kind, like *Nature,* nor can its aggressiveness be attributed to the tensions of a particular occasion, like that of "The American Scholar" and the "Address." The significance of its structural similarity to those works emerges all the more clearly because of the difference in its ostensible subject. In fact, almost any essay would do for a rather exhaustive (I hope not exhausting) investigation of the cycle of antithetical personae that generates an Emersonian essay, in which I will ask more insistently what motivates the shifts from one attitude to another. The kinds of transitions that become problematic in "The Poet" are the sudden plunges from sublimity to irony, the abrupt substitutions of nature and instinct for self-conscious human authors, and the manifestations of the usual figures—the needy reader, the creative reader, the anxious young poet, the poet in his apotheosis as liberating god. Although sorting out these roles becomes more difficult the more closely one looks at the essays, an intensive reading of "The Poet" confirms, as well as complicates, the patterns we have traced in earlier works. It enables us to analyze with greater precision the defensive and aggressive functions of Emerson's irony, his repetitions, and his contradictions.

Emerson defines his initial stance in "The Poet" by two oppositions: first, us versus them, that is, the speaker and his audience versus the "selfish and sensual" "umpires of taste" and second, us as distinct from him, the Poet. Emerson stands over conventional critics, his selfish inferiors, but, as a reader himself, looks up to the heroic poet. Three similes in the first paragraph instigate this hierarchical self-definition. The worthless cultivation of "amateurs" is merely local, "as if you should rub a log of dry wood in one spot to produce fire, all the rest remaining cold." Next "We"—Emerson and ourselves—possess sparks of the spirit only "as fire is put into a pan to be carried about." But, finally, as "children of the fire" we may aspire to join the "highest minds of the world" which attain "accurate adjustment" (W.III.3–4).

In the opening movement of the essay, then, we know Emerson first by what he is against—what Bishop calls "enemy values"— and second by what he lacks and desires.[1] False critics, referred to abstractly as "Criticism . . . infested with a cant of materialism," are his antagonists. Their knowledge consists only of "some study of rules and particulars, or some limited judgment of color or form . . . exercised for amusement or for show." Emerson, as the true critic, occupies the middle ground between "them" and "Him." He damns the unnamed contemporary poet (who the journals show to be Tennyson [JMN.VII.471]) with the faint praise of resembling "the landscape-garden of a modern house." Yet he remains, like us, a listener and reader. We "need an interpreter," he confesses, including himself among the needy: "Too feeble fall the impressions of nature on *us* to make *us* artists." We who "miswrite the poem" admit the superiority of "men of more delicate ear"; unlike contemporary wits, we "know that the secret of the world is profound, but who or what shall be our interpreter, *we* know not" (W.III. 3–9,11. emphasis added). As Bishop finely intuits, there is in this prose—as perhaps in all prose—"a latent connection among aggression, writing, and identity." Affirmation of Emerson's "new self," Bishop observes, necessitates opponents: "One's identity is found by distinguishing a self from those who are not oneself."[2] Emerson, like the general he pictured in the Divinity School "Address," is "not himself until the battle [begins] to go against him"; he is one of those men "who rise refreshed on hearing a threat" (CW.I.91–92).

The speaker's position in the hierarchy between "theologians" and "the highest minds" is revealed stylistically as Emerson's rhetoric moves from diminution to dilation:

Theologians think it a pretty air-castle to talk of the spiritual meaning of a ship or a cloud, of a city or a contract, but they prefer to come again to the solid ground of historical evidence. . . . But the highest minds of the world have never ceased to explore the double meaning, or shall I say the quadruple or the centuple or much more manifold meaning, of every sensuous fact. (W.III.4)

The scornful miniaturization of "a pretty air-castle" yields to the explosive multiplication of meanings available to the poet. Similarly, the "recent writer of lyrics" has a head that resembles "a music-box of delicate tones," whereas the "eternal man" of superhuman dimensions stands "out of our low limitations" like a mountain peak (W.III.9).

Emerson's position as the man in the middle accounts for many such tonal variations. As critic, he argues and insists; as aspiring poet, he yearns. He belittles heroes and sages as "secondaries and servants; as sitters or models in the studio of a painter, or as assistants who bring building-materials to an architect." Yet this is followed by the humility of his own failure: "[W]e hear those primal warblings and attempt to write them down, but we lose ever and anon a word or a verse and substitute something of our own, and thus miswrite the poem." In the first role, he speaks as "emperor in his own right"; in the second, as "any permissive potentate" (W.III.8,7). These oscillations correspond to his changing relationships with his reader; when he is needy, his "we" includes us; when he is strong, his "I" excludes us. There is no question, I think, that the latter condition gives him greater pleasure. He strikes out rhetorically at an opponent, be it idea, feeling, or person. The recoil from this encounter moves him from the desire for power toward the exercise of it. The essay gets underway with an attack on "umpires of taste" that carries Emerson to his true subject, the "man of Beauty." Barely restrained scorn for the "recent writer of lyrics" and other "men of talents" catapults him into an entirely different mood in which he imagines a thought so "passionate and alive" that it constitutes a "metre-making argument." He does not yet think this thought; his is still the passion of deprivation, not

of possession. Nevertheless, the energetic rebound from the encounter with critics carries him onward and upward to "the aurora
of a sunrise which was to put out all the stars" (W.III.4, 9–10).
Sublimity is the effect of aggression, and also, as we shall see, of
reading.

The memory of the auroras is one of the essay's high points,
"high" both stylistically and by virtue of the sublime emotions it
describes. Emerson mentions the appearance of the aurora borealis
in September 1839, in his journal (JMN.VII.238–39). It was a
fairly recent memory when he wrote the entry that forms the kernel
of this passage. The journal editors speculate that William Ellery
Channing the younger, who was visiting Emerson at the time, is
the subject of this entry (JMN.VII.463n.). In that case, the "youth
who sat near me at table" of the essay would really have been a
youth who was a guest at his table. Instead of involving two young
men of about the same age, as the essay passage implies, the an-
ecdote concerns Emerson at thirty-nine and Channing at twenty-
four. Furthermore, Emerson had serious reservations about Channing's ability. The essay, then, by setting the memory in the distant
past of his own youth, invents a naïve Emerson. The quasi-paternal
relationship that in fact prevailed between Emerson and Channing
is reversed; Channing becomes the primary author, Emerson the
reader of vast authorial ambitions. In the essay version, Emerson's
heightened rhetoric is caused by his distance from the light. He
has received the "good news" second hand: "I remember when I
was young how much I was moved one morning by tidings that
genius had appeared in a youth who sat near me at table." He
seems not even to have actually read the "hundreds of lines" then
composed. Even the poet "could not tell whether that which was
in him was therein told." Emerson hears an account of the writing
of a poem: a much-mediated vision. Yet his metaphors claim that
for him, as well as for the youth, "all was changed." Space and
time are reordered: "Boston seemed to be at twice the distance
it had the night before . . . Rome, —what was Rome?" Loci of
past and present authority fall away. As verbs shift into the
present tense ("These stony moments are still sparkling and
animated!") he experiences directly the new heaven and new

earth that a few sentences before were known only by report (*W*.III.10–11).

The justly famous auroras are the central metaphor for imagination in this passage. "Tidings" of good news, the silencing of the oracles, the advent of a world-changing youth draw on Gospel accounts of the Nativity. The nocturnal occasion—"all night . . . these fine auroras have been streaming"—recalls the shepherds' vigil rewarded by an angelic visitation, the "sunrise which . . . put out all the stars." Complicating the Nativity imagery with mythological associations, the auroras become sacred fires burning before oracles or, perhaps, the oracle itself as the voice or "fires" of nature. The metaphoric sequence ends magnificently in an image of the human face reminiscent of Blake's engraving "Glad Day": "all night, from every pore, these fine auroras have been streaming" (*W*.III.10–11).

The vision of nativity granted to Emerson is apparently as radical as that experienced by his "poet." His response depends on a suppressed syllogism: if genius can strike another here and now, it can strike me, too. The poet is ecstatic over his poem; Emerson, the reader, ecstatic with ambition. In the auroras passage, the reader senses his potential superiority to the poet. "Plutarch and Shakespeare . . . and Homer" had been his teachers; the sources of his culture had been as remote as Greece, Rome, and England. The change to the present tense accentuates precisely that aspect of the occasion that so overjoys Emerson: "poetry has been written *this very day*. . . . [T]hat wonderful spirit *has not expired!*" (*W*.III. 10–11, emphasis added). He forgets the other youth and puts himself in his place. The signs of power—light, fire, oracular voices—attest to the strength of his aspiration. The mere thought that "the spirit" has not died out, that he might be part of an unbroken apostolic succession reaching back to Homer, stimulates a fantasy of Orphic and prophetic powers. Exposure to poetic achievement so inflames Emerson's desire for literary greatness that he imaginatively elides his own development. Without having written anything, he attains the "condition of true naming" (*W*.III.16). The actual poem then composed matters only insofar as it proves that power is accessible.

But the rhetoric that bears witness to influx quickly recoils in the opposite direction. The rising sun gives way to collapse, the optative mood to self-mockery. The next paragraph breaks in half with the "but" in "Such is the hope, but the fruition is postponed." Suddenly the future, not the past, is remote. Emerson is betrayed, allegedly by the man who soars only as high as "a fowl or a flying fish," but also, Icaruslike, by his own desire for "the all-piercing, all-feeding and ocular air of heaven" (W.III.12). The absurd poet, flapping his stubby wings, is as much a victim of this desire as his follower.

Emerson's shifts in tone and stance are usually brought about by antithetical or negative reactions. The triple epithet—"all-piercing, all-feeding . . . ocular"—offers a clue as to the antagonist that makes possible the shift from sublimity to humor here. Personified as a transparent eyeball looking downward, the aggressor seems to be the air itself. "Piercing" describes the power of vision and "all-feeding" the nourishing quality of a manna-bestowing heaven. Yet "piercing" can also mean "wounding" and "all-feeding" suggests "devouring." Like Blake's sky god Urizen, this is an image of the sublime conceived as an external objective rather than discovered within by that key Emersonian motion, surprise. Desire that is too self-conscious ends up reflecting on itself from a distance. Under the scrutiny of the "objective" mind, the yearning for transcendence appears ridiculous. The speaker parodies his own aspiration: "I shall mount above these clouds and opaque airs in which I live" becomes "this winged man . . . whirls me into mists, then leaps and frisks about with me as it were from cloud to cloud." Emerson hears the winged man "still affirming that he is bound heavenward," a deft ironic touch. Colloquialisms—"I tumble down . . . into my old nooks"—effect a stylistic descent and convey his comic disillusion before he asserts it outright: "I . . . have lost my faith in the possibility of any guide who can lead me thither where I would be" (W.III.12–13). All this reads like an echo and a parody of Hugh Blair, who, with serious misgivings, popularized the Romantic sublime:

The Poet is out of sight, in a moment. He gets up into the clouds; becomes *so abrupt in his transitions; so eccentric and irregular* in his motions, and of course *so obscure,* that we essay in vaine to follow him, or to partake of his raptures.[3]

The "of course" is priceless.

Every transcendental flight in "The Poet" is similarly denied or negated, usually at once, by "descents of the spirit . . . as fraught with ecstasy as any ascent Emerson could make," and often fraught with humor, as well.[4] The pattern strongly suggests that descent is caused by ascent. The reflex is skeptical rather than nihilistic; inventive and witty, not despairing. As readings of two or three subsequent passages will show, Emerson's reversals or inversions of sublimity are characterized by playful images (fowl and flying fish), a comic stance ("tumbling down"), and an ironic tone ("being myself a novice"). Here, the fantasy of poethood cannot stand the return of reflection. One way of conceiving of Emerson's task in the essays is as an effort to find a sublime that does not dissolve under the scrutiny of the critical, self-conscious mind.

Directly following his "tumble" into disappointment, Emerson entertains "new hope," and we wonder if the cycle of ascent and descent is about to repeat itself. However, this part of the essay (paragraphs 10–24) exhibits tendencies somewhat different from those of the opening section. A new element appears: nature, the world of "things." This permits Emerson to avoid an excessive imaginative investment in mortal writers. He turns away from poets who mislead their "victims" to seek a guarantee for the poetic office in the earth itself: Nature "has insured the poet's fidelity to his office of announcement and affirming . . . by the beauty of things." For the moment, Emerson theorizes that art originates in nature instead of in the poetic imagination. But power, although attributed to nature, still takes linguistic forms. Everything signifies. Men who take advantage of nature's offer of a "picture-language" are rewarded with "a second, wonderful value," the "new and higher beauty" conferred by expression (*W.*III.13). Meaning is intensified as symbolic parts join to form wholes symbolic to the second power. Images express ideas; body reveals spirit; form conveys character. The reader and would-be poet beholds a redundancy of signifiers: images, symbols, beauty, language. Significance need not be created, for it surrounds us. In shifting from poet to nature, Emerson has substituted text for author—a strategy that temporarily relieves him from considerable anxiety.

"Everything signifies" has as its corollary "every man is so far a poet as to be susceptible of these enchantments of nature." Insofar as one is a "susceptible" reader of nature, one is a poet. Where "all men have the thoughts whereof the universe is the celebration," democracy prevails among men and objects alike. "Nature" is a leveling agent who demotes winged pretenders while elevating mean subjects and low language. If poetry is defined as responsiveness to things, not just "men of leisure and cultivation" but also "hunters, farmers, grooms and butchers" are potential artists. A characteristic "not more . . . than" construction suggests the presence of shadowy authorial opponents: "The schools of poets and philosophers are not more intoxicated with their symbols than the populace with theirs" (W.III.15–16). The extended fable of collaboration between egalitarian society and nature is Emerson's revenge on the anti-democratic, over-educated poet.

After the first celebration of nature, we seem to encounter a detour, but the accidental discovery of the immanent "secret of the world" reveals one of the advantages of setting nature up as artist. A favorite passage from Spenser's "Hymn to Beauty" precipitates a new cognition or, since Emerson knows at once where he is, a recognition:

> Here we find ourselves suddenly not in a critical speculation
> but in a holy place, and should go very warily and reverently.
> We stand before the secret of the world, there where Being
> passes into Appearance and Unity into Variety. (W.III.14)[5]

The change in "place" is actually a change in *topos*, for it describes the shift from "critical speculation" to "holy," that is, Miltonic and Biblical, tones; from analysis to sublimity. We can only discover the holy place inadvertently; we "find ourselves suddenly" arrested. This is how we escape critical speculation. Surprise evades the dangers of self-consciousness, particularly the excess of hope which led to the too-strenuous and disillusioning pursuit of the "winged man." Emerson surrenders the initiative to what he calls "nature" in order for the world to take him by surprise; truth seems holier for being found, not earned.

As long as nature possesses the language-making power, the structures of sentences and paragraphs tend toward parallel repetitions and away from distinctions or oppositions. Emerson's demonstration of democratic symbolism takes the form of a series of equations in which the forceful voice of individual ambition yields to the language of the common man and of nature itself: "the north wind . . . rain . . . stone and wood and iron. . . . Lowell goes in a loom, and Lynn in a shoe, and Salem in a ship. . . . [T]he cider-barrel, the log-cabin, the hickory-stick, the palmetto" (W.III.16). But the lull in Emerson's rhetoric of aggression is only temporary. Among the *sententiae* that compose the interchangeable parts of the paragraph beginning "Beyond this universality of the symbolic language," one stands out: "We can come to use [symbols] yet with a terrible simplicity." Such heightenings signal, or effect, the re-entrance of the poet. Catalogues have filled the world with words, facts, and men, but these begin to vanish. Simplicity is realized as he "disposes very easily of the most disagreeable facts." The sense of accelerating motion (nature adopts them "very fast") and hyperbole ("the fact of mechanics has not gained a grain's weight"; "[l]ife . . . can dwarf any and every circumstance") create a rhetorical updraft (W.III.17–19). The winged man is once more among us.

With him come the combative distinctions of the opening paragraphs. The poet who purportedly heals "dislocation and detachment" also brings them into being. In this part of the essay, the motif of the circle represents the poet's relationship to others. The beehive and the "geometrical web" are images of the symmetrical whole that forms around him wherever he unifies by his "insight" a landscape that appears "broken up." Nature's "vital circles" repeat the poet's appropriating gesture. It persists through the "centred mind," the "curve of the sphere," and the situation of the country boy who centers himself in the city as the poet has in the landscape. The circle can be a figure of either inclusion or exclusion, depending upon one's point of view. Initially it incorporates "millions" of "particulars," as the poet draws nature into his gravitational field. When he begins to dominate, however, its circumference excludes the speaker of the essay and us, its readers. We are "intelligent" but not original; we "inhabit symbols," but do not recognize them. The poet is the active agent who "turns the world to glass"; we are the spectators to whom he "shows . . . all things" in their correct order. He is "nearer" to the center than we are, and shares the fluidity of the world's molten core while the objects we perceive stand "dumb and inanimate" at the petrified surface (W.III.18–21).

The distinction between "us" and "Him" signals a resurgence of the poet's authority at the cost of nature's—and at the cost of Emerson, the reader. This is one of the intriguing moments when Emerson seems to elect inferiority or to prefer vicarious to direct gratification. An act of aggression establishes the poet's dominance; the world is "put under the mind for verb and noun." Things fall "under" his mind, both as subjects live "under" their ruler and as we view a cell "under" a magnifying glass. Perception becomes a metaphor for power, as it always does in Emerson's writings. In a synaesthetic celebration of several kinds of power, he asserts that perception makes possible control, expression, and kinesis. "[T]hat better perception" discovers perpetual motion, first in thought, then in things. Emerson blurs the distinction between the "stability of the thought" and the "fugacity of the symbol" with the notion of "multiform" thought. Energy is contagious, a force "within . . . every creature . . . impelling it to ascend into a higher form." Instinct and rhetoric combine in speech that "flows with the flowing of nature." This influx brings about the predicted condition of "terrible simplicity," but the achievement of transparency definitively casts "us"—including Emerson—in a subordinate role: "As the eyes of Lyncaeus were said to see through the earth, so the poet turns the world to glass, and shows us all things in their right series and procession." This is the holy place where the poet "alone" witnesses "metamorphosis," the "secret of the world." He is "one step nearer to things" than his readers (W.III.20–21). Once again, Emerson experiences a moment of sublime vision at the cost of dependency. The trappings of the Romantic sublime here do not result in the elevation of the reader over the author who has overimpressed him. The linearity of the catalogue—"sex, nutriment, gestation, birth, growth"— gives way to vertical motion as particulars pass "into the soul of man, to suffer there a change and reappear a new and higher fact." "[A]stronomy, chemistry, vegetation and animation" are realigned on the sublime axis of height and depth: "[the poet] knows why the plain or meadow of space was strown with these flowers we call suns and moons and stars; why the great deep is adorned with animals, with men, and gods." The last sentence of the paragraph grows out of the first. The mind that put the world under it becomes the poet who rides "the horses of thought" (W.III.21). In the space between the two metaphors, thought has subsumed things and taken flight.

Just as the conquest of nature by the poet is at hand, Emerson reverts to the theory of poetry as natural process. He apparently feels no need to reconcile what seem to us competing claims. Language making is first willed, then as automatic as the growth of "a leaf out of a tree." The poet's authority as "Namer" is taken over by a mother who "baptizes herself." Emerson delights at one moment in the "detachment or boundary" established by names; at another, in attachment or continuity when naming is redefined as "a second nature, grown out of the first as a leaf out of a tree" (W.III.21–22). This was a familiar paradox even in Shakespeare's time—*vide* Polixenes and Perdita on nature's art.[6] The peculiarity of Emerson's version is that he will neither recognize the paradox nor resolve it. Man and nature, as creators, do have substantive differences in "The Poet," however. As I suggested earlier, the poet is self-conscious and nature, as sheer process, is not. There seems to be a trade-off. The attributes of power—vision, motion, voice—accrue mostly to the poet. Nature bears no burden of consciousness, but her powers of transformation are less radical. The strain of poethood seems to make Emerson want an unreflective, nonhuman, and wholly natural art. When nature is dominant, on the other hand, he grows restless with her benign organic forces and yearns for his antithetical hero. "Nature" frequently appears to stand for an intermittent, saving forgetfulness. Here it no doubt saves the speaker from the bathetic collapse that resulted from his first episode of enthusiastic soaring.

Emerson's attitude toward nature here is somewhat different from the "nostalgia" attributed by de Man to Romantic poets, despite the fact that de Man describes their similarly "alternating feelings of attraction and repulsion . . . towards nature."[7] Emerson's rhetoric reveals more clearly than theirs his awareness that nature's authorship is a fiction. We hardly need ask ourselves whether he means that names literally grow out of nature "as a leaf out of a tree"; we know to take this as hyperbole. Throughout "The Poet," the rhapsodic status of his assertions is obvious:

> What we call nature is a certain self-regulated motion or change; and nature does all things by her own hands, and does not leave another to baptize her but baptizes herself; and this through the metamorphosis again. (*W*.III.22)

The repetitive "and-and-and" construction of this sentence expresses enthusiasm without demanding our rational assent, and Emerson's acknowledgment of the figurative meaning of "what we call nature" conveys his sophisticated awareness of its metaphoric quality.

After substituting nature for the poet, Emerson suddenly—but not, by now, surprisingly—reintroduces the human author. He calls upon the Orphic poet, whom his argument has just rendered unnecessary, a repeated gesture that indicates how little sentiment he really has for nature. He would have us believe that the words of the Orphic poet which follow are especially persuasive, uttered by one possessing particular authority. In *Nature,* the voice of the Orphic poet is a serious, heightened one. In "The Poet," however, as in other essays, Emerson is more skeptical about Orphic powers. This bard sounds too much like the disillusioned speaker earlier in the essay to be convincingly sublime. As before, our expectations of sublimity are aroused, then deflated by parodic images, a comic fall, and a humorous tone. Quantitative extremes ("billions of spores," "two rods off") and hyperbolic adjectives ("a fearless, sleepless, deathless progeny") sound comical, not weighty. "[V]ivacious offspring" of the poet take to the air, beating their emblematic wings; the "new self" has become outrageously plural. Emerson keeps his brood alive with *ad hoc* allegorizing. Suddenly we have not one flock but two. The songs "flying immortal from their mortal parent" are pursued by "clamorous flights of censures, which swarm in far greater numbers and threaten to devour them." This time, instead of Emerson tumbling down into his old nooks, critics "fall plump down and rot." "Censures," not desirous emulators, pursue the poet. Their motive is not aspiration but attack, and their ensuing collapse is thus thoroughly deserved. With villains substituted for victims, the airborne songs "ascend and leap and pierce into the deeps of infinite time" unscathed (W.III. 23–24).

The Orphic poet is fair game; Emerson has little patience with expert testimony, even of his own invention. The Poet waxes hyperbolical until Emerson's skeptical reflex reacts and his own overstatements strike him as funny. The longer he dwells on a thought—particularly a "sublime" thought—the more susceptible he becomes to laughter. Hence Emerson's climaxes are often comical. In this instance, I think it is the mechanical aspect of nature's activity that begins to amuse him. He parodies his own complicated metaphoric apparatus of fungus, gills, spores, and sowing in the anatomical details of the flying melodies and their "plump" pursuers. He uses the devices of allegory to ridicule the excesses of allegory itself. The object of his humor is the Orphic speaker of the parable. Nature and poems mockingly collaborate to escape poet and critics. The device of the Orphic poet is a witty turn against the wrong kind of sublimity.

As we continue to read through "The Poet," we find that the essay repeats itself. Certain tones and attitudes generate each other in predictable ways: the desire for and the exercise of power, the celebration of and skepticism about the hero-poet, sublime transcendence and ironic descent. Alternation between these, not a developing argument of "dialectical" synthesis, accounts for the progress of the essay. Each repetition is also a variation, however, so the cumulative effect is expansive, not reductive. We learn the full implications of each stance and motion. More importantly, we learn that there is, finally, no resolution; such motions are unending. In the paragraph following the bard's speech, another one of these cycles begins. Emerson first returns to the theme of "organic" expression. Objects automatically generate the poems of which they are the subjects. But almost immediately, authorial inspiration revives and nature yields to the supernatural. Language appears that we will associate with the poet at the height of his powers as liberating god. Metaphors of transparency ("making things translucid to others") and excess ("intellect doubled on itself") are part of this mood, as is the occasional touch of Old Testament grandeur ("his speech is thunder, his thought is law"). Motion accelerates. Metamorphosis "does not stop"; following and suffering, flowing and circulating speed up until the poet's "centrifugal tendency" is great enough to fling him "out into free space" (W.III.25–28). Organic process gradually gives way to instantaneous and unnatural change described as magic, madness, and drunkenness. The speaker once more participates vicariously in inspiration. As eyewitness, Emerson again interprets the work of art as a prophecy of his own poem. This time, he is not defended by irony. His youthful memory of the unnamed sculptor repeats the previous account of the auroras. "I knew in my younger days" echoes "I remember when I was young," and the dawn that imbues Phosphorus recalls the auroral light. Like the youth who "could tell nothing but that all was changed," the sculptor is "unable to tell directly what made him happy or unhappy, but by wonderful indirections he could tell" (W.III.24).

Through a complex sequence of similes, the poet's power begins to grow. Passive Lockean perception ("in the sun, objects paint their images on the retina of the eye") is likened to the way things "paint a . . . copy of their essence in his mind." Then "the metamorphosis of things into higher organic forms" illustrates "their change into melodies." Finally, the eye's reflection of form is analogous to the musical image of "its daemon or soul." Emerson uses the word "daemon" to mean an attendant spirit or genius. But the daemon's stance "over everything" betrays a power that belongs to other connotations of the daemonic, a "field of force" occupied by the "more than rational energy of imagination."[8] Daemonization—taking the daemon that stands over nature into his own

y"—is the poet's reward for his boldness in entering that
'his speech is thunder, his thought is law, and his words
iversally intelligible as the plants and animals." The quest
traditionally routed through the underworld is implicit in the
movement "into" and "through": "new passages are opened for
us into nature; the mind flows into and through things hardest and
highest, and the metamorphosis is possible." The "passage out into
free space" follows the journey down into the earth (W.III.25,
27–28).

We encounter the following dynamic, then. The "possessed and
conscious intellect" of the aspiring poet wants to augment "his
privacy of power as an individual man." His goal is to know the
world directly, which means, for Emerson, to control matter ("he
disposes of disagreeable facts"), other men (as liberator, teacher,
language maker), and, ultimately, time. Perceiving "a great public
power" out there in "things," he sees the world as the object of
his desire. He defines the "Not Me" (CW.I.8) as what the self
would be: ethereal, auroral, divine. Although the poet flows out
into and mingles with things, his identity does not dissolve. On
the contrary, he absorbs nature into himself. Speaking for and as
the Not Me, he mediates between it and all other men. What looks
like loss is aggrandizement. Emerson's hero acknowledges power
other than his own only to "take advantage of it" (W.III.26, 28).
He risks losing his soul in order to gain the whole world. The
inebriation caused by a heady draught of "instinct" calls for re-
strictions, as though Emerson seeks to discipline his dream of
power. No "spurious mode of attaining freedom" is permitted;
these lead into "baser places" where poets are "punished for that
advantage they won, by a dissipation and deterioration" (a phrase
that condemns both aggression and substance abuse). The habit of
living "on a key so low that the common influences . . . delight
him" protects the poet from an excess or the wrong kind of imaginative stimulation. Midway between the bare common of *Nature*
and the bleak rocks of "Experience," "the lonely waste of the
pinewoods" is an appropriate setting for the "radiance of wisdom"
in "The Poet" (W.III.28–29).[9]

Throughout these paragraphs, the speaker of the essay has been vicariously benefiting from the poet-hero's progress. After all, it has been a characteristic of the sublime since Longinus that the mind of the reader "swells in transport and inward pride, as if what was only heard had been the product of its own invention."[10] Having himself escaped from "the custody of that body in which he is pent up, and of that jail-yard of individual relations in which he is enclosed," the poet leads his readers "out of a cave or cellar into the open air." As the poet resigned himself to the Not Me, we yield to him and are similarly compensated. The mind of the "beholder" is liberated: "Men have really got a new sense and found within their world another world, or nest of worlds; for the metamorphosis once seen, we divine that it does not stop" (W.III.28, 30). A list of representative metaphors follows (W.III.30–31). Having described the consequences of reading poetry, Emerson now offers us a practical demonstration.

The experience of reading, however, reminds him how much he dislikes this secondary role (which he nevertheless has consistently elected). If "tropes" are liberating, books are oppressive. In the next paragraph, he argues that freedom is given to us *in* books in order that we may be free *from* them.

> An imaginative book renders us much more service at first, by stimulating us through its tropes, than afterward when we arrive at the precise sense of the author. I think nothing is of any value in books excepting the transcendental and extraordinary. If a man is inflamed and carried away by his thought, to that degree that he forgets the authors and the public and heeds only this one dream which holds him like an insanity, let me read his paper, and you may have all the arguments and histories and criticism. (W.III.32)

That "I think" arrogantly dismisses everything except "the transcendental and extraordinary" in a tone encountered here for the first time in the essay, the unmistakable hubris of the reader's sublime. The initial distinction between "tropes" and "the precise sense of the author" quickly stiffens into the opposition between "this one dream which holds him like an insanity" and "all the arguments and histories and criticism," though even here Emerson tends to forget his own strength as reader in his contemplation of the writer. Strengthened by vicarious liberation, the first person voice tries itself against an opponent in the familiar "us versus them" tactic. The sharpening antithesis and growing outrageousness of tone go together. Emerson's self-enjoyment derives from the exhilarating clarification of his stance that the antagonist permits. Put another way, friction between the speaker and books that presume to instruct him generates the energy that inflames and carries away this pronouncement. "We" disappears in favor of the unabashed "I." The apotheosis of the reader-critic displaces the poet just recently deified. Emerson excepts from his general denunciation only the author who "forgets the authors and the public." That is, he reads in order to have his own rebellious readings confirmed. While he avows that his admiration for a pantheon of writers is exempt from the general curse, the breezy tone in which he declares that "all the value" of this group is "the certificate we have of the departure from routine" still thrills to its own audaciousness. The closing *fortissimo* suggests that the "emotion" with which a reader responds to a trope is an empathetic fantasy of origination. Feeling like a creator, he usurps the poet's Orphic powers:

> the magic of liberty . . . puts the world like a ball in our hands. How cheap even the liberty then seems; how mean to study, when an emotion communicates to the intellect the power to sap and upheave nature; how great the perspective! nations, times, systems, enter and disappear like threads in tapestry of large figure and many colors; dream delivers us to dream, and while the drunkenness lasts we will sell our bed, our philosophy, our religion, in our opulence. (W.III. 32–33)

Emerson never feels so free as when he is rejecting "nations, times, systems," "arguments, and histories, and criticism." His poetics are polemical; freedom is always freedom *from* and power, always power *over*.

But once again, Emerson voluntarily renounces his goal just as it is achieved. This habit of abandoning authority once he has it saves his will to power from brutality. Before the superman can oppress anyone, he resigns and joins the revolution that would have resisted him. After an apparent victory, the Orphic reader surrenders. Again "fruition is postponed" (W.III.12). Suddenly "the poor shepherd, who . . . perishes in a drift within a few feet of his cottage door" is an "emblem of the state of man." Drunken opulence has left the speaker washed up on "the brink of the waters of life." Spatial metaphors situate us once more on the periphery of a circle of which the circumference is everywhere, the center nowhere: "The inaccessibleness of every thought but that we are in, is wonderful. . . . [Y]ou are as remote when you are nearest as when you are farthest." Deprivation revives desire and the tone of affectionate longing: "we [readers] love the poet, the inventor, who in any form whether in an ode or in an action or in looks and behavior has yielded us a new thought" (W.III.33).

Desire reinstates the hierarchical distance between reader and poet which, as we could have predicted, leads Emerson to discover a new opponent. He attacks the literal-minded reader or writer. The crucifying "mystic" "nails a symbol to one sense" and so makes it "too stark and solid." The poet, with his unfailing powers of invention, is unperturbed by the temporary nature of his productions. His faith in himself is so immense that any one symbol is "held lightly" (W.III.34–35). The mystic, on the other hand, is capable of only one good idea which he anxiously and possessively insists on. To dramatize the distinction and reprove the mystic's heavy-handed symbolism, Swedenborg materializes. Readers of "Swedenborg, or The Mystic" cannot help but find it strange that he should be deployed as a corrective to mysticism, for in *Representative Men*, Emerson attributes to him precisely the tedious fixity here ascribed to mystics (W.IV.132). Emerson habitually mocks the literal-mindedness of Swedenborg while conceding the "literary value" of his "epical parables" (CW.I.68).[11] "I commended him as a great poet," he reports in a journal entry of July 1842. This was hardly good enough for Sampson Reed, who "wished, that if I admired the poetry I should feel it as a fact." But Emerson dismissed Swedenborg's beliefs as "Absurd." " 'Otherworld?' I reply, 'there is no other world; here or nowhere is the whole fact.' " In the end, though, Emerson resolves, "I can readily enough translate his rhetoric into mine" (*JMN*.VIII.183).

We have an example of such translation in "The Poet." Pieces of visions from Swedenborg's writings are joined into Emersonian "rhetoric." His adaptation results in some stylistic peculiarities. The nonparallelism between figs and grapes, between affirming a truth and a blossoming twig, between gnashing and thumping and disputing voices is bewildering; so is the imagery of dragons in heavenly light and men in a cabin. The visions become progressively more alarming as we shift disconcertingly between distance and nearness, inside and outside. Whose point of view do we share? Swedenborg? The protagonists of his visions (who "to each other . . . appeared as men")? The reader? Or Emerson, who wonders how others perceive him? When the poet inspires "awe and terror" because of the quality of "perception in him," every point of view finally postulates a perspective beyond itself (*W*.III.36). Emerson seems to have committed the intellectual sin he would later attribute to Swedenborg, that is, "a confounding of planes . . . which is dislocation and chaos" (*W*.IV.140).

The result is closer to farce than poetry. Emerson betrays not the slightest hint of a smile; indeed, he apparently assumes that he has shown us sublimity itself when he calls Swedenborg "an object of awe and terror." Awful and terrible, it should be noted, by virtue of a potentially comic doubleness: "men may wear one aspect to themselves and their companions and a different aspect to higher intelligences." At such moments, "[t]he question Emerson raises," writes Barbara Packer, "is not primarily what he means by these bizarre associations, but whether or not he was aware of how funny they sound."[12] After the annunciation of Swedenborg's awful aspect, the writing gets even funnier. To see men as dragons is one thing, but priests as "dead horses"? In a moment of slight detachment, irony enters and "instantly" Emerson comically re-imagines the material to which he has just alluded. "Epical parable" is repeated as joke:

> instantly the mind inquires whether these fishes under the
> bridge, yonder oxen in the pasture, those dogs in the yard,

are immutably fishes, oxen, and dogs, or only so appear to
me, and perchance to themselves appear upright men; and
whether I appear as a man to all eyes. (W.III.36)

Yet Emerson does not admit his own humor even now. He presents,
still in the key of high seriousness, Brahmins and Pythagoras, wheat
and caterpillars, until he arrives at a restatement of the first sentence of the paragraph, which invested Swedenborg with the full
regalia of the poet. We are left, in Packer's words, with "the Tyger
of Wrath as Cheshire Cat."[13]

This adaptation of Swedenborg's cosmic fantasies is the third
ironic episode in "The Poet," along with the fables of the "winged
man" and of the "clamorous flights of censures." Taken together,
these passages give us an insight into the relationship of irony and
the sublime in Emerson's prose. Such episodes, and the many
others like them scattered throughout the essays, resemble the
closing paragraph of "Intellect" as it originally appeared in the
journals. Its development illuminates the motivation of Emerson's
ironic fables.

Of these unquiet daemons that fly or gleam across the brain
what trait can I hope to draw in my sketch book? Wonderful
seemed to me as I read in Plotinus the calm & grand air of
these few cherubim—great spiritual lords who have walked
in the world—they of the old religion—dwelling in a worship
that makes the sanctities of Christianity parvenues & merely
popular; for "necessity is in intellect, but persuasion in soul."
This band of grandees Hermes, Heraclitus, Empedocles, Plato,
Plotinus, Olympiodorus, Proclus, Synesius, & the rest, have
somewhat so vast in their logic, so primary in their thinking,
that it seems antecedent to all the ordinary distinctions of
rhetoric & literature, & to be at once poetry & music &
dancing & astronomy & mathematics. I am present at the
sowing of the seed of the world. With a geometry of sunbeams
the Soul lays the foundations of nature. The truth & grandeur
of their thought is proved by its scope & applicability; for it
commands more even than our dear old bibles of Moses &
Swedenborg the entire Schedule & inventory of things for its

illustration. But what marks its elevation & has a comic look to us if we are not very good when we read, is the innocent serenity with which these babe-like Jupiters sit in their clouds & from age to age prattle to each other and to no contemporary; perfectly assured that their speech is intelligible & the most natural thing in the world, they emit volume after volume without one moment's heed of the universal astonishment of the poor human race below, who do not comprehend a sentence. . . . The angels are so enamoured of the language that is spoken in heaven that they will not distort their lips with the hissing & unmusical dialects of men but speak their own whether there be any near, who can understand it or not. (*JMN*.VII.413–14)

The journal entry opens with a Miltonic flourish in rather hushed tones of desire, wonder, and praise appropriate to a subject both "vast" and "primary." Once again we hear the "holy place" motif in a vision of Being "antecedent" to Appearances—"I am present at the sowing of the seed of the world." With the reference to "our dear old bibles of Moses and Swedenborg," though, gravity gives way. The very next sentence begins with a pivotal "But" which confesses the "comic look" of what Emerson has just imagined. Comic, that is, "if we are not very good when we read." Irony is a delicious sin, then, a temptation the "good" reader and, surely, the "good" writer must try to resist.

This temptation perhaps besets Emerson more often than usual when Swedenborg is his subject. (In the published version of "Intellect," interestingly enough, the reference to the "bibles of Moses and Swedenborg" drops out and Emerson's laughter is more decorous [*CW*.II.204–5].) Emerson regards Swedenborg's visions as exercises in point of view that can be enjoyed as intellectual play, whatever the author's intentions. Add his mixed feelings about Swedenborg, and it is not surprising that the impulse to irony frequently prevails. It prevails far too often to be accounted for by his response to a single writer, however. The fact that the representative mind of "Intellect" undergoes a metamorphosis from high seriousness to high good humor suggests that the ironic moment is central to Emerson's literary philosophy and method. The Transcendentalist is, by his own definition, an ironist. His analysis of "The Comic," the best possible gloss on his ironic passages, bears this out:

> [T]he best of all jokes is the sympathetic contemplation of things by the understanding from the philosopher's point of view.

> This is the radical joke of life and then of literature. The presence of the ideal of right and of truth . . . makes the yawning delinquencies of practice remorseful to the conscience, tragic to the interest, but droll to the intellect.

> [T]he occasion of laughter is some keeping of the word to the ear and eye, while it is broken to the soul. (W.VIII. 153,154,157)

This definition of humor shows why Emerson laughs at Swedenborg's "confounding of planes." "The comic" is profoundly ironic, generated by several points of view belonging to different faculties that come into play together: conscience, interest, and intellect; Understanding and Reason ("the philosopher's point of view"); ear, eye, and soul. "Yawning" discrepancies in the responses of the various faculties provoke laughter. In each case, the superior faculty laughs. The philosophical sense and the soul are amused by what the understanding, eye, and ear take seriously. (The superiority of intellect to conscience is questionable, however.) Humor requires an "ideal of right and truth." The more high-minded we are, the more likely we are to find life comical, since our soul is that much more remote from our senses.[14] If the higher faculties mock the lower, however, the lower also expose the higher. In comic moments, the soul acknowledges the understanding, whereas in sublime moments, the soul defeats the understanding. It is the "truth and grandeur" of Emerson's "band of grandees" in "Intellect" which trigger the ensuing parody, suggesting that the lower faculties can function as the antagonists. As the syntax reveals, "what marks . . . elevation" is what "has a comic look." Clearly, irony is essential to Emerson's oscillation between the mood of awed desire and that of irreverent self-aggrandizement. It shatters monolithic perceptions and frees the observer into laughter.

The apparent inadvertence of Emerson's irony is thus deceptive. Irony is one of the intentions of an art of multiple points of view and tones of voice. The argument that Emerson is a consciously ironic writer accommodates the accidental genesis of any given passage. In its full range of meanings, irony pervades Emerson's works. Its essential "halfness" or "break" recurs in his theory of transition and in stylistic discontinuities. Repetition, the chance for second thoughts, also precipitates irony. Finally, as the reference to the comic sense as a reader's affliction implies, irony strikes when Emerson contemplates the works of other writers. Since the "transcendental and extraordinary" never fill a whole book, the reader inevitably perceives the author's "yawning delinquencies of practice" that miss the soul and impress only the lower faculties. The very structure of the act of reading involves assent on one "plane" and mockery on another. Emerson thus grounds his theory of literary influence in this bifurcated response to past masters.

The essay's final movement represents this double, or ironic, reading in dramatic terms as it repeats the central action of the work: deprivation provokes critical distinctions that bring about an influx of power. Emerson as reader displaces his poet-hero, only to close by invoking him once more. He begins the closing section by recapitulating his call for assistance. The poet of America, "the timely man," is late in arriving. ("The principal event in chronology," as Emerson told us once before, "is postponed.") "We" delay the emergence of the poet within us: "We do not with sufficient plainness or sufficient profoundness address ourselves to life, nor dare we chaunt our own times and social circumstances. If we filled the day with bravery, we should not shrink from celebrating it." The speaker as representative reader turns against himself, and this gesture begins his metamorphosis. The call for a "genius" to recognize "the value of our incomparable materials" initiates this recognition (W.III.37). An "astonishingly prideful figure presents itself unabashedly as the very figure of the ideal poet for which it calls," Porter observes. "*It summons itself.*"[15] I would revise this. What really materializes out of Emerson's evasive arrogance is not the poet, but the critic. He finds his own version of the American poem inadequate, but denies that anyone has yet produced a better one. Outraged and outrageous, he dismisses all of European literature:

> If I have not found that . . . which I seek, neither could I aid myself to fix the idea of the poet by reading now and then in Chalmer's collection of five centuries of English poets. These are more wits than poets, though there have been poets among them. But when we adhere to the ideal of the poet, we have our difficulties even with Milton and Homer. Milton is too literary, and Homer too literal and historical.

The American provincial regards five centuries of English poetry as an anthology into which he dips "now and then"; his revenge is an "ideal" that no poet who has ever lived can match. In a demonstration of the aggressive uses of criticism, Emerson's British and classical competitors are dispatched by a theoretical double bind which rules them either too literary or not literary enough. The mask of the humble critic ("I am not wise enough for a national criticism") cannot hide the speaker's egotism. Acting as archangel to the poet's Adam, he assumes the privileged role of mediator who discharges an "errand from the muse to the poet concerning his art" (W.III.38).

Emerson chooses not to end at the height of his critical powers. The poet once more becomes the central figure. He is in the throes of a painful adolescence. If Emerson yields to the poet, then it is to a youthful one whose anxieties are very close to those of Emerson-as-reader. Emerson lyrically reimagines the poet's development as quest romance, then as pastoral. These somewhat fanciful treatments effect a rhetorical *diminuendo;* more importantly, they recapitulate the frustrations Emerson experienced as a maturing writer. The older speaker who looks to the poet for revelation and the struggling youth represent two phases of Emerson's development. Even as the hero of the essay is displayed in the soft colors of pastoral and romance, he strives to find a voice that will shatter the nostalgic style which praises him.

In the first fable, the quest romance, poets "found or put themselves" (an interesting equivocation) "in certain conditions . . . exciting to [their] intellect." Encountering these "conditions" suggests tales in which the hero lies down to sleep under an enchanted tree, drinks from magical waters (tasting "this immortal ichor"), or trespasses half-deliberately on haunted ground (the journal passage reads "I see the beckoning of this Ghost" [*JMN*.IX.71]). A vision initiates the quest: "He hears a voice, he sees a beckoning . . . he pursues a beauty, half seen, which flies before him." The "charm" of his own "original and beautiful" utterances lures him further on his way until the strangeness he desires is his, at least, in "our way of talking." The quest fable is clearly an allegory of the creative, agonistic release of what is "in me, and shall out." Pursuit of an external object changes to the ejaculation of "thought . . . as Logos." Like the young Emerson, the poet is rendered speechless by external and internal constraints; he is both "balked" and "dumb." He perceives the audience by whom he is "hissed and hooted" as the antagonist with whom he is to "strive." Convinced nightly in solitude of his capacity to conduct a "whole river of electricity," he finds himself blocked during the day in public. Afraid of the force of his own imagination and unwilling to appear shamelessly egotistical (they go together), he hides the ambition that rages within him. Belief in his own potency and aggression toward a perceived oppressor once again generate each other. When the poet accepts his own power, antagonism evaporates momentarily. He reconciles himself to the world by imaginatively absorbing it: "All the creatures by pairs and by tribes pour into his mind as into a Noah's ark, to come forth again to people a new world" (*W*.III.39–40).[16]

The Biblical story of nature saved from the Flood becomes a fable of nature pouring into the mind *as* flood and undergoing there an imaginative transvaluation. In the closing paragraphs of the essay, the Biblical landscape of rain, flood, covenantal rainbow, and greening trees repeats and naturalizes the drama of desire, agon, and power. Instead of dreaming electric dreams, the poet lies "close hid with nature," smitten with "an old shame before the holy ideal." A hint of harshness remains in his sentence; he "must pass for a fool and a churl for a long season" in the eyes of Capitol and

Exchange. In the end, though, the poet dwells harmoniously with his fellow creatures in an "actual world." The landlord metaphor seems to describe stewardship and at-homeness rather than dominance. "Impressions" do not flood the poet's mind, but "fall like summer rain, copious, but not troublesome." The rain recurs in the gentle parody of the Eucharist that closes the essay: "[T]here is Beauty, plenteous as rain, shed for thee." This benign image of plenitude without excess signals the transformation of the "liberating god" into the "well-beloved flower" of Pan (W.III.41–42).

The peculiar repetition that ends "The Poet" tells us a good deal about Emerson's conception of closure in his prose works. Our feeling that the essay is winding down is achieved entirely by rhetorical and imagistic means. The closing episodes recall earlier passages: dumbness attributed to "some obstruction or . . . excess of phlegm in our constitution"; the poet "isolated among his contemporaries by truth and by his art, but with this consolation . . . that they will draw all men sooner or later"; the solitary who rejects Boston and New York for "the lonely waste of the pine woods." These elements recur in the closing allegories of trial, but there is no reason why these repetitions should be more meaningful than the many earlier ones. The idiom of supernatural romance acts as a foil for the quieter, naturalistic fable that follows. The shift into a more soothing tone and setting confirms our sensation of closure. This sensation depends in part on the illusion that the generative oppositions which have sustained the essay have been healed. We have had this sensation before in "The Poet" and should know by now that it is only a temporary resting place. Even as we are seduced by the trappings of sublimity—the long apostrophes ("Doubt not, O poet, but persist"), the prophetic mood ("the ideal shall be real to thee"), archaisms, and Biblical resonances ("thou shalt")—we recognize them for the conventional flourishes they are (W.III.6,5,29,40–42). The gratuitousness of the ending reminds one of the conclusion to "Fate." In three paragraphs all beginning "Let us build altars to the Blessed Unity" or "to the Beautiful Necessity," Emerson pulls out the same peroratorical stops (W.VIII.48–49). Burke's phrase, "the machinery of transcendence," expresses our sense that at such moments Emerson lowers on us the stylistic equivalent of *deus ex machina*.[17] The ostentatiousness of the coda betrays its arbitrary character. It has been imposed on a text that could continue its oscillations indefinitely.

The concluding pages of "The Poet" verify what the rest of the essay has already taught us. Emerson composes by depicting the stages of his own development. But his prose is by no means autobiographical, for the essayistic representation of his progress is significantly different from his personal reminiscences. Emerson became a writer by identifying criticism with power and by making reading necessary to writing. En route to these discoveries, he made himself miserable. In essays like "The Poet," he chooses to relive the particular exasperations of his twenties. The repetition apparently is motivated by his desire to repeat the movement from deprived ambition to aggressive criticism. The fact that he repeatedly chooses positions disagreeable in themselves strongly suggests that his greatest pleasure is in the willing reenactment, freely and playfully dramatized, of slow and painful change.

"QUOTATION AND

ORIGINALITY"

The dynamics of influence and interpretation that organize Emerson's earlier works appear also in the 1859 lecture published with little revision as "Quotation and Originality." For our purposes, the most important thing about this piece is the persistence of structures that had emerged twenty years before. Such stability argues for the constitutive role of these dynamics in Emerson's prose; once formulated, they are a permanent feature. The central terms of "Quotation and Originality" are attributes and operations (like those of the essays on "Love," "Art," "Fate") not protagonists ("The Poet," "The American Scholar," *Representative Men*), but this is a negligible difference. All of Emerson's essays assign essentially the same operations to essentially the same performers. In addition to its value as evidence of the staying power of Emerson's designs, "Quotation and Originality" is, of course, intriguing because of its manifest content. As the title indicates, it makes explicit the theories of interpretation dramatized in so many other works, and thus provides an appropriate gloss on and summary of the readings in this section. It makes clear, in a casual way, the role of the higher criticism in Emerson's development of a general hermeneutics; its ambiguous anecdotes of duplicitous quoters contribute to our ongoing exploration of Emerson's irony; and, most significantly, it offers a sustained discussion of literary influence, although "Quotation and Originality" is not one of Emerson's great rages against tradition. While it exhibits his characteristic shifts among the roles of reader, critic, and writer, it is less aggressive than many essays. It may be that he is so deeply committed to the method of quotation by this time that he cannot get fully aroused against it. The earlier work or author, the antagonist, is more a part of himself. Nevertheless, his pleasure in repeated sequences of self-deprecation, desire, and aggression that issue in the momentary dominance of the reader-as-writer persists.

The opening image, a violently reductive allegory, lets us know at once that Emerson has mixed feelings about his subject. In one of the grotesque parables that so delight him, he points out "the extreme content" which "flies, aphides, gnats . . . innumerable parasites, and even . . . infant mammals" take in "suction." "If we go into a library or news-room," he continues, "we see that same function on a higher plane, performed with like ardor, with equal impatience of interruption, indicating the sweetness of the act. In the highest civilization the book is still the highest delight (W.VIII.177). The shift from "suction" to "sweetness," from "parasites" to readers, deflates the pretensions of "civilization" by reminding us of our uncontrollable instinctual need for bookish pleasures. At the same time, that need is made to appear disgusting.

After this cautionary irony, the essay begins in earnest with the appearance of one of Emerson's typically modest personae, whose subject is the great, but not entirely original, man. "All minds quote" but the "great man" most of all; "in proportion to the spontaneous power should be the assimilating power." Quotation is not limited to actual verbal citation. As Emerson enumerates modern inventions that resemble or were suggested by ancient ones, "quotation" comes to signify any known historical connection: "We quote . . . arts, sciences, religion, customs, and laws; nay, we quote temples and houses, tables and chairs." When we comprehend an institution or an idea well enough to trace it back to prior forms, then we call its later reappearance "quotation." Since every event has discoverable antecedents, the past becomes an endless series of quotations. The word is a synonym for history itself: "There is imitation, model and suggestion, to the very arch-angels, if we knew their history." "There is something mortifying in this perpetual circle," the essayist remarks somberly. It "argues a very small capital of invention." He includes himself among the dependent: "In this delay and vacancy of thought, we . . . [seek] the wisdom of others to fill the time." Having eliminated the possibility of individual creativity, the only way he can account for the ongoing activity of writing is by a theory of intertextuality. The search for an ancient, original text drives us backwards in an infinite regress of reading.

> The first book tyrannizes over the second. Read Tasso, and you think of Virgil; read Virgil, and you think of Homer; and Milton forces you to reflect how narrow are the limits of human invention. The "Paradise Lost" had never existed but for these precursors.

The avowed indebtedness to Emerson of our latest theorist of influence, Harold Bloom, is amply justified by passages like this, in which Emerson uses influence to define a canon and calls attention to the "tyranny" of "precursors." Emerson goes on to reveal the relationship of this vision to Biblical criticism:

> if we find in India or Arabia a book out of our horizon of thought and tradition, we are soon taught by new researches in its native country to discover its foregoers, and its latent, but real connection with our own Bibles. (W.VIII.178–80)

Comparative mythology establishes the "foregoers" of literary works, then connects them to each other through their common ancestors. The author breaks apart into multiple sources and his book into quotations. The process of critical fragmentation, as we have seen in other essays, is a prerequisite for creative reading. Emerson has generalized the procedures of the higher criticism to demystify all written works.

In the next portion of "Quotation and Originality," still part of the long opening movement that traces the derivative present back to an original past, Emerson applies this mode of criticism. He begins with illustrative genealogies of individual writers. Plato originated Christianity's "evangelical phrases"; "Hegel pre-exists in Proclus"; "Rabelais is the source of many a proverb, story, and jest"; Dante "absorbed" St. Bonaventura and Thomas Aquinas (W.VIII.180–81). From the idea of authors as embodiments of tradition, Emerson proceeds to the logical consequence of this approach, the notion of collective authorship. "Mythology is no man's work" but every man contributes to it: "the legend is tossed from believer to poet, from poet to believer, everybody adding a grace or dropping a fault or rounding the form, until it gets an ideal truth." Anonymous folk creation is endless quotation, which ensures myth's universal meaning and purges it of egotism. "Religious literature," too, is "the work of the whole communion of worshippers"; the Bible is the supreme example of man's collective inspiration. Once again, the literary interpreter has gone to school to the higher critics and the mythologists, but he invests these forms of criticism with his own anti-authoritarian motives: "[W]hatever undue reverence may have been claimed for [the Bible] by the prestige of philonic inspiration, the stronger tendency we are describing [collective authorship] is likely to undo." The suspicious critic successfully challenges more pious readers' control of the interpretive marketplace. The passage continues:

> What divines had assumed as the distinctive revelations of Christianity, theologic criticism has matched by exact parallelisms from the Stoics and poets of Greece and Rome. Later, when Confucius and the Indian scriptures were made known, no claim to monopoly of ethical wisdom could be thought of; and the surprising results of the new researches into the history of Egypt have opened to us the deep debt of the churches of Rome and England to the Egyptian hierology. (W. VIII. 182)

Here Emerson exhibits a clear grasp of analogues of his own position. Comparative or "parallel" investigations by "theologic critics" put an end to the Christian "monopoly" of "ethical wisdom" by showing its "deep debt" to other traditions. More than any Biblical scholar, Emerson perceives the general theory of influence implicit in the higher criticism. Using it, he can challenge the ethical pretensions of any authors and literatures by exposing their resemblance, and thus their debt, to earlier writings.

At this point, without abandoning the stance of judicious reader, he shifts his focus to the author who must live in and with this culture of indebtedness. Writers adapt to it, he suggests, by perfecting a sleight of tone that makes quotation sound like originality. Borrowing is "honest enough" when its dishonesty goes unnoticed:

"A great man quotes bravely. . . . What he quotes, he fills with his own voice and humor, and the whole cyclopaedia of his table-talk is presently believed to be his own." Successful quotation involves a kind of illusion or deception. Famous men of all eras have passed off borrowed material as their own and enhanced their reputations by doing so. Undetected fraud is the test of rightful appropriation. If one can utter a quotation in one's "own voice and humor," runs Emerson's argument, then the borrowing is legitimate. Webster's "three rules" for young men "are none the worse for being already told, in the last generation, of Sheridan; and we find in Grimm's Mémoires that Sheridan got them from the witty D'Argenson; who, no doubt, if we could consult him, could tell of whom he first heard them told" (W.VIII.183). In these jocose "begats," we hear the smile of the cat right after it has swallowed the canary, of the author after he has assimilated his precursor. As legitimate trickery, quotation is an ironic tactic detected only by the ironic critic. Again, irony appears with the perceived gap between wisdom and egotism. It is the tone in which we knowingly appreciate the subterfuges of success and thus defend ourselves against them. If we see through an author's fraud, he has less power over us. Irony once more demystifies sublime effects.

Emerson drifts away from the dilemmas of authors to the subject of proverbs, ballads, and fables of "doubtful paternity." That phrase, "doubtful paternity," is a telling one. It indicates not condemnation, but relief, and suggests why, whenever the presence of known authors—acknowledged fathers—becomes too palpable, the theme of collective authorship recurs in the essays. Emerson pursues this theme with appropriately "doubtful" examples, claiming influence where there is only a general affinity of idea:

> Rabelais's dying words, "I am going to see the great Perhaps" . . . only repeats the "IF" inscribed on the portal of the temple at Delphi. Goethe's favorite phrase, "the open secret," translates Aristotle's answer to Alexander, "These books are published and not published." . . . Wordworth's hero acting "on the plan which pleased his childish thought,"

is Schiller's "Tell him to reverence the dreams of his youth," and earlier, Bacon's "*Consilia juventutis plus divinitatis habent.*" (*W.*VIII.185)

The very speciousness of these connections demonstrates that paternity is always doubtful. Luckily for the nineteenth century, no thought can be attributed to only one author. In the domain of literary influence, there are no copyright laws to protect past writers and regulate present ones.

With a reprise of the lessons of comparative mythology ("only within this century . . . [have] England and America discovered that their nursery-tales . . . are the property of all the nations descended from the Aryan race"), the first movement of the essay appears to come to an end. After having dissolved the authorial subject several times into a chain of anonymous texts, the speaker faces the consequences of this procedure for himself as an author. Recognizing that his own arguments prove him to be unoriginal, he protests. Emerson's outburst conflates all the fables of the fall which the Orphic poet had cited in *Nature*, interpolated below in brackets, and adds a new one—quotation:

> Now shall we say that only the first men were well alive, and the existing generation is invalided and degenerate? ["Man is the dwarf of himself."] Is all literature eavesdropping, and all art . . . imitation? our life a custom, and our body borrowed, like a beggar's dinner, from a hundred charities? A more subtle and severe criticism might suggest that some dislocation has befallen the race ["the axis of vision is not aligned with the axis of things"]; that men are off their centre; that multitudes of men do not live with Nature, but behold it as exiles ["That indescribably small interval is as good as a thousand miles, and has forever severed the practical unity"].

Suddenly quotation is a symptom of the remoteness of truth, not truth's vehicle. It does not mediate between, but divides man and nature. "Quotation confesses inferiority," he announces in a new tone. "Quotation" no longer designates historical consciousness but stock responses, the absence of self-reliance:

People go out to look at sunrises and sunsets who do not recognize their own . . . but know that it is foreign to them. As they do by books, so they *quote* the sunset and the star, and do not make them theirs. Worse yet, they live as foreigners in the world of truth, and quote thoughts, and thus disown them. (*W.*VIII.187–88)

Emerson's tone becomes judgmental as he turns against the inferior role of the reader. He represents alienated readers as different from himself. "[O]ur life" and "our body" give way accusingly to "they live," the change in pronoun dramatizing "their" foreignness. He is also contemptuous of the writer who reveals his "unguarded devotion" to earlier authors. "If Lord Bacon appears . . . in the preface, I go and read the Instauration instead of the new book," he threatens. The grotesque fable of parasitism which opened the essay returns, more darkly interpreted according to the law of compensation:

The mischief is quickly punished. . . . Admirable mimics have nothing of their own. In every kind of parasite, when Nature has finished an aphis, a teredo or a vampire bat,—an excellent sucking-pipe to tap another animal, or a mistletoe or dodder among plants,—the self-supplying organs wither and dwindle, as being superfluous. (*W.*VIII.187–88)

Having distanced himself from inferior quotation by using the parasitical writer as scapegoat (to mix zoological metaphors), Emerson tries once more to define the conditions of legitimate quotation. He continues to oscillate between regretting and accepting parasitism. "[T]here are certain considerations which go far to qualify a reproach too grave," he begins judiciously. An economic metaphor describes a rare vision of equality between past and present authors or between author and reader: "The capitalist . . . is as hungry to lend as the consumer to borrow" and "the transaction is honorable to both." After all, quotation, as joint authorship, is an expression of "coöperation," of "our social nature." These are only fleeting wishes, however. Quickly Emerson returns to his usual vocabulary of power relations: "Each man is a hero and an oracle to somebody, and to that person whatever he says has an enhanced value. . . . [M]en of extraordinary genius acquire an almost absolute ascendant over their nearest companions." And then we are back on the side of the creative reader. Quotation is a form of criticism that makes certain elements of the past visible for the first time. "Many will read the book before one thinks of quoting a passage," and (quoting Landor on Shakespeare) that one is "more original than his originals" (W.VIII.189–91).

No amount of rationalization can suppress Emerson's uneasiness about the dishonesty of quoting, however. The quoter "is like the false Amphitryon; although the stranger, it is always he who has the air of being master of the house." The false Amphitryon (in this quotation from Dubuc) is, of course, Zeus—authentic power manifested as imitation. Wordsworth, like a false Amphitryon, passed off De Quincey's remarks as his own in De Quincey's presence. "On the whole," Emerson comments ambiguously, "we like the valor of it." He describes Wordsworth's action as proof that "truth is the property of no individual, but is the treasure of all man," denying the shameless egotism of the gesture. "[I]nasmuch as any writer has ascended to a just view of man's condition, he has adopted this tone," a tone of ostensible impersonality. "Tone," however, is Emerson's word for the impact of personal presence. The "tone" of Wordsworth and the other writers whose behavior he describes is one of instinctive self-regard. Emerson keeps trying to discriminate between morally legitimate and reprehensible forms of quotation. Altruistic motives make all the difference to the reader, "the simple seeker." "The nobler the truth or sentiment, the less imports the question of authorship." When the author is inspired by idealism, the tone of his quotations has "valor." Furthermore, Emerson warns, a selfish motive is betrayed by a discontinuous style. Egotistical quotation leads to textual gaps: "some steep transition, some sudden alternation of temperature, or of point of view, betrays the foreign interpolation" (W.VIII.192–93). Emerson's definition of moral borrowing seems to condemn, not justify, Wordsworth's repetition of De Quincey's *bons mots* apparently for social effect. Furthermore, Emerson criticizes a style precisely like his own. As we shall see in later chapters, he knew full well that his prose was characterized by discontinuity and conspicuous transitions, often caused by interpolations of "foreign," that is, quoted, material. These spasms of unconvincing high-mindedness suggest his discomfort with evidences of self-love in other writers which, when he acknowledges them as his own strategies, come in for enthusiastic praise.

When he has tried, unpersuasively, to idealize the quoter's motivation, he must account for the peculiar power of the quotation itself. It takes on the intentionality of the writer who is being used. Emerson meditates on the way allusions can retroactively alter our perception of a work (much as T. S. Eliot would do in "Tradition and the Individual Talent"[1]): "The passages of Shakspeare that we most prize were never quoted until within this century; and Milton's prose and Burke, even, have their best fame within it." The quotation interprets its creator "as if the charm belonged to the word and not to the life of thought which . . . enforced it." Quotation is one of the "tricks . . . fine words play with us." But Emerson knows that the charm of the word is an illusion, and that the power of quotation derives from the presence of one author in another's text: "another's thoughts have a certain advantage with us simply because they are another's." Alienation and majesty come together in quotation. Otherness signifies authority, just as authority signifies otherness. Consequently, "the high poets" are quoted "in the manner in which Scripture is quoted in our churches . . . with honoring emphasis." But a literary criticism analogous to Biblical criticism diminishes quotation's power. The book that is the object of much scholarship is less threatening, even a little quaint. The "citation of a passage" by a "historian of literature," Emerson observes drily, "carries the sentimental value of a college diploma" (W.VIII.193–95, 202, 195).

The extreme instability of Emerson's attitude toward writers who quote other writers arises from the double function of quotation. Quotation elicits the reader's awe, but when exposed as "mask" and "trick," makes possible the reader's defense and revenge. The speaker's rapidly alternating opinions in "Quotation and Originality" represent different phases of the reader's life cycle we have traced in other works. Now the essay shifts once again from negating the power of quotation to recommending it. Despite the efforts of criticism, the impact of borrowed material is so great that writers seek to imitate the *effect* of quotation even in original work, "ascribing their own sentence to an imaginary person, in order to give it weight." Although he knows that "many men can write better under a mask than for themselves," he immediately denigrates this strategy as "a sort of dramatizing talent . . . without the least original eloquence" (W.VIII.196). Here Emerson describes but does not defend his own "dramatizing" method in speaking through the Orphic poet or, in the journals, through the pseudonym of "Osman" (see *JMN*.VIII.4–5n.), and also in the self-quotation and the quotation of quotations that composing from his journals entailed. We must assume that the functional equality in his own prose of original and derived material contributes to the unstable distinctions between invention and quotation in this essay. The emphasis on the authorial subject in this part of "Quotation and Originality" predictably brings about a reaction against it in renewed praise of collective authorship. We live "in a circle of intelligences that [reaches] . . . back to the first geometer, bard, mason. . . . [E]very individual is only a momentary fixation of what was yesterday another's, is to-day his, and will belong to a third to-morrow." However, the next paragraph begins, "But there remains the indefeasible persistency of the individual to be himself." The threat posed by Emerson as reader/critic to his own authorial integrity finally provokes the defense of originality which was aborted earlier: "To all that can be said of the preponderance of the Past, the single word Genius is a sufficient reply. . . . The divine never quotes, but is, and creates" (W.VIII.199–201).

Present inspiration "makes the Past forgotten," and no one practices that forgetting or knows its importance better than Emerson. Creativity "implies Will"—the will to forget, the will to power: "Genius believes its faintest presentiment against the testimony of all history." Emerson's turn to faith in the possibility of originality is a compromise solution. Originality involves the displacement of an objective condition by a subjective one; it equates "being" with being one's self. However, the writer is both history's object and its subject; he creates and feels himself created. His will triumphs by a willed yielding:

> If to [Will] the sentiment of piety be added, if the thinker feels that the thought most strictly his own is not his own, and recognizes the perpetual suggestions of the Supreme Intellect, the oldest thoughts become new and fertile whilst he speaks them. (W.VIII.201–202)

Looking with "piety" toward the "Supreme Intellect" is a version of the alienated majesty that allows one to discover one's own strength only when it is externalized in or projected onto another writer. Because the oversoul manifests itself in all men and diffuses power in collective authorship, any single man is prevented from appearing intimidating. Emerson can experience his power as an external force without engaging in a contest with particular authors.

Emerson's own literary biography testifies to the truth of his insights into the necessary pretenses of quotation and reminds us of the reflexivity of this essay. His early journals show how the writer discovers his gift by reifying it in the quotation, which he sees as the manifestation of another's power over him. The feeling of being ravished by other geniuses that pervades the early journals survives in his tendency to prefer himself in the guise of his quoted sources, "ascribing [his] own sentence to an imaginary person." In order to effect the substitution of self for other, an initial error must be committed and corrected. Awed by another writer's thought, Emerson discovers that it is his own. This is the essential trick of quotation: a moment of unconscious projection is necessary to bring about the full consciousness that can confess its prior self-deceptions:

> The Intellect goes out of the Individual, & floats over its own being, & regards its own being always as a foreign fact, & not as I & mine. *I & mine* cannot see the Wonder of their existence. This the Intellect always ponders. (JMN.V.446–47)

Emerson's theorizing in "Quotation and Originality" and elsewhere brings together many of the elements we have been investigating. We can begin to understand how and why the higher criticism, a theory of influence and reading, is connected to poetry, a literature of irony and sublimity. Both turn on the drama of self and other, which has as one of its crucial scenes the confrontation of the self *as* other. To summarize, then, the young reader, looking on past masters, wants to emulate their achievement. To him, these authors and their books seem surrounded by the halo of genius. He invokes the muses of the ancients to inspire him, and the great authors enter him in his acts of imitation. But the glory of literature is the reader's projection of his own power and desire. He sees what he wants to be; he feels the effect he wants to produce. He experiences the other author as an overwhelming, aggressive presence whose voice invades him and makes him its instrument.

Emulation results in crisis. The reader is so fully receptive to the whole literary universe that he is overcome by the sheer quantity of books. His integrity is threatened, not by a single influence, but by an incomprehensible multitude. Imitation of a past that is present to him as chaotic fragments seems impossible. Several defensive reactions may occur. He can accept the plenitude of earlier works and turn them against each other. This reaction is evident in the way Emerson uses German writers against British ones, for example, or, in *Representative Men*, the way he uses one man's strengths to show up another's weaknesses. Frequently, he denies the existence of other writers with the theory of collective or anonymous authorship. More aggressively, he claims that civilization is himself writ large. As reader, he bestows meaning on what he reads, recognizes it as an extension of himself, and absorbs it into himself. To quote another is an act of narcissistic mirroring, whether one is, at that instant, more in love with oneself or with one's reflection. In another crisis brought about by self-consciousness, which quickly catches up with such strategies, the subject finds that the discovery of resemblance results in an appallingly solipsistic universe. Distinctions between self and other, reader and text, present and past are lost. The glory of art, arising from its otherness, cannot long survive identification. This stage corresponds to the reader's inability to "continue the sentence" begun by other writers. The claim of identity breaks down when he does not produce a work of epic stature. What looks and feels like failure restores the dualism necessary for sublimity. The book once again becomes the other, and the power of its author over the reader returns. The stage again is set for invocation.

More important than any momentarily stationary position in this cycle is the passage between positions. This is the sublime and/or ironic turn celebrated by Emerson as "transition" and "metamorphosis." The ability always to break out of either a dominant or a subordinate stance, not dominance itself, is what brings about the sensation of power. Ultimately, he desires freedom more than control. Transition is the moment of forgetfulness that produces the discontinuity so characteristic of his prose. In order to have the feeling of newness and change, he must deny repetition, refusing to acknowledge that his reactions are patterned. On the surface, Freud's dictum holds; we repeat because we will not remember.[2] But Emerson's tone of ironic naïveté admits a half-knowledge of recurrence which convinces us that we are not dreaming his repetitions.[3]

· III ·

STRUCTURES WITHIN
THE ESSAYS

INTRODUCTION

Many fragments remain to us among his works by which
we may see the manner in which all his works were written.
Works of this sort which consist of detached observations
and to which the mind has not imparted a system of its
own, are never ended. . . . [T]o make [his] works complete,
he must live to the end of the world. (EL.I.335)

This passage, from Emerson's 1835 lecture on Bacon, a figure
prominent in his speculations on method, suggests that there is a
causal relationship between unsystematic thinking and a fragmented style. Bacon's unfinished works—"fragments"—betray
the essential incompleteness of all his productions. His works are
never finished, meaning both "never ended" and unpolished, because they "consist of detailed observations" strung together in
an open-ended series and not endowed with the closure of "a
system." This is an astute, if worried, commentary on Emerson's
own prose, and describes the idiosyncrasies that readers since
Emerson have often faulted. His essays seem fragmentary because
comprised of detached observations. And, as Emerson has intuited
here, fragmentation implies repetition. A series of percepts, all of
equal ontological status, will inevitably strike us as fragmented.
The sense of unity depends on the subordination of observations
to system; without this hierarchical organization, we have a collection of interchangeable parts. "To write a fragment," therefore,
"is to write *in* fragments."[1] If writing is discontinuous, without
system, it will be repetitive. Conversely, if one repeats by always
composing the same kind of statement, then one's prose will be
disjunctive. Regardless of his periodic spasms of regret about the
texture of his rhetoric, Emerson knew, as we should, that fragmentation and repetition organized his kind of eloquence.

The connection between repetition and discontinuity, and the
implications of this connection, are the subjects of the third and

final phase of my reading of Emerson's works. The personifications of critical maneuvers we have observed throughout the essays have required our attention to the phenomena of repetition, sudden changes of tone and opinion, allusion, and metaphoric coloring. But now our focus changes from the overall structure of the essays to more local relationships among the fragments from which they are constructed. We look not at a repeated cycle of attitudes presented argumentatively or through brief narratives but at repetition of a more obvious kind: actual restatements within paragraphs and the repetition of certain techniques in lists of metaphors and strings of anecdotes, quotations, and fables. The minutiae of Emerson's style, however, are generated by the same tensions as the essay's drama of multiple personae. The defensive interpretation of influences and the competition between irony and the sublime are as active in these arrangements of the prose as they are in Emerson's interpretive strategies. In order to discern these tendencies, we must shift our attention from the figure of the reader in the text to reactions of readers of the text, Emerson and ourselves.

The first chapter of this section is an etiology of the paragraph focusing on Emerson's habits of composition and revision. Once the relationship between repetition and discontinuity in the writing process has been established and described, the question of its effect on the reader leads us to our dual response of ironic skepticism and sublime assent. When, in the following chapter, we turn to Emerson's self-interpretations, we find that when he reads his own works, he, too, registers an uneasy response. Through a recurring complex of metaphors, he represents his prose in terms of discrete objects and metamorphic energy, in other words, as a series of transitions between fragments. Although his preference is clearly for antagonistic differences rather than organic integrations, Emerson, like all true Romantics, alternately celebrates discontinuity and wishes it could be teleologically resolved. In both moods, he assigns figurative values to fragmentation, discontinuity, and repetition, so that stylistic attributes are absorbed into his complex self-mythologizing. In the final chapter, the problem of the status of his metaphors, their intention and meaning, requires an investigation of his metaphors for metaphor. In its most characteristic, serial form, Emerson's figurative language reintroduces the problematics of influence. His metaphors are almost always allusive. The comparative interpretations that discover the repetitions in history turn the past into a supply of analogous figures. The local repetitions of Emerson's rhetoric, like the cyclical structure of the essays, reenact his overcoming of tradition. The point of these final chapters, then, is to show that the interpretive processes which are dramatized in the tones and poses of the essays also organize our progress through words, sentences, and paragraphs. The reader must work out for herself or himself the anxieties and pleasures of an Emersonian development.

· 7 ·

REPETITION

Emerson's prose is organized by "discontinuous adjacency."[1] Contiguous sentences are paraphrases of or substitutes for each other. This kind of repetition causes sentences to feel randomly arranged, like interchangeable parts. It creates "the most fragmentary result," as Emerson well knew, "paragraphs incompressible each sentence an infinitely repellent particle" (CEC.185). Our problem will be to discover what causes his—and our—sensations of excess and disorientation. What is the source and meaning of the energy manifested as "jets and projectiles of thought"?[2] How is repetition of content related to the discontinuous quality that enabled a later anthologist to isolate "Philosograms" ("Over Two Hundred Pungent Sayings of 'The Sage of Concord' ") as well as, in another volume, "Two Thousand Quotable Thoughts" and "Many Virile Epigrams" by the same author?[3]

As we know, Emerson's essays were not so much composed as assembled in a patently "synthetic" process.[4] The process began with "the fortuitous order of the journal," that assemblage of "disjointed dreams, audacities, unsystematic irresponsible lampoons of systems, and all matter of rambling reveries" (CEC.272).[5] He reworked this raw material in abbreviated collections, whole notebooks of transcriptions from earlier journals, and revisions of individual passages.[6] Emerson's indexing system undoubtedly reinforced the repetitive structure of the journals, since subject headings guided him to multiple variations on a single theme. By tracing the evolution of selected paragraphs through some or all of these phases, we can find, in what he retained and emphasized and what he edited out, evidence of his intentions. I want to demonstrate in some detail first, that repetition is not an accident, but the con-

sciously elected form of his mature prose; and second, that discontinuity is the deliberate result of repetition.

In 1847, Emerson put together a typical cluster of related passages under the heading "Transition." The letter-number codes
in the text are his own cross-references; the numbers in parentheses
to the right are mine.

Intellect detaches   (1)
All things grew, every detachment only prepares a new
detachment   Individ[ual] under Genera
Intellect sees these

   Οι ρεοντες[7]   Transition

           Intellect detaches   (2)
              In the most decided manner
We touch crimes, depths, mischance & are yet safe
Also with heights, virtues, heroes we find an interval

Intellect detaches the person. In any & every low company   (3)
he is always salvable. He turns his Gyges ring & disappears
from them at will.
      'Tis a patent of nobility. Ali Buonaparte

   Intellect contemplates Detachment   (4)

  Detachment of all things
  All things let go hands
Intell[ect] shares the detachment it sees   (5)
       makes an interval
       detaches the Person & is a patent of nobility

      Advantage
      CKN[ewcomb] good company
      luxury
      emphasis not laid on persons, & facts.

      Disadvantage
      spoils virtue

action
even conversation

But all this detachment is the preparation for Transition, which is the organic destiny of the mind.
    Life is transitive

        The moment of Transition in history. CD 48
Value of a trope that the hearer is one.
Certainly, the great law of nature will work here; that the more transit, the more continuity; or, we are immortal by force of transits.
We ask a selfish immortality, Nature replies by steeping us in the sea which girds the seven worlds, & makes us free of them all
——

at any pitch a higher pitch   O 176

What we call the universe of today is only a symptom or omen

        I see the law of the world to be transition.
Our power lies in that, CD 48 as, when the knees straighten, there is said to be a certain infinite of Power, which is availed of in the Power Press—

transit in rhetoric,
        in nature. natura
        in time
        in ascension of state

Every atom is on its way onward, the universe circulates in thought.
Every thought is passagére[?] in

    Power passes from races of men as from pears. JK last page
                                        (JMN.X.159–61)

Examining the provenance of these notes shows Emerson engaged in the potentially unending process of self-quotation and self-interpretation familiar to all students of the journals. These

· 162 ·

deceptively rough jottings not only carry forward earlier journal entries, but refer to passages already incorporated into lectures and/or essays. For example, the line "value of a trope that the hearer is one" apparently refers to a journal entry on "Transit" (*JMN*.X.44) which would be partially utilized later in "Eloquence" (*W*.VIII.127). That journal entry is followed immediately by a note in which he reminds himself that he had *already* touched on the subject of "transit" in "The Poet." As we pursue the sources of a single line, we discover a receding horizon. A journal entry used in "The Poet" is echoed in a later journal, then in the 1847 collation, then in "Eloquence." There are cross-references to three other journal entries in the "Transition" collation. The two references to "CD 48" take us to an 1847 journal entry used in "Power" (*W*.VI. 70–71):

> Every thing good in nature & the world is in that moment of transition, the foam hangs but a moment on the wave; the sun himself does not pause on the meridian; literature becomes criticism, nervousness & a gnawing when the first musical triumphant strain has waked the echoes. (*JMN*.X.82)

A rather cryptic observation on the elusiveness of "Truth" and "the ideal" found at "O 176" glosses "At any pitch a higher pitch" (*JMN*.IX.405–406). Finally, Emerson remembers or finds "JK last page." "Power passes from races of men as from pears" directs us to a paragraph appearing twice in the journals in which this startling simile is explained. He compares races of men to "the St. Michael's pear tree" that "wears out and will have an end." Man "vegetates, thrives & multiplies, usurps all the soul & nutriment, & so kills the weaker races . . . but his doom was in nature as well as his thrift, & overtakes him at last" (*JMN*.VII.90; X.404). As we see Emerson browsing through his journals, noting relevant passages and commenting on them ("Certainly, the great law of nature will work here"), we are aware of the various, not the repetitive, character of his observations. But when he pauses to clarify what has accumulated, he perceives the serial structure of his notes and condenses them to expose that structure: "transit in rhetoric / in nature . . . / in time / in ascension of state." As

I and other critics do, he explains his repetitions by reducing them to a common denominator, "transit." He has been seeking "twenty fables with one moral," actively interpreting his own history in order to subdue its chaotic diversity (CW.II.8).

The reduction of diversity to unity does not account for the genesis of Emerson's repetitions, however, though it may describe his later reading of them. If we go back to the passages I have numbered (1) through (5) at the beginning of the "Transition" collation, we can observe repetitive improvisation in progress. Citations from earlier journals generate new variants, alternatives, equivalents, analogues of or metaphors for each other. These additions take the form of exposition, illustration, hyperbole, or free association.[8] In the first group of phrases, he elaborates the premise "Intellect detaches" by apposition. Detachment is growth, which he defines in turn as continuous preparation for "a new detachment." In addition, or alternatively, detachment is the mental act of classification, the perception of "Individ[uals] under Genera." Each phrase is both a partial definition and a restatement of "Intellect detaches." Emerson reiterates his proposition while making its syntax more complex: Intellect detaches / Intellect contemplates detachment / Intellect shares the detachment it sees. The degree of repetition is obviously disproportionate to the minor additions of meaning.

In grouping (2), the same phrase is similarly extended. The fourth line adds a complementary catalogue ("Also with heights, virtues," and so on) to the third line but can stand in for it as well. For example, we understand what "safe" means here by substituting the homologous word in the next line. "Interval" is equivalent only because parallel, for it is different in proper meaning, connotation, and part of speech.

The third cluster of phrases restates the refrain "Intellect detaches." "We touch crimes . . . & are yet safe" is paraphrased as "in . . . low company he is always salvable." The germs of three illustrative fables follow this line, featuring, respectively, the possessor of the "Gyges ring," "Ali," and "Buonaparte." With no trouble at all, we can imagine a typical Emersonian paragraph of analogous parables.

In segment (4), "Intellect contemplates detachment" is completed by "Detachment of all things," then rendered figuratively, "All things let go hands." The fifth segment, too, both reiterates and augments its first line by several paraphrases of it: "shares the detachment" *means* "makes an interval" *which is* a "patent of nobility." The repetitive structure of these notes persists in the paragraphs they become in the lectures assembled by James Cabot as "Natural History of Intellect" (*W*.XII. "Notes," 421–25). The "interval" becomes the subject of a later paragraph, but the refrain is still "Intellect detaches." It is of the greatest significance that the "method of restatement" is *more* pronounced in the assembled lectures than in the journal.[9] Journal notations grew into lecture paragraphs by the addition of more repetitions. The lines retained from the 1847 "Transition" entry in the lecture (and included in the notes to "Natural History of Intellect") are underlined:

This is the first property of the Intellect I am to point out: the mind detaches. . . .

In speaking of identity, I said, All things grow; in a living mind the thoughts live and grow, and what happens in the vegetable happens to them. There are always individuals under generals; not stagnant, not childless, but everything alive reproduces, and each has its progeny which fast emerge into light; or what seemed one truth presently multiplies itself into many.

Of course this detachment the intellect contemplates. The intellect forever watches, foresees this detachment. 'T is an infinite series. Every detachment prepares a new detachment. Of course the prophecy becomes habitual and reaches to all things. Having seen one thing that once was firmament enter into the kingdom of growth and change, the conclusion is irresistible, there is no fixture in the universe. Everything was moved, did spin, and will spin again. This changes once for all his view of things. Things appear as seeds of an immense future. Whilst the dull man always [lives] in a finished world, the thinker always finds himself in the early ages; the world lies to him in heaps.

<u>The intellect that sees the interval partakes of it.</u> (W.XII.38, 435,44)

Between the already repetitive clauses of 1847, Emerson fits new variations, as though to bridge gaps. However, the impression of discontinuity is reinforced, not eliminated. Rearranging one of the paragraphs just quoted clarifies its structure:

> all things grow
> in a living mind the thoughts live and grow
> what happens in the vegetable happens to them
> not stagnant, not childless
> everything alive reproduces
> each has its progeny
> what seemed one truth multiplies itself into many

The first three clauses stem from the classification of "individuals under generals": minds and vegetables are subcategories of "all things" and analogues of each other. A chain of associated words creates the series: "grow"—"live and grow"—"childless"—"re-produces"—"progeny"—"multiplies." Synonyms also generate part of the next paragraph: the intellect "contemplates," "watches," "foresees." "Everything was moved, did spin, and will spin again" is not so much a new application of the law of "infinite series" as a figurative restatement of "there is no fixture in the universe." "Seeds of an immense future" and the thinker who "finds himself in the early ages" are metaphors as well as deductions. Emerson's tropes further his logic but also exceed and complicate it. The rich figurative texture of these paragraphs, which appears to vary, conceal, or soften their repetitive structure, actually constitutes it.

This process of composition by repetition results in the familiar rhetoric of the published works. If we return to "The Poet," a convenient source of examples because it has received our closest reading, we find that the essay is organized by repetition within paragraphs as well as by the repetition of the antithetical cycles blocked out in Part II. Analogous restatement is not motivated by the desire to convert contradiction into "dialectical synthesis." Opposites are repeated without being reconciled. "The Poet," we

recall, opens by situating the speaker between "sensual" critics
and the Poet. Virtually every sentence in the first paragraph extends the polarity. "Whatever is elegant" is juxtaposed to "beautiful souls," "fair pictures" to "acts . . . like fair pictures." "[F]ire"
and "cold," "form" and "soul," "We" and "our bodies," "Time
and its creatures" and the "ideal and beautiful," are irreconcilable.
The paragraph constituted by the theme of antagonism is formally
no different from those which celebrate identity.

The second paragraph of "The Poet" sets forth another dualistic
series. This time the two terms are related by quantitative comparison: partial man/the complete man; private wealth/common-
wealth; himself/more himself than he is; he received/but they more;
man is half himself/the other half is his expression. Again, repetition strengthens the distinction between part and whole rather
than subsuming the "partial" into the "complete" (*W*.III.3–4).

In paragraph 10 of "The Poet," all sentences either restate the
opening assertion that nature's worthier impulses protect the poetic
office or enumerate those impulses. The third and fourth sentences
paraphrase parts of the first. A simile (the carpenter's cord) and
a quotation, which works both as restatement and as *exemplum*,
illustrate the idea of nature's linguistic significance. What sounds
like explanation ("because Nature is a symbol") is the occasion
for further repetition, and a concrete example (the line drawn in
the sand) initiates the series of correspondent pairs that issues in
the quotation from Spenser. The paragraph closes with a contin-
uation of that series, the Being-Appearance, Unity-Variety dual-
ities. Whether the sentences are metaphors, allusions, or assertions,
they set forth the same relationship.

The nature of the repeated content does not substantially alter
the tendency of repetition to generate ambivalence in the reader.
The sheer plenitude of synonyms makes us more aware of difference
than of likeness. Emerson's variations have the cumulative effect
of breaking up "what seemed one truth . . . into many" subtly
differentiated truths (*W*.XII.435). In the 1847 journal entry,
Emerson suggests that an "infinite series" gives rise to incessant
"detachment"; repetition is the "[w]ave which severs whom it
bears / From the thing which he compares" (*W*.XII.[2]). Each of

the paragraphs cited constitutes a diacritical system. Like a thesaurus, a list of words that purport to be interchangeable extends the meaning of any one term. At the same time, we perceive connotative differences that prevent the words from being truly equivalent. Furthermore, because synonyms or analogues are parallel rather than truly sequential within the paragraph, conventional links between them, the "signals of *identity*" and "*transition*" which move expository prose forward, are either missing altogether or are deprived of their proper function.[10] Repetition displaces or subverts logical transitions between sentences and opens the way for Emerson's "astonishing variety of logic-confounding devices":

> conflation of apparent opposites, chiasmus, clefting that fragments assertions, switching of tenses that blurs time distinction, interchanging of singular and plural entities, transforming of multiples to single elements in defiance of syntactic logic, and word-order inversion. . . . In addition . . . redundancy almost of an incantatory nature, violations of subject-verb convention . . . abrupt and unannounced shifts from cause to effect, agent to receiver . . . passivization, mixing of abstract and concrete imagery.[11]

These discrepancies originate in Emerson's compositional habits. The jolts and jars, losses of balance, and recoveries that we experience in pursuing him through one of his essays are due largely to small syntactic, grammatical, and tonal inconsistencies between passages that were "found separate" (*JMN.V.*39). But the survival of these gaps in his published prose is intentional and purposeful. As he writes in one of his more swashbuckling justifications of his procedure, "if you desire to arrest attention, to surprise, do not give me facts in the order of cause & effect, but drop one or two links in the chair, & give me with a cause, an effect two or three times removed" (*JMN.VII.*90). By retaining baffling transitions in the finished product, he creates a rhetoric of linguistic, not theological, apostasy.[12]

The impression of discontinuity is strengthened by the way repetition within paragraphs affects the transitions between them, "his perilous passages from paragraph to paragraph of manuscript," as Alcott put it.[13] The flow of an essay slows almost to a halt as the paragraph spreads out in a pool of analogies. When Emerson begins a new paragraph, therefore, he conspicuously reestablishes linearity in order to compensate for its temporary suspension. The impulse that led him to construct outlines and chapter plans for *Nature* has not died out. The conservative attention to coherence, however, is deceptive, as always. Paragraphs begin with a spate of demonstrative adjectives, conjunctions, and conjunctive adverbs, signals inserted "so that a reader can easily see the kind of relation that's implied between one statement and the next one."[14] But the very transitions that purport to clarify are often as disconcerting as the omission or skewing of connectives within paragraphs. His signals are oddly unrelated to content. Words that should indicate a change of subject introduce continuations; demonstratives that require an antecedent announce new thoughts. He nods in the direction of the conventions of nonfictional prose, then shapes the essay to his own antithetical and associative patterns.

The first sentence of the twelfth paragraph of "The Poet," for example, conspicuously refers back—but to what? What are "these waters" over which we hover "with a religious regard"? I argued in my chapter on "The Poet" that this alludes to the "holy place" previously mentioned; the connection of both passages to Genesis supports that conclusion, I think. But this reading is not immediate or obvious. A number of possibilities suggest themselves and must be considered before we settle on one of them. The truths articulated in the preceding paragraph seem to be designated collectively as deep waters over which the reader "hovers." Or the waters may be one of these truths, the "brute and dark" mystery we perceive in phenomena when our corresponding faculties are not yet active. The phrase is divided between "these," the demonstrative adjective that insists on continuity, and the metaphoric vehicle, "waters," with no apparent tenor (W.III.15).

Proceeding to the next paragraph, we again encounter the demonstrative and the assertion of continuity: "The inwardness and mystery of this attachment drive men of every class to the use of emblems." "This attachment" has too many antecedents. Almost every sentence in the paragraph before attests to our attachment to or "fascination" with nature. After a moment it occurs to us that we are to carry forward the general theme of "attachment" rather than to remember a single antecedent. Similarly, there is no obvious referent for the demonstrative at the beginning of paragraph 20: "This insight, which expresses itself by what is called Imagination, is a very high sort of seeing" (*W*.III.16,26).

If Emerson signals identity where we expect transition, he indicates transition where we expect identity. In the paragraph beginning "But the quality of the imagination is to flow, and not to freeze," "but" prepares us for a contrast with what has just been stated. There is no mention of fixity in the preceding paragraph to be rejected, however. "But not to freeze" may modify the "immorality" of imaginative works, distinguishing permanence from stasis. Still, the content seems to call for a signal of continuity, not contrast. A similar "but" occurs after the speech of the Orphic poet: "So far the bard taught me, using his freer speech. But nature has a higher end in the production of new individuals than security, namely ascension, or the passage of the soul into higher forms." The bard has, in fact, just concluded an allegory of ascension: "the melodies of the poet ascend and leap and pierce into the deeps of infinite time" (*W*.III.34,24). At moments like these, gaps are simultaneously widened and bridged. Neither fully parallel nor linearly related, paragraphs intersect incidentally in a skewed, oblique way. The unnerving passages between them result from the same motives as the somewhat different transitions between sentences. Emerson makes imperfect connections (masked by a conventional manner) for the sake of the mental sensation of leaping between fragments. The further apart statements are, so to speak, the more aware the mind is of its power in moving from one to the next. Emerson's delight in the electrical charge of each "repellent particle" is equaled only by the energy of the "impertinent associations" that span the distance between them. Alcott, sensitive to the kinetics of Emerson's language, commented: "Each period is self-poised; there may be a chasm of years between the opening passage and the last written, and there is endless time in the composition. Jewels all! separate stars. You may have them in a galaxy, if you like, or view them separate and apart."[15]

The joys of such a style are closely related to its aggressiveness, as pleasure always is in Emerson's prose. In order to clarify the link between repetition and aggression, I want to read, carefully, one more passage from "The Poet."

> For the Universe has three children, born at one time, which reappear under different names in every system of thought, whether they be called cause, operation and effect; or, more poetically, Jove, Pluto, Neptune; or, theologically, the Father, the Spirit and the Son; but which we will call here the Knower, the Doer and the Sayer. These stand respectively for the love of truth, for the love of good, and for the love of beauty. These three are equal. Each is that which he is, essentially, so that he cannot be surmounted or analyzed, and each of these three has the power of the others latent in him and his own, patent. (W.III.6–7)

This strikes me, somewhat incidentally, as a parody of Coleridge's meditation on the Trinity in *Aids to Reflection.* Coleridge translates Father, Son, and Holy Ghost into Substantive, Verb, Participle, then into thesis or position, antithesis or opposition, synthesis or equilibrium.[16] The passage from "The Poet" also resembles one of Emerson's journal entries of 1835:

> The Germans believe in the necessary Trinity of God,—the Infinite; the finite, & the passage from Inf. into Fin.; or, the Creation. It is typified in the act of thinking. Whilst we contemplate we are infinite; the thought we express is partial & finite; the expression is the third part & is equivalent to the act of Creation. Unity says Schelling is barren. Duality is necessary to the existence of the World. Shall I say then that the galvanic action of metals foreshows from afar the God head, the zinc the metal & the acid; or the marriage of plants the pollen, the ovary, & the junction? (JMN.V.30)

Here, Emerson conflates the Coleridgean Trinity with Schelling's dialectic. Then, characteristically, his tone alters and he imagines material equivalents of this system: "the galvanic action of metals" and "the marriage of plants" are similarly tripartite and thus "[fore-show] from afar the God head." He comes down to earth as Coleridge does not and is well aware of the incongruity between zinc and the Godhead, as the slightly arch "Shall I say then" indicates. He is conscious of the play of translation, and the resulting detachment contrasts sharply with Coleridge's seriousness.

In the same spirit, the paragraph from "The Poet" names and renames a trinity in the languages of several "system[s] of thought" or kinds of knowledge. The initial metaphysical terms (cause, operation, effect) are paraphrased "more poetically" (Jove, Pluto, Neptune), next "theologically" (Father, Spirit, Son). Then Emerson invents his own names (Knower, Doer, Sayer), and ends by equating these with affective responses to different moral objects (truth, good, beauty). Religion, myth, philosophy, morals, and psychology are equivalent and interchangeable—and figurative. How does a paragraph like this affect the reader? Where so many labels can be applied, can any of them be definitive? Emerson instructs us in relativity. Ironic juxtaposition diminishes every term. If "the Father, the Spirit and the Son" are just other names for the essences once called "Jove, Pluto, Neptune," then Christianity ceases to be superior to pagan mythology. They have equal value, which may mean no value, as systems of belief. He apparently validates even the patently fictive names by linking them to conduct and feelings, explaining myths as the actions of doing, knowing, and saying, and these as results of the attraction to truth, good, and beauty. But even the psychological ground of fable turns into an infinite regression which, if it amplifies meaning by showing the relationships among disparate terms, drains away meaning by making the reader skeptical. Repetition can, as Kierkegaard knew, lead both to "the negative feeling which is the passion of the absurd" and to "the positive feeling, 'Behold, all things have become new.' "[17] Earlier, in trying to describe the journal notes on "Transition" and the essay paragraphs they became, I distinguished several kinds of repetition: classification, or the listing of "individuals under genera"; word association that generates a chain of synonyms; metaphoric variations; self-paraphrase that both repeats and elaborates an initial statement; quotation and allusion. Each kind of repetition would seem to have a separate motive. But these repetitions, despite their differences, precipitate the same dual response in the reader, who feels as though he has been asked a question to which the only answers are "none" or "all of the above."

Our skepticism results from perceiving the repeated elements as substitutes for one another implicitly connected by "or." This "or" does not indicate a forced choice (either/or), but an excess of equally valid alternatives:

or, more poetically . . . *or* theologically

science always goes abreast with the just elevation of the man . . . *or* the state of science is an idea of our self-knowledge.

The beauty of the fable proves the importance of the sense; to the poet, and to all others; *or* if you please, every man is so far a poet as to be susceptible of these enchantments of nature. (*W*.III.6–7,14–15)

In addition to whatever undercutting occurs as a result of interaction between specific terms, such as the challenge "Jove, Pluto, Neptune" pose to "the Father, the Spirit and the Son," the act of substitution, the act of "or," itself creates disjunction. Repetition forces us to take out one interchangeable part and insert another. To adopt Emerson's terminology, it creates the "interval," "break in continuity," or "gap" necessary for "the Comic." This is the act of "detachment" that makes possible "transition"—to use the key terms of the next chapter. Such intervals affect the reader by intensifying the figurative or fictive quality of language and thus diminishing its capacity for true and final naming.

When repetitions are related by addition, however, by an implied "and," the original statement is persuasively extended, enriched, and complicated. We rise above the local difficulties of the catalogue and feel its terms cumulatively gather into hyperbole. We feel that conviction, not doubt, has motivated its redundancies. If we are aware of contradictions, we are likely to interpret them as expressions of multiple possibilities rather than as self-negating positions. The energy of the prose is prolific, not destructive. In a sense, we reenact the phases of the mathematical sublime: our disorientation in the face of a series or scattering of elements is resolved by and into the mind's sense of apprehensive power. Fragments point us toward an unavailable wholeness of vision and become identified with the intuition of completeness they precipitate.[18] In Benjamin's grim evaluation, what we do at such moments is "to pile up fragments ceaselessly, without any strict idea of a goal, and, in the unremitting expectation of a miracle . . . take the repetition of stereotypes for a process of intensification."[19]

Although I have described the ironic and sublime responses to Emerson's paragraphs in either/or fashion for the sake of distinguishing them, we typically experience a mixture of the two. It is the sensation of slipping or wavering between doubt and conviction that characterizes one's reading of Emerson. This mixed reaction is another version of the competition between ironic and sublime tones, only now it is located in us, not depicted in the text. Such sensations are not peculiar to the twentieth-century reader. Emerson's own figurative representations of his prose portray it as radically fragmented, and his evaluations are as unstable as ours. At one moment, discontinuity exhilarates him; at another, it plunges him into despair. Variations in affect, furthermore, are complicated by his equivocations on the relative priority of reading and writing, self-consciousness and surprise.

DETACHMENT AND
TRANSITION

I have followed Emerson's example in describing in Romantic terms the sensations produced by reading his prose. For just as he knowingly reflects on his anti-authoritarian hermeneutics in certain of his fables, so he represents, in other parables, ideas about composition and style that utilize a variety of Romantic aesthetic notions. The relationship between the drama of interpretation enacted throughout the essays and the thematic values Emerson ascribes to stylistic features is very close. His fluctuating emotions about the nature and extent of the author's intellectual control of his tradition are repeated in allegories about the interaction between words and thoughts, discontinuity and teleology, purposiveness and surprise. He manages to convince me, at least, that his style successfully gratifies his desire for both conscious power over his material and the feeling of being surprised by it. He addresses our sense of the apparent randomness of his prose by repeatedly telling us what randomness signifies; he advances but also skeptically criticizes periodic claims to order. Such meditations focus on the metaphoric opposition of objects and energy and, analogously, of detachment and transition.

These patterns emerge in a characteristic fable. Emerson justifies his own practice of assembling essays from journal entries by attributing this method to all artists. Initially, he praises stylistic discontinuity resulting from the separate origins of a work's parts:

> by a multitude of trials & a thousand rejections & the using
> & perusing of what was already written . . . a poem made

that shall thrill the world by the mere juxtaposition & inter-action of lines & sentences that singly would have been of little worth & short date. Rightly is this art named compo-sition & the composition has manifold the effect of the com-ponent parts. The orator is nowise equal to the evoking on a new subject of this brilliant chain of sentiments, facts, illus-trations whereby he now fires himself & you. Every link in this living chain he found separate; one, ten years ago; one, last week; some of them he found in his father's house or at school when a boy; some of them by his losses; some of them by his sickness; some by his sins. The Webster with whom you talk admires the oration almost as much as you do, & knows himself to be nowise equal, unarmed, that is, without this tool of Synthesis to the splendid effect which he is yet well pleased you should impute to him.

No hands could make a watch. The hands brought dry sticks together & struck the flint with iron or rubbed sticks for fire & melted the ore & with stones made crow bar & hammer these again helped to make chisel & file, rasp & saw, piston & boiler, & so the watch & the steam engine are made, which the hands could never have produced & these again are new tools to make still more recondite & prolific instruments. So do the collated thoughts beget more & the artificially com-bined individuals have in addition to their own a quite new collective power. The main is made up of many islands, the state of many men. The poem of many thoughts each of which, in its turn, filled the whole sky of the poet was day & Being to him. (*JMN.V.39–40*)

Journal keeping—"the using & perusing of what was . . . written . . . ten years ago" or "last week"—initiates the "art named composition." Sentences record "sentiments, facts, illus-trations" that have been lifted out of the continuum of experience, have "filled the whole sky of the poet," were "day & Being to him." The author must link these in a "living chain" without diminishing their individual integrity as moments. The separate genesis of "lines & sentences" makes possible juxtaposition, in which they creatively clash with each other and generate the "power" that "fires" the reader or listener.

This parable metaphorically represents the interaction of subject matter and imagination as the symbiotic relationship between objects and energy. Fragments of experience ("sentiments, facts, illustrations") and of prose ("lines & sentences") correspond to raw materials: dry sticks, flint, iron, stones, tools. Authorial intelligence is represented by energy: hands, fire, steam. The "living chain" of imaginative prose is a chain reaction between the two. Later in the passage, the ocean's flow, a collective political will, the poet's active mind transform into new wholes isolated islands, men, and thoughts. But Emerson's metaphor undergoes a significant change as he feels his way through this meditation. "Mere juxtaposition" gives way to "Synthesis" and an allegory of technological progress. He begins by celebrating the "splendid effect" of random combination. But open-ended process becomes teleological through shifts in metaphor. Oscillation becomes progressive, as in the famous dictum from "Self-Reliance": "Power . . . resides in the moment of transition from a past to a new state, in the shooting of the gulf, in the darting to an aim" (CW.II.40). The privileged term ceases to be "transition" and becomes "aim."

In a lecture of the same year as the "tool of Synthesis" passage, Emerson criticizes Bacon's failure to use that tool:

> Bacon's method is not within the work itself, but without. This might be expected in his *Natural History* but . . . in his *Essays* it is the same. All his work lies along the ground a vast unfinished city. He did not arrange but unceasingly collect facts. His own Intellect often acts little on what he collects. Very much stands as he found it—mere lists of facts. . . . The fire has hardly passed over it and given it fusion and a new order from his mind. It is sand without lime . . . thrown together; the order of a shop and not that of a tree or an animal where perfect assimilation has taken place and all the parts have a perfect unity. (*EL*.I.335)

Again we find the dichotomy between matter and fire, "facts" and intellect. Their ideal relationship is the organic fusion of a tree's or an animal's "perfect assimilation." The opposite image of a "vast unfinished city" bears witness to repeated beginnings never completed, a nightmare vision of the technological miracles praised in the other passage. Nostalgia for the organic enters in response to an unending series like the desire for the unifying absolute of the sublime. We glimpse the anxiety that frequently leads Emerson to recommend organic synthesis rather than the contrived alternation that potentially leads to "mere lists."

The impulse to sheer away from the constructed nature of his own work surfaces in his equivocations on the writer's self-consciousness. The idea that "composition" involves "a multitude of trials & a thousand rejections & the using & perusing of what was already written" implies that revision is the most creative phase of writing. Our examination of Emerson's own methods bears this out. Yet he then claims that his successes are inadvertent. The author "admires the oration almost as much as you do & knows himself to be nowise equal . . . to the splendid effect which he is yet well pleased you should impute to him." The passage shuffles between method and accident, intention and automatism, as he attributes energy to the artist's own mind, then to a spirit within or behind things. "Juxtaposition" generates sparks that surprise even the author. Tools—emblems of human inventiveness—produce effects beyond his control. The brilliant synopsis of technological development from the Stone Age to the Industrial Revolution conveys our perpetual unpreparedness in the face of our "recondite and prolific instruments."

The journal entry written at Nantasket Beach in July 1841 and partly quoted in my introduction brings together with marvelous complexity Emerson's simultaneous desire for knowledge and power, which he represents as repetition and surprise:

> We have two needs Being & Organization. See how much pains we take here in Plato's dialogues to set in order the One Fact in two or three or four steps & renew as oft as we can the pleasure the eternal surprise [sic] of coming at the last fact as children run up steps to jump down or up a hill to coast down on sleds or run far for one slide or as we get

fishing tackle & go many miles to a watering place to catch
fish and having caught one & learned the whole mystery we
still repeat the process for the same result though perhaps the
fish are thrown overboard at the last. The merchant plays
,the same game on Change, the card lover at whist, and what
else does the scholar? He knows how the poetry he knows
how the novel or the demonstration will affect him no new
result but the oldest of all, yet he still craves a new book &
bathes himself anew with the plunge at the last. The young
men here this morning who have tried all the six or seven
things to be done, namely, the sail, the bowling alley, the ride
to Hull, and to Cohasset, the bath & the spyglass, they are
in a rage just now to *do* something these itching fingers, this
short activity, these nerves, this plasticity or creativeness accompanies forever & ever the profound Being. (*JMN*.VIII.
12–13)

Emerson's explanation posits an economy of psychic forces. The
last sentence suggests that repetition is a discharge of energy. Young
men "in a rage . . . to *do* something" are flooded with the su-
prapersonal force of Being, of which they are not conscious and
which is consequently beyond their control. They "rage" because
they have not yet discovered the pleasures of recurrence. But if
they are governed by involuntary motion ("itching fingers" and
"nerves"), the scholar "organizes" the pure dynamism of Being
by *electing* to repeat himself. Repetition is a complex episode in
which consciousness manages to surprise itself—a perfectly ironic
and perfectly sublime event. As always in Emerson's writings,
surprise is a conscious strategy to replicate unself-consciousness,
a borderline state contained in the oxymoron, "eternal surprize."
The reader "knows the poetry . . . will affect him" with "the
oldest of all results" yet "bathes himself anew." An instantaneous
change of state yields a split second of illusory newness which,
later, he knows as renewal. It is as though there is a momentary
lag when memory has not yet caught up to sensation.

As Nietzsche proclaimed in "The Use and Abuse of History"
(1873), one of his most Emersonian polemics, "Forgetfulness is a

property of all action."[1] Emerson was quite right to assert, in "Memory," "We forget . . . according to beautiful laws" (*W*.XII.107). He clearly attributes repetition to the workings of a pleasure principle; he repeats to "renew . . . the pleasure, the eternal surprize." "This metonymy, or seeing the same sense in things so diverse, gives a *pure pleasure*," he writes elsewhere. "Every one of a million times we find a charm in the metamorphosis" (*W*.VIII.25; emphasis added). Pleasure is a compound of motion and power. The mind's leap in repeated transition is play for its own sake. As with the card player's or financier's calculations, the winnings are irrelevant; "perhaps the fish are thrown overboard at last." Stevens, writing against Freud, would later celebrate the same pleasure in repetition and difference: "Two things of opposite nature seem to depend / On one another. . . . This is the origin of change / . . . cold copulars embrace / and forth the particulars of rapture come" ("Notes toward a Supreme Fiction," Part II, canto iv, 11.1–6).[2]

Emerson's need for a distance or difference between subject and object, mind and world, reveals how unlike Coleridge he was. Despite the importance of Coleridge to his intellectual development, he never absorbed the English Romantic's desire to interinvolve subject and object organically; rather, he thrives on the almost conflictual difference between them. In another parable, which favors teleology over sheer transition, the action of energy on matter once again represents imaginative process. "Is not poetry the little chamber in the brain," he asks, "where is generated the explosive force which, by gentle shocks, sets in action the intellectual world?" He answers himself by illustrating how consciousness takes up nature and converts it into words in a process which both requires and frees the mind's energy:

> the beholding and co-energizing mind sees the same refining and ascent to the third, the seventh or the tenth power of the daily accidents which the senses report, and which make the raw material of knowledge. It was sensation; when memory came, it was experience; when mind acted, it was knowledge; when mind acted on it as knowledge, it was thought.

"Explosive force" acts on "raw material." When objects are "melted" in the "Promethean alembics" of the mind, they "come out men, and then, melted again, come out words, without any abatement, but with an exaltation of power!" (W.VIII.64, 24, 16).

Emerson summarizes his metaphoric system in "Experience": "A subject and an object,—it takes so much to make the galvanic circle complete." The authorial subject is "the conductor of the whole river of electricity" (W.III.80, 40). His objects are fragments of writing, the "boulders" or "infinitely repellent particles" that he knows make for his "lapidary style" (CEC.185, 303). Emerson's journal entries are substantial, even material, entities. Each of his sentences is "a cube, standing on its bottom like a die, essential and immortal" (J.IX.423). It is while writing to Carlyle that he most often objectifies his language. Usually these metaphors are self-deprecating, part of the exchange of apologies and curiously mutual stylistic insults sprinkled throughout their letters. "I dot evermore in my endless journal," he reports, "a line on every unknowable in nature; but the arrangement loiters long, & I get a brick kiln instead of a house." The "little raft" of *Essays, First Series* is "only boards & logs tied together." Carlyle agrees. His correspondent's sentences do not "rightly stick to their foregoers and their followers: the paragraph [is] not as a beaten *ingot*, but as a beautiful square bag of *duck-shot* held together by canvas!" (CEC.278, 291, 371).

Emerson restates the metaphor of objects and energy cognitively in terms of the mind's acts of "detachment" and "transition," two of the key terms of his poetics. His artist's first task is identifying and fixing the points between which he will move. "And thou shalt serve the god Terminus, the bounding Intellect, & love Boundary or Form," he instructs the poet (JMN.VIII.405). In the following selection from "Art," the starting point can be object, thought, or word, so long as it be detached:

> The virtue of art lies in detachment, in sequestering one object from the embarrassing variety. Until one thing comes out from the connection of things, there can be enjoyment, contemplation, but no thought. . . . It is the habit of certain minds

to give an all-excluding fulness to the object, the thought, the
word, they alight upon, and to make that for the time the
deputy of the world. . . . The power . . . to magnify by
detaching is the essence of rhetoric in the hands of the orator
and the poet. (CW.II.211)

Rhetorical power originates in an epiphanic experience of the object
when the poet's attentiveness climaxes in a moment of "all-excluding fulness." Having made "a pigment of thought . . . palpable
and objective," the artist can launch himself toward another position. The "fact" created by objectification becomes a "fulcrum":
"Transition is the attitude of power. A fact is only a fulcrum of
the spirit. It is the terminus of a past thought, but only a means
now of new sallies of the imagination and new progress of wisdom"
(W.XII.59).

Emerson's ambivalence about detachment is characteristic of
Romantic notions of creative thought. Coleridge attributes something like the powers of detachment and transition to the imagination. The secondary imagination, we recall,

> dissolves, diffuses, dissipates, in order to re-create; or where
> this process is rendered impossible, yet still, at all events, it
> struggles to realize and to unify. It is essentially *vital*, even as
> all objects (as objects) are essentially fixed and dead.[3]

Coleridge is pessimistic about the possibility of total "recreation."
He implies (more darkly than is usually noticed), that "this process" is frequently "rendered impossible." Still, when the imagination cannot win, it should "at all events" struggle with its material.
If the Coleridgean imagination fails, what remains is Emerson's
terminology of energy (vitality), "fixed and dead" objects, and the
continuous oscillation (struggle) between them. Coleridge prefers
to focus on the successful acts of re-creation that effect unity in
poems, nations, and Christians. But his vision of what happens
when the secondary imagination breaks down seems to prophesy
the poet who detaches objects rather than dissolves them and jux-
taposes thoughts and things instead of "diffusing" them. Emerson's
habit of distinguishing objects from energy reverses the strategy of

most English Romantics, who envisioned language as living matter or incarnate spirit.[4] He desires the contest between idealizing mind and recalcitrant objects which, to Coleridge, was a poor second best. Like a good American, he identifies power with struggle, self-reliance with rebellion. The poet as liberator cannot afford to "diffuse" his adversary.

In his emphasis on detachment and objectification, Emerson comes closer to the German Romantics than to the English. Detachment was frequently discussed as both a perceptual and an historical phenomenon, "the path along which the individual, as well as the race, must pass." For Schiller, disunity is the moral equivalent of the fall of man. In the naïve state, man enjoyed "an undivided sensuous unity." But "once [he] has passed into the state of civilization," art "divides and cleaves him in two."[5] Detachment is agonizingly felt as self-division but is absolutely essential for art. For Schelling, detachment, "definiteness of form," is "never negation but always an affirmation." It is not an historical process but an attribute of nature and the works that seek to represent her: "without bound the boundlessness could not be manifested . . . if unity is to be made palpable, this can only be done through singularity, isolation and conflict."[6]

The notion of the detached fragment leads Emerson, as it led Schlegel, to a celebration of irony. Emerson's translation of "Witz" is "whim of will." He characterizes the fragment as an aggressive, self-reliant individual. It is no accident that in "Fate," his exemplar of the sublime is a human fragment, a baby. "I know not what the word *sublime* means," he writes in that essay, "if it be not the intimations, in this infant, of a terrific force. . . . A little whim of will to be free gallantly contending against the universe of chemistry!" (*W*.VI.29). Compression increases energy, and diminution is an index of heroism, it seems, in people as in prose. The speaker of "Experience" expects to be admired for telling us, "I know better than to claim any completeness for my picture. I am a fragment, and this is a fragment of me" (*W*.III.83).[7] Emerson's irony informs the peculiarly blithe tone of many passages in "Fate": "The way of Providence is a little rude." "The more of these drones perish, the better for the hive." "[I]t would be . . . the speediest way of deciding the vote, to put the selectmen or the mayor and aldermen at the hay-scales." "The German and Irish millions, like the Negro, have a great deal of guano in their destiny" (W.VI.7, 14, 16). This essay, which is supposed to express the darkening mood of Emerson's middle and later years, is, in fact, dryly humorous. The tension between the themes of repetition (the determinism of fate) and of discontinuity (the human will that defies necessity) results in a celebration of sublime irony:

> here they are, side by side, god and devil, mind and matter, king and conspirator, belt and spasm, riding peacefully together in the brain of every man.

> A man must ride alternately on the horses of his private and his public nature, as the equestrians in the circus throw themselves nimbly from horse to horse, or plant one foot on the back of one and the other foot on the back of the other. (W.VI.22–23, 47)

In "The Comic," we recall, the "double consciousness" exposes "the radical joke of life, and then of literature." The simultaneous perception of freedom and fate is a "radical joke," not tragic knowledge.

In intensifying the struggle between mind and matter, Emerson drew on quite a different set of sources, nineteenth-century varieties of linguistic fundamentalism and primitivistic conceptions of the word. In Swedenborgian cosmology, ideas and words tend toward the condition of matter but remain sharply distinguished from each other, for correspondence requires a triple parallelism of nature, thought, and language. The French Swedenborgian, Oegger, for example, advanced a theory of literal correspondence between nature and Scripture, even providing a table of "Hieroglyphic Keys" to facilitate a reading of nature's text.[8] Sampson Reed dreamed of an ideal state of language in which ideas are one with words and words "one with things." Human language "being as it were resolved into its original elements, will lose itself in nature."[9] It is but a short step from the correspondence of words and things to conceiving of words as thinglike. Attributing substance to words implies that ideas, too, are discrete entities.

Emerson's conception of detachment combines or reacts to elements of all these speculations. From the philosophers, he receives the fundamental notion of detachment as the origin of art and, like them, regards it as both loss and gain. In order to emphasize transition between detached perceptions, he increases the materiality of thoughts and words. Swedenborgianism provides a convenient vocabulary for this, although Emerson's "transition," as a differentiating movement, undoes the Swedenborgians' correspondential links. The demand for objects to react against comes from an antithetical rather than synthetic or Coleridgean imagination. Emerson's need to represent the unlikeness of words and mind (objects and energy) reveals the crucial role of difference in repetition. What is repeated is the "struggle" between different qualities, which strongly suggests that the motive for repetition is antagonism.

One result of Emerson's conception of the encounter between mind and matter is that every object comes to stand for the term, "matter." The aggressive imagination turns the world into a collection of metaphors, all vehicles for the same tenor. The alternating current of transition can take place between any two places, things, or persons, if sufficiently detached:

> Our strength is transitional, alternating; or, shall I say, a thread of two strands. The sea-shore, sea seen from shore, shore seen from sea; the taste of two metals in contact; and our enlarged powers at the approach and at the departure of a friend; the experience of poetic creativeness, which is not found in staying at home, nor yet in travelling, but in transitions from one to the other, which must therefore be adroitly managed to present as much transitional surface as possible. (W.IV.55–56)

Sea and shore, two metals, two persons must be separate. When the artist moves through the spaces created by detachment, he cannot be precisely located. He evades those who would define him and in this elusive freedom discovers the "enlarged powers" which make possible "the experience of poetic creativeness." Yet his termini are related by resemblance. Intellect masters an "embarrassing variety" of objects by discovering that they typify the same thing. Intense scrutiny transforms the object into a figure for the world's "central nature." The underlying affinity between the end points of transition permits Emerson to conceive of transition as metaphor making.

> The metamorphosis of nature shows itself in nothing more than this that there is no word in our language that cannot become typical to us of nature by giving it emphasis. . . . The world is a Dancer; it is a Rosary; it is a Torrent; it is a Boat; a Mist; a Spider's Snare; it is what you will, and the metaphor will hold, and it will give the imagination keen pleasure. . . . [T]he ear instantly hears, & the spirit leaps to the trope. (*JMN*.VIII.23)

"Emphasis"—that is, detachment or objectification—makes any word "typical . . . of Nature." Detachment entails the perception of the inherently metaphoric character of words and things which, thus fixed, become the objects between which "metamorphosis" occurs. (We remember the connection, in the "Transition" collation, between "transit" and "trope" in the mind of the reader [*JMN*.X.160].) In "Prospects" at the end of *Nature*, Emerson announces that the mystery of man's life lies in the "tyrannizing unity in his constitution, which evermore separates and classifies things, endeavoring to reduce the most diverse to one form" (*CW*.I.39–40). This splendidly succinct definition, which ricochets between unity and separation, reduction and diversity, under the pressure of his drive to embrace them simultaneously, shows us what metaphor does. A unifying impulse separates in order to conform what has been sundered to its own vision of unity. Imagination thus generates discontinuities that only it can heal, a solipsist exulting in its own deconstructive and reconstructive powers. We can see how metaphor fits into the paradigm of language as objectification that "separates and classifies" and as "tyrannizing, endeavoring" energy. This energy enables the writer to contain opposites in the close verbal quarters of a metaphor, where their interaction generates the "explosive force" of language (*W*.VIII.64).

The physics of detachment and transition replicates the strategy we observed at the outset of "The Poet" and other essays. Emerson sets himself against one figure in order to propel himself toward another. He attacks, we found, not in order to attain the object of his desire, but to restore or strengthen his self-regard. In opposition, he feels free, distinct, and individual. His theory of transition accomplishes the same thing. With a remarkable awareness of the thematics of style, he makes fixity a necessary attribute of figurative language. The sensation of power comes in the transition between one momentarily frozen percept and the next, in the instant of undoing their artificial importance. "Man is made for conflict, not for rest," he exclaims. "In action is his power; not in his goals but in his transitions man is great" (W.XII.60). In acting to connect two objects, intellect becomes aware of its own energy. Self-consciousness, in turn, brings on "an exaltation" or redundancy "of power" (W.VIII.16). The mind discovers that it is greater than the thoughts it entertains; between two ideas is a field of force that contains them both. By continuously separating and rejoining consciousness and its contents, energy and matter, Emerson simultaneously enjoys freedom from and mastery of facts.

The association of transition with power is, of course, conventional. Sudden, even violent transitions between the parts of the ode (turn, counter-turn, stand) had long been thought to be essential to the reader's astonishment and wonder. In the Romantic lyric, the association between discontinuity and greatness persists. Blair found it difficult to condone the fact that the sublime poet is "so abrupt in his transitions; so eccentric and irregular in his motions." But Wordsworth hoped his readers would find in "the transitions and the impassioned music of the versification" of "Tintern Abbey" "the principal requisites" of the ode.[10]

Although in Emerson's formula perpetual transition seems to be brought about by an unlimited supply of metaphoric vehicles, the availability of these vehicles actually depends on the author's "ulterior intellectual perception": "*once seen* . . . [metamorphosis] does not stop" (W.III.20, 30; emphasis added). Metaphor is not a property of the object but of the observer who perceives the independence of the thought on the symbol, the stability of the thought, the accidency and fugacity of the symbol. As the eyes of Lyncaeus were said to see through the earth, so the poet turns the world to glass, and shows us all things in their right series and procession. (W.III.20)

The metaphoric chain reaction is an ongoing act of mastering the object world. Once things are seen through, we are free from them; that is why symbols have the "power of emancipation" and "liberty" for all men (W.III.30, 32). Since any word or image can "represent the world," and since transition can occur between any two words or images, the chain reaction can go on forever, fueled by an infinite number of possible substitutions. Emerson "deprives himself of any brake on the transmutation of form," but this is not what bothers him.[11] When he knows himself capable of transition, he can contemplate the possibility of its endless repetition with perfect equanimity. But a series of unrelated objects not bound by organizing energy, the "vast unfinished city" that "lies along the ground," is a different matter. At one moment, detachment is "the measure of all intellectual power" (W.XII.39) and at another, an "immense deduction from power" (W.XII.44). Pessimistic versions of his fable of mind show us detachment without transition. In these passages, we can trace how he alters his parable to compensate for transit's frequent cessation.

In the absence of energy, solid objects become oppressive. "[I]t is the inert effort of each thought having formed itself into a circular wave of circumstance . . . to heap itself on that ridge, and to solidify and hem in the life." The writer cannot muster sufficient force to overcome the inertia of his raw material. "Alas for this infirm faith," Emerson laments, "this will not strenuous, this vast ebb of a vast flow!" (CW.II.180–82). He feels that enormous intervals, as well as hypostasis, prevent him from making contact with his material and thus from manipulating it in transitional play. For example, the writings that make up "Natural History of Intellect," from which I cited passages that show his delight in the mind's detaching power, also contain passages like these:

the discontinuity which perception effects between the mind and the object paralyzes the will. . . . That indescribably small interval is as good as a thousand miles, and has forever severed the practical unity. . . . Affection blends, intellect disjoins subject and object. For weal or woe we clear ourselves from the thing we contemplate. We grieve but are not the grief; we love but are not love.

[C]ontinuity is for the great. . . . what we want is consecutiveness. 'T is with us a flash of light, then a long darkness, then a flash again. Ah! could we turn these fugitive sparkles into an astronomy of Copernican worlds. (W.XII.44, 52–53)

In good Romantic fashion, he blames self-consciousness ("perception" or "intellect") for his debility. An "indescribably small interval" appears immense ("as good as a thousand miles") because the will to span it is paralyzed. The verbal result of this condition is the remoteness of words from things; its visual effect, the lack of coincidence between "the axis of vision" and "the axis of things" (CW.I.43).

Frequently, he represents the curse of detachment in compressed synopses of the passage from a naïve to a sentimental condition. In his little cosmogony in *Nature* ("Man is the dwarf of himself"), the Orphic poet describes an "interval" that is both spatial and temporal:

having made for himself this huge shell, his waters retired; he no longer fills the veins and veinlets; he is shrunk to a drop. He sees that the structure still fits him, but fits him colossally. Say, rather, once it fitted him, now it corresponds to him from far and on high. (CW.I.42)

The same parable that describes the poor fit of man to nature illustrates his linguistic predicament:

Language clothes nature as the air clothes the earth, taking the exact form & pressure of every object. Only words that are new fit exactly the thing, those that are old like old scoriae that have been long exposed to the air & sunshine have lost the sharpness of their mould & fit loosely. (*JMN.V.246*)

The yearning to eliminate all distance whatsoever by taking "the exact form and pressure" of the world is the opposite of the enjoyment of voluntary detachment Emerson recommends elsewhere.

These last two passages exhibit the structure of the "alienated majesty" motif in its diachronic manifestations (*CW.II.27*). When Emerson longs for something, he tends to locate it in the past or future. He may draw, in the first instance, on fables of the Fall, Romantic primitivism, and theories of an original language in which words were one with things. In the second case, he makes use of the prophetic conventions and millennial imagery found in the closing paragraphs of "The Poet." He is fully aware that these mythic projections are representations of inaccessible mental states. With considerable humor, he pictures the nostalgic impulse as a mildly senile but benevolent old man:

> The Spirit of Humanity finds it curious & good to leave the arm-chair of its old age . . . & go back to the scenes of Auld Lang Syne, to the old mansion house of Asia . . . where the faculties first opened, where youth first triumphed in the elasticity of strength & spirits & where the ways of Civilization & thought (*then* deemed *infinite*) were first explored.

"It may be," he comments after this flight of fancy, "this emotion will be only occasionally felt for though the grandeur is real, it is ever present, as the firmament is forever magnificent but is only felt to be so when our own spirits are fresh" (*JMN.II.218*). Even as a very young man (this was written when he was twenty-one) he understood the dynamics of desire well enough to know that it projects its objects in time and space: "the world lacks unity and lies broken and in heaps . . . because man is disunited with himself" (*CW.I.43*).

But this awareness does not defend him against feeling that the condition of detachment unredeemed by transition is one of loss. Loss, in turn, activates the desire for future resolution he has criticized as a wishful illusion. He compensates for the failure of transitional energy by introducing teleology into his fables, as we have already seen. Separate insights, images, and sentences are defined, not as the termini of energetic oscillation, but as parts evolving in the direction of wholeness. The unifying element is an anticipated retrospection, as hope replaces power:

> I write anecdotes of the intellect; a sort of Farmer's Almanac of mental moods. . . .

> I cannot myself use that systematic form which is reckoned essential in treating the science of the mind. But if one can say so without arrogance, I might suggest that he who contents himself with dotting a fragmentary curve, recording only what facts he has observed, without attempting to arrange them within one outline, follows a system also—a system as grand as any other, though he does not interfere with its vast curves by prematurely forcing them into a circle or ellipse, but only draws that arc which he clearly sees, or perhaps at a later observation a remote curve of the same orbit, and waits for a new opportunity, well assured that these observed arcs will consist with each other. (W.XII.11)

Keeping an "Almanac" of daily "anecdotes" demonstrates his faith that life is taking shape, that time itself bestows form. When self-reliance wavers, future closure gives the present its significance. Transition originates in freely willed detachment. Its reward is the sensation of mastery that occurs in the rapid apprehension of unlikeness when, as in all forms of the sublime, the mind recognizes its superiority to its objects. When incapable of transition, Emerson feels that he has lost control. Detachment has been imposed, not elected. The movement between dissimilar elements is not his own, aggressive and quick, but the impersonal, slow purposiveness of nature or of the soul's instinct.

The fluctuation between the two versions of detachment and transition repeats the alternating moods of desire and power analyzed in Part II. Emerson is proud of his bravely unconventional prose and scorns the critic who would protest. In this he is right in line with theorists and practitioners of the sublime who, beginning with Longinus, have legitimated breaking the rules of style.[12] But at times, he looks on discontinuity as failure. To the extent that he shares them, he feels himself at the mercy of his readers' expectations of thematic unity and stylistic continuity. One of the most complex manifestations of Emerson's ambivalence occurs in a journal entry recorded in the fall of 1841. The heading indicates that its purported theme is "Criticism," not the act of criticizing, as it turns out, but the effect of criticism on the writer (one is tempted to say "victim"). The passage begins by recounting a dream or dreamlike fable and proceeds to interpret it:

> Into one of the chambers of hell came a man with his head under his arm, then several men carrying their heads under their arms. Well I suppose a man will come to that in his time also to put up his brain & his heart neatly in a box to carry, and put his irritabilities aloof from him as a fact, out of which the interpretation of the dream was also to be extorted. But why do I write another line, since my best friends assure me that in every line I repeat myself? Yet the God must be obeyed even to ridicule. The criticism of the public is, as I have often noted, much in advance of its invention. The ear is not to be cheated. A continuous effect cannot be produced by discontinuous thought and when the eye cannot detect the juncture of the skilful mosaic, the Spirit is apprised of disunion simply by the failure to affect the Spirit. This other thing I will also concede,—that the man Fingal is rather too swiftly plastic, or, shall I say, works more in the spirit of a cabinet maker, than of an architect. The thought which strikes him as great & Dantesque, & opens an abyss, he instantly presents to another transformed into a chamber or a neat parlor, and degrades ideas. (JMN.VIII.95–96)

The passage exhibits two kinds of detachment or "disunion" which correspond to two visions of hell. The effect of criticism is the same as the effect of man's fall into self-consciousness. "[A]n intellectual man has the power to go out of himself and see himself as an object," he writes in "Powers and Laws of Thought." "Intellectual perception severs once for all the man from the things with which he converses" (*W*.XII.44). Criticism exacerbates these operations and causes the artist to perform them on himself. He literally contains himself, boxing up his brain, his heart, and his anger. He has betaken himself voluntarily to a hell where his punishment reenacts his sin. Assuming that style is a true image of spirit, he accepts decapitation as an image of psychic "disunion" that no rhetorical surface can mask. He attempts to excise the organ that he blames for provoking criticism by disassociating himself from his irritabilities (putting them "aloof"), but this only creates more drastic division. Having been censured for excessive repetitiveness, he confronts duplicates of himself: "a man with his head under his arm" turns into "several men carrying their heads under their arms."

Emerson defends himself against criticism by agreeing with it. He accepts the judgment of his "best friends" and "the public," which he credits with critical astuteness "much in advance of its inventions." The irritability which he disavows is almost certainly exasperation at such friendly advice. The question "why do I write another line," and his answer, "The God must be obeyed," show him to be restless in his acquiescence. But the reference to Fingal (a figure for Emerson) occasions more self-criticism, and he confesses to being fanciful rather than imaginative. But even as he chastises his "too swiftly plastic" talent, his "god" inspires "the thought which strikes him as great and Dantesque and opens an abyss." Having imagined the hell of criticism, he recalls the hell Dante created. The wish to match Dante's powers, suppressed throughout as he tries to make concessions to his critics, breaks out in an acknowledgment of the thrill of disunion and the sublimity of the abyss. But what came to him as a sublime image, he receives "in the spirit of a cabinet maker." In the end, he boxes up inspiration as he boxed up his brain and heart in the "dream."

Two models of imagination, composition, and reading, each with radically different criteria for success, are implicit in this entry. According to the dominant conventional view, "discontinuous thought," an imaginative flaw, produces a regrettably discontinuous prose. Even where disjunction is not manifested stylistically, the "failure to affect the reader's Spirit" betrays the author's spiritual condition. Penetrating the rhetorical surface, spirit speaks to spirit; the reader is disappointed and the writer exposed. Reacting to this condition, the artist goes to the other extreme, producing graceful, "plastic" prose with all the aesthetic virtues of a "neat parlor." The reference to a "Dantesque thought" suggests an opposite interpretation of the same facts. The poet does indeed think discontinuously—his idea "opens an abyss." But as Dante's readers find his abyss to be sublime, so Emerson recognizes his thought as "great." In this light, the urge to domesticate and decorate with an excessively continuous style "degrades" the vision of the abyss. Both reader and writer would prefer less unity and more power.

This exercise in defensive self-interpretation is a meditation on the compositional habits we examined in the last chapter. Repetition and discontinuity are genetically related, and their effects are clearly intentional. But they result in a form of sublimity that defies conventional expectations of continuity and resolution. The thought of failing in the judgment of his public and anxiety about his mind's power to control and organize its material (which is to say, the thought of failure, period) makes sublimity a source of distress as well as of gratification. Emerson works out his mixed feelings by inventing elaborate metaphoric representations of his style which are alternately defensive and desirous. In the reading of his dream, he rebels against the expectations of the conventional reviewer and insists that his text is inspired. The author turns interpreter and retroactively makes the dream in which he was damned represent an imaginative victory; he changes it from an image of his failure into a figure for his will.

· 9 ·

FIGURATIVE LANGUAGE

There is a sense in which we have done nothing but explore Emerson's figurative language. Our subjects, after all, have been his self-mythologizing in the antithetical voices of the essays and his metaphoric representations of writing itself. But in order fully to appreciate the way his ideas about figuration serve his desire for metamorphosis, we need to look more closely at his rhetoric and theories of rhetoric. For, as with other techniques, figurative language takes on thematic values in the self-interpretations which constitute his prose.

Emerson blithely disregards the precise meanings of the usual terms for rhetorical figures. In the few pages of the "Language" chapter of *Nature*, for example, he uses the following as approximate synonyms: sign, symbol, analogy, figure, type, image, allegory, metaphor (*CW*.I.17–22). Although he sometimes associates "fables, parables, and allegories" (*CW*.I.22) in one subcategory and usually reserves "analogy" for the correspondence between mind and world, he uses the rest of the terms interchangeably to designate natural facts, words, and rhetorical figures. We find the same fluidity in the vocabulary of "The Poet," by which time he has moved beyond his early correspondential definitions of figurative language. In that essay, the "use of symbols" and of "tropes, fables, oracles and all poetic forms" is defined as "metamorphosis" (*W*.III.30). His definitions are too casual for his readers to discriminate finely among them or to apply them systematically to his writing. In practice, Emerson uses two principal kinds of figures—short and long. For descriptive convenience in the discussions of his style which follow, I use the term "metaphor" for metaphor, simile, and variants thereof, that is, for compressed figures of no more than a couple of sentences, usually structured as an equation turning on the copula: x is y. I use "fable" for units of a paragraph or more, the narrative passages that could also be called allegory or parable.

A large part of this chapter is devoted to showing that Emerson's metaphors and fables are structurally similar. Both figures are in essence plural, rarely appearing singly. As with other forms of repetition, the focal point is the movement from one figure to another of the same kind; "trope" and "transition" are inseparable. Taken to extremes, these conceptions of metaphor and fable lead to similar dangers (though neither Emerson nor his reader need always perceive them as such): the complete divorce of words from things and of history from fact. The feeling-tone and hence the meanings of the two figurative modes are not identical, however. Metaphor is Emerson's epiphany, the moment when he revels in the instantaneous change that accelerates beyond self-consciousness. The transitions of fable, on the other hand, result from the insights of comparative criticism. Fable is a mature critique of his adolescent love of romance.

METAPHOR

In selecting examples of Emerson's use of metaphor, I looked for its plural form, the condition toward which his single metaphors tend. Three of the best illustrations are passages about metaphor. Like so many of Emerson's rhetorical displays, his figurative exhibitions tend to be reflexive. There is virtually no difference or time lag between the performative and the interpretive moment. Treating something as a metaphor is proof, for Emerson, of the mind's theoretical power. Figuration is the effect of interpretation, therefore, not its cause or occasion. The first example, from *Nature*, typifies Emerson's earliest practice:

> Every appearance in nature corresponds to some state of the mind, and that state of mind can only be described by presenting that natural appearance as its picture. An enraged man is a lion, a cunning man is a fox, a firm man is a rock, a

learned man is a torch. A lamb is innocence; a snake is subtle spite; flowers express to us the delicate affections. Light and darkness are our familiar expression for knowledge and ignorance; and heat for love. Visible distance behind and before us, is respectively our image of memory and hope. (CW.I.18)

In this passage, a "natural appearance" is paired with "a state of mind" in a strict one-to-one correspondence of vehicle and tenor. This bipartite structure is a throwback to eighteenth-century language theories. Locke postulated that abstract signifiers derive from literal ones; names for ideas are synthesized by the mind from the names for images of things or "sensible ideas."[1] Language theorists subsequently adapted the Lockean hypothesis to the defense of passionate figuration.[2] Their conclusions were summed up by Blair, who writes that early men were, from "want of proper and precise terms, obliged to have recourse to circumlocution, metaphor, comparison, and all those substituted forms of expression, which give a poetical air to language." For substitution to result in a "poetical air," it requires poetical thought, the "power of a warm imagination to suggest lively images."[3] Emerson appropriated such accounts of primitive peoples whose every insight was a figure of speech and who instinctively symbolized moral ideas. Half-imitating, half-parodying them, he writes: "An enraged man is a lion; a cunning man is a fox," and so on. Most unlike Locke, Emerson grafts the doctrine of correspondence, which insists on the meaningful symbolic relation between image and idea, onto the theory of the metaphoric origins of language.

Emerson's outline of the life cycle of symbols in *Nature* takes the form of a logical proof that quite illogically conflates notions of Locke and of the Swedenborgians:

Every word which is used to express a moral or intellectual fact, if traced to its root, is found to be borrowed from some material appearance.

Every appearance in nature corresponds to some state of the mind, and that state of the mind can only be described by presenting that natural appearance as its picture.

The corruption of man is followed by the corruption of language. (*CW*.I.18, 20)

In terms of intellectual history, these statements seem irresponsible, but they serve Emerson's purposes. According to this series of postulates, the names of sensory phenomena come to signify abstract ideas. The abstract words thus created express the spiritual realities also symbolized by nature. And so abstraction takes us back to the real origin of language, not in nature, but in the realm of the ideal. The circle is complete: facts represent the ideal; the names of facts, used figuratively (that is, abstractly) become ideal once again. According to this reasoning, words and things are concrete and abstract, figurative and literal, at different stages of their history. Words and objects persist through time though their functions vary as Emerson assigns literal and figurative meaning to different phases. This makes logically possible the condition Emerson seeks to justify, that is, constant change.

The style of a later passage on "tropes" is quite different. It is the paragraph from "The Poet" in which Emerson tries to prove the power of metaphor by mustering a list of examples:

I will not now consider how much this makes the charm of algebra and the mathematics, which also have their tropes, but it is felt in every definition; as when Aristotle defines *space* to be an immovable vessel in which things are contained;—or when Plato defines a *line* to be a flowing point; or *figure* to be a bound of solid; and many the like. What a joyful sense of freedom we have when Vitruvius announces the old opinion of artists that no architect can build any house well who does not know something of anatomy. When Socrates, in Charmides, tells us that the soul is cured of its maladies by certain incantations, and that these incantations are beautiful reasons, from which temperance is generated in souls; when Plato calls the world an animal, and Timaeus affirms that the plants also are animals; or affirms a man to be a heavenly tree, growing with his root, which is his head, upward; and, as George Chapman, following him, writes,

"So in our tree of man, whose nervie root

Springs in his top;"—
when Orpheus speaks of hoariness as "that white flower which marks extreme old age"; when Proclus calls the universe the statue of the intellect; when Chaucer, in his praise of "Gentilesse," compares good blood in mean condition to fire, which, though carried to the darkest house betwixt this and the mount of Caucasus, will yet hold its natural office and burn as bright as if twenty thousand men did it behold; when John saw, in the Apocalypse, the ruin of the world through evil, and the stars fall from heaven as the fig tree casteth her untimely fruit; when Aesop reports the whole catalogue of common daily relations through the masquerade of birds and beasts;— we take the cheerful hint of the immortality of our essence and its versatile habit and escapes, as when the gypsies say of themselves "it is in vain to hang them, they cannot die." (W.III.30–31)

In this passage, metaphor is definitional: x is y. But the two parts of a definition do not necessarily conform to the matter/spirit, fact/idea dichotomy of the preceding passage. Mathematical concepts— line and point—are defined in terms of each other. Two states of mind ("reasons," "temperance") or two natural facts (plants and animals) illuminate each other. Which is signifier and which is signified? The two-part structure gives way to more complex comparisons such as that among plants, animals, and men; to Chaucer's long, detailed heroic simile; and to John's apocalyptic vision. Correspondence is in the process of becoming field or series; differences between paired terms blur as they move toward equivalent degrees of meaningfulness. Most readers would agree, I think, that the examples of metaphor Emerson cites here do not deliver the sensations he promises. He insists that tropes offer "charm," the "joyful sense of freedom," and "the cheerful hint of . . . immortality." Yet rather than being exhilarated, we are likely to find his selection somewhat dull. What intensity does build up is due to the artful placement of the more sublime selections at the end. His anticipation of our excitement embarrasses us as the passage runs on through its fourteen examples. It is precisely the number of examples, not their content, that gives him joy, however. Metaphor is no longer a static equation, but perpetual transition. The metaphor itself is less important than the movement from it to the next.

The use of quotations and allusions as exemplary metaphors is significant. As Emerson reads eighteenth-century language theory, any word is a "fossil" (W.III.22) which has been taken from its original site and rearranged in a new context. Our present use of words is a kind of quotation resonant with primitive associations. "Let [a man] speak a word," he writes, "only to say 'chair,' 'table,' 'fire,' 'bread,'—What are these but quotations from some ancient savage?" (JMN.VII.236). In a complex way, words make us aware of other authors. We notice how carefully he distinguishes the word's charm from the motivating subject, the "life of thought," behind it:

> Every word . . . has once been used happily. The ear, caught by that felicity, retains it, and it is used again and again, as if the charm belonged to the word and not to the life of thought which so enforced it. (W.VIII.193)

Since metaphor is word substitution, it is, according to his definition, also quotation substitution. Not only are present words, ideas, and facts equivalent and interchangeable, but so are fragments of the past. When he illustrates the advantage of tropes by quoting other writers' metaphors, he is only making more conspicuous the allusiveness of any metaphor. To say that every word is a trope is to say that every word is an allusion, for the history of language is the evolution from literal to figurative meaning; a word in its later abstract or metaphoric stage always carries with it an earlier concrete usage.

For my final example, I cite a journal entry of 1841, partially cited earlier:

> The Metamorphosis of nature shows itself in nothing more than this that there is no word in our language that cannot become typical to us of nature by giving it emphasis. The world is a Dancer; it is a Rosary; it is a Torrent; it is a Boat;

a Mist; a Spider's Snare; it is what you will; and the metaphor will hold, & it will give the imagination keen pleasure. Swifter than light the World converts itself into that thing you name & all things find their right place under this new and capricious classification. . . . [The soul] derives as grand a joy from symbolizing the Godhead or his Universe under the form of a moth or a gnat as of a Lord of Hosts. Must I call the heaven & the earth a maypole & country fair with booths or an anthill or an old coat in order to give you the shock of pleasure which the imagination loves and the sense of spiritual greatness? Call it a blossom, a rod, a wreath of parsley, a tamarisk-crown, a cock, a sparrow, the ear instantly hears & the spirit leaps to the trope; and hence it is that men of eloquence like Chatham have found a Dictionary very suggestive reading when they were disposed to speak. (JMN.VIII.23)

Here, dualistic metaphor disappears altogether. Trope is neither correspondential nor definitional but serial. The model is not the single lexical entry of a word and its definition, but the dictionary itself. The dictionary roughly "corresponds" to the universe; "the World converts itself into that thing you name." But pleasure derives from the substitution of signifiers not, as before, from the double vision that apprehends signifier and signified together. Metaphor now calls attention to the difference in meaning between two words, rather than to the ontological difference between fact and idea, object and representation. The metaphoric series appears relatively late in Emerson's prose, after *Nature,* but from hen on coexists with, though it always criticizes, the dualistic variety.

The theory of metaphor implicit in the metaphoric series is based on the mind's joy in conversion rather than on an intrinsic affinity between a symbol and its meaning. Metaphor is tantamount to name changing; conversely, all names are metaphors, whether those names be "Jove, Apollo, Neptune," as in the "Trinity" paragraph from "The Poet," or "Dancer," "Rosary," "Torrent," "Snare." Since virtually any name will do, trope is indeed "capricious." Each name momentarily detaches an aspect of the world. A minimal degree of representation survives as we quickly have to imagine *how* the world resembles a blossom, a rod, a tamarisk-crown. But we are less conscious of blossoms and rods than of the sensation of the difference between them as we entertain first one, then another set of visual and tactile qualities. The changes in meaning are expressed as verbs, usually the copula ("The World is a Dancer; it is a Rosary," and so on). But these transitions are more aggressive than verbs of being indicate. The real verbs are those of active change; the world "converts itself into," or, more accurately, we convert the world into, one word after another. In the noun-verb-noun structure of metaphor, we encounter the alternation between detachment and transition that characterizes Emerson's style generally. Metaphor is another manifestation of his delight in alternately establishing and escaping solidity. The "shock of pleasure" occurs as the metaphor's "hold" is released and "[s]wifter than light the World converts itself into that thing you name." Then the mind takes "hold" again in a new "classification."

Correspondential metaphor, the kind found in the first passage cited, is the linguistic equivalent of the fortunate fall. The literal use of the word is historically earlier and closer to nature than its abstract or figurative application. But when a fact stands for a thought or the name of an object becomes the name of an intangible quality, it is given over to a higher "use"; it serves the soul. In synchronic terms, the interval between the line of words and the line of things is compensated for by realignment which renders nature transparent to spirit. Both the spatial and the temporal versions value spirit more highly than words, for a sense of loss can be assuaged only by spiritualizing language. Emerson's serial metaphors mark his acceptance of the mind's power to derive pleasure from language itself.

In his celebration of serial metaphor, Emerson attributes the production of meaning to the apparently random interaction of words instead of to the intentions of subjects. The qualities he ascribes to language, however, are precisely those that benefit the subject. According to Bloom's fable, Emerson's "every trope burns away context, and when enough context [literary, societal, and historical] has been dissolved, a pragmatic fresh center appears."

The self inhabits the vacuum from which influence has thus been emptied out:

> his vision of self-reliance is one that cheerfully concedes the final reliance of the self upon the self, its condition of perfect sphericity, in which it knows and glories in its ultimate defense or trick, which is that it must be misinterpreted by every other self whatsoever.[4]

I revise this as follows. While I think Emerson does conceive of and use figurative language as a defense against literary influence, I do not find that he does so by "burning away" the traces of intertextuality. He lives at the center of a universe full of tropes that remain within his imagination's field of force even as they collide, adhere, and form themselves into new worlds. Before this universe existed, its elements belonged to other systems. The entropy of the old galaxy and the mastering gravitational field of the new star combined to pull material out of its original "context" and into Emerson's prose. His enjoyment derives not from doing away with context, but from remembering how it was undone. Hence the allusive character of tropes discussed earlier. It is this memory, the self-consciousness of power, which puts the subject at the center and words at the periphery of the Emersonian cosmos.

Emerson's celebration of perpetual figurative motion is the result of the critique of the symbol which he had developed well before *Nature*. Implicit in "The Lord's Supper" is a vision of history and nature as a symbolic continuum in the process of transformation. Honoring the Eucharist above all other symbols misinterprets not only that event but the metamorphic quality of history: "we . . . have preserved this rite and insisted upon perpetuating one symbolical act of Christ whilst we have totally neglected all others." True Christianity is manifested in activity and change:

> A passage read from [Christ's] discourses, a moving provocation to works like his, any act or meeting which tends to awaken a pure thought, a flow of love, an original design of virtue, I call a worthy, a true commemoration. (*W*.XI.11, 20)

Worshiping symbols, "the dead scurf of Hebrew antiquity" (W.VIII.35), results in the opposite of life, motion, and flexibility. It brings about a "formal religion" in which veneration hardens into idol-worship, authority stiffens into tyranny, the spirit dies out and leaves the dead letter: "The whole world was full of idols and ordinances. The Jewish was a religion of forms; it was all body; it had no life" (W.XI.22). The danger of symbols is hypostasis.

Emerson's criticism of symbols was aimed first at the Eucharist, then, in the Divinity School "Address," at miracles. In the latter, the argument proceeds by means of similar metaphoric contrasts. The rigidity of the "formalist" whose prayers "smite and offend us" is juxtaposed to the "beautiful meteor of the snow" as death is to life, stasis to motion. An "eastern monarchy of a Christianity" opposes the "life" which makes existing forms "plastic and new." The appearance of symbols marks the beginning of a "Cultus" and the end of change and freedom (CW.I.85–86, 82, 92).

Later, he directed the same arguments against Swedenborg. His response to the Swedenborgian doctrine of symbols is divided between praise and blame. Initially, that doctrine seems to promise a universal democracy of signs in which it will be impossible to elevate any one symbol to oppressive ritual status: "Every thing is Protean in his [Swedenborg's] eye. . . . the eternal flux of things goes always on there is no material kernal only a spiritual center" (JMN.VIII.221). Emerson's habit of associating a radically semiotic vision and perpetual flux is clear in "The Poet," where he remarks of Swedenborg, "I do not know the man in history to whom things stood so uniformly for words. Before him the metamorphosis continually plays" (W.III.35). Inevitably, Emerson was disillusioned. Symbolic plenitude, he found, does not prevent rigidity or "exaggeration" (W.IV.123, 28). Indeed, because the Swedenborgians permit only one meaning per fact, their system was even more stifling than the orthodoxies it replaced. The restriction of interpretive freedom resulted from a denial of truly figurative meaning. Emerson's argument with Sampson Reed about whether to read Swedenborg's works as "fact" or "poetry," we recall, turned on the issue of whether objects have fixed meanings or manifold significances. When the link between fact and idea is determined by the nature of things, the symbol can only be taken literally. In Emerson's cosmos, by contrast, metamorphosis and figuration go together. The free play of the mind continually generates new meanings for facts without ever pausing to sanctify them.

Emerson's mature theory of the symbol receives full expression in "The Poet." The Neoplatonic, Swedenborgian, and primitivistic clichés of *Nature* still abound:

Things admit of being used as symbols because nature is a symbol, in the whole, and in every part.

. . . there is no fact in nature which does not carry the whole sense of nature.

. . . each word was at first a stroke of genius, and obtained currency because for the moment it symbolized the world to the first speaker and to the hearer. (W.III.13, 17, 21–22)

These static equations, however, are very different from the idea of figuration that subsumes them. They add up to the conclusion that everything can stand for everything else and that, where all is symbolic, symbols are arbitrary. The poet "perceives the independency of the thought on the symbol, the stability of the thought, the accidency and fugacity of the symbol." He knows that what matters is the mind's motion among symbols, "the flowing or metamorphosis." Metaphors of fluidity dramatize the poet's willingness to let go of each symbol in order to embrace the next: "following with his eyes the life, [he] uses the forms which express that life, and so his speech flows with the flowing of nature." Metaphor is metamorphosis, "the power to sap and upheave nature," "the ethereal tides" that "roll and circulate" through the poet, a "passage out into free space." Since there is no end of symbols, men find "within their world another world, or nest of worlds . . . the metamorphosis once seen . . . does not stop" (W.III.20–33).

In "The Poet," these assertions culminate in the critique of mysticism that would reappear in *Representative Men:*

the difference betwixt the poet and the mystic, [is] that the last nails a symbol to one sense, which was a true sense for a moment, but soon becomes old and false. For all symbols are fluxional; all language is vehicular and transitive, and is good, as ferries and horses are, for conveyance, not as farms and houses are, for homestead. Mysticism consists in the mistaking of an accidental and individual symbol for an universal one. . . . [Symbols] must be held lightly, and be very willingly translated into the equivalent terms which others use. . . . [A]ll religious error consisted in making the symbol too stark and solid, and was at last nothing but an excess of the organ of language. (W.III.34–35)

Subsequently Swedenborg is accused of precisely this error: "He fastens each natural object to a theologic notion . . . and poorly tethers every symbol to a several ecclesiastical sense. The slippery Proteus is not so easily caught." And Emerson goes on to summarize the attributes of the only cosmos in which metamorphosis can take place:

In nature, each individual symbol plays innumerable parts, as each particle of matter circulates in turn through every system. The central identity enables any one symbol to express successively all the qualities and shades of real being. (W.IV.121)

The necessary link between metaphor and metamorphosis is clarified in Wallace Stevens' reprise of Emerson's poetics in "Three Academic Pieces." Like Emerson, he justifies his theory of metaphor with a theory of nature, which he relates analogically to the imagination. Nature's "universe of reproduction is not an assembly line but an incessant creation," he begins. "Because this is so in nature it is so in metaphor," which is "a symbol for . . . the creation of resemblance by the imagination." The automatic reproduction of the assembly line has the appalling consequence of reducing resemblance to repetition. The insistence by Emerson and Stevens that tropes are transformations resists precisely this anxiety about repetition. For both of them, "metamorphosis might be a better word" than "metaphor." As nature is "incessant creation," so its images, "perceptions of resemblance [metaphors/metamorphoses] are effortless accelerations." Poetry is metaphor, and metaphor is energy and change:

[It] is almost incredibly the outcome of figures of speech or, which is the same thing, the outcome of the operation of one imagination on the other through the instrumentality of the figures. To identify poetry and metaphor or metamorphosis is merely to abbreviate the last remark.

Stevens concludes, "it is not too extravagant to think of . . . the repetitions of resemblance as a source of the ideal." Because the "ideal" of metamorphosis arises from a horror of automatism, it is always found in conjunction with the thought of repetition.

But Stevens imagines an alternative rationale for repetition in the same essay. Reinterpreting the Narcissus myth, he strongly contests Freud and grounds repetition in the pleasure principle (this despite his unconvincing demurrer that narcissism is not the cause but only "an evidence" or symptom of our anticipation of pleasure). Whereas Freud had connected repetition to the death drive in opposition to the sexual and ego instincts, including narcissism, Stevens argues that narcissism motivates repetition and thus metaphor:[5]

Narcissus did not expect, when he looked in the stream, to find in his hair a serpent coiled to strike, nor, when he looked in his own eyes there, to be met by a look of hate, nor, in general, to discover himself at the center of an inexplicable ugliness from which he would be bound to avert himself. On the contrary, he sought out his image everywhere because it was the principle of his nature to . . . expect to find pleasure in what he found.

"So strong is that expectation" of pleasure, Stevens continues, "that we find nothing else."[6] For him, as for Emerson, repetition— which always takes the form of figuration—is inextricably bound up with a myth of the self. His two justifications of repetition— our need for change and our pleasure in our image—come together in the Emersonian dynamic of "alienated majesty." We interpret (under the illusion that we are discovering) art and nature as aspects of ourselves and take pleasure in the image that confirms our expectation. But because change cannot occur when narcissism is carried to the point of solipsism, the world must still preserve its externality and otherness. It must continuously offer the poet material for metamorphic transformation.

FABLE

Ultimately, Emerson seeks the same pleasures and encounters the same dangers in fable that he finds in metaphor and other repetitive techniques. Fables, too, appear in series and provide the kinetic thrill of the transition from one element to the next; they, too, threaten to blur significant differences. But most of them have a rather different feeling and point from Emerson's shorter forms of figurative language. Rather than letting tradition be implied by the primitive origins of words, in the fables he imitates the forms of tradition's constituent narratives—myth, romance, legend—so as to remind us that the nineteenth century is in the process of criticizing and rewriting historiography. Emerson's use of these materials thus constitutes a sophisticated "modern" reading of past cultures. His fables are fragments of myth and science that show how the latter is subverted by its equivalence to the former.

These fables begin in the present and dilate into past and future. Many of Emerson's little narratives originate in the bipartite, definitional statements of simile and metaphor: "a man is a god in ruins"; "Man is the dwarf of himself" (CW.I.42); "Genius is the activity which repairs the decays of things" (W.III.22); "The reason why we feel one man's presence and do not feel another's is as simple as gravity" (W.III.95); "Nature is the incarnation of a thought, and turns to a thought again, as ice becomes water or gas" (W.III.196). A metaphor suggests a narrative, and the result is fable. For example, the equation, "Conversation is a game of circles" is reimagined as episode: "We all stand waiting, empty. . . . Then cometh the god and converts the statues into fiery men" (CW.II.184). Another passage on conversation begins as analogy ("as when"). The metaphor then introduced of "a new . . . region" turns into a narrative of discovery that subsumes simile ("as it were . . . as if"):

I do not at once arrive at satisfactions, *as when,* being thirsty, I drink water; or go to the fire, being cold; no! but I am first apprised of my vicinity to a new and excellent region of life. . . . [T]his region gives . . . sign of itself, *as it were* in flashes of light, in sudden discoveries of its profound beauty and repose, *as if* the clouds . . . parted at intervals and showed the approaching traveller the inland mountains. (W.III.71; emphasis added)

Even when the fable does not originate in metaphor per se, it begins with a statement about a present condition which becomes attached to a past *when* statement modulates into narrative. The poet who finds himself "not near enough to his object," for instance, participates in a complex event: "this is but outskirt and a far-off reflection and echo of the triumph that has passed by and is now at its glancing splendor and heyday, perchance in the neighboring fields" ("Nature"; W.III.192). The spatial metaphor of distance is not enough to describe alienation; the temporal dimension is needed to communicate the sense of something just missed. Similarly, the circle turns to narrative as Emerson imagines an elastic geometric figure which acts out the "life of man." This animate circle "rushes . . . outwards," the wave of circumstance tends to "heap itself . . . solidify . . . and hem in," the soul "bursts" its restraints and "expands," the deep "runs up into a high wave" (CW.II.180–81). Natural law possesses an intention that "bursts over the boundary" dividing science from trope. Again and again, a figure of speech calls up a story. In "Nature," the assertion "Every act hath some falsehood of exaggeration in it" becomes fable as soon as prosopopeia has created a protagonist, Nature:

And when now and then comes along some sad, sharp-eyed man, who sees how paltry a game is played, and refuses to play but blabs the secret . . . the wary Nature sends a new troop of fairer forms. (W.III.185)

As in "The Poet," personifying nature initiates a history of the life cycle of the species from "seed" to poem (W.III.22–24).

These witty allegories are presented as arguments, explanations, or illustrations that support the introductory metaphoric assertion. When we examine the development of such incessant explanatory parables, however, we discover that they do not result in—and probably do not intend—clarification and comprehensibility; the purported explanation of a prior statement complicates rather than simplifies things. An energy other than that of logic creates multiple fables, and multiplicity causes each constituent myth to undermine all the others. These fragmentary histories are another instance of analogous propositions discontinuously related, like the paragraph structures analyzed in Chapter 7 or the metaphoric series discussed in the first part of this chapter.

Fable's tendency to multiply is evident in the geographic parable about conversation with "a profound mind" cited above ("I am at first apprised of my vicinity to a new and excellent region"). This region is valorized by a plethora of images drawn from literary, religious, and national mythologies. As the speaker explores the country, he finds the stock pastoral scene of "eternal meadows . . . where flocks graze and shepherds pipe and dance," the "sunbright Mecca of the desert," and "this new yet unapproachable America" (W.III.71–72). Similarly, in the quasi-scientific fable in "Character," Emerson translates the statement "Truth is the summit of being" into several natural equivalents, not all consistent with each other:

> All individual natures stand in a scale, according to the purity of this element in them. The will of the pure runs down from them into other natures, as water runs down from a higher into a lower vessel. This natural force is no more to be withstood than any other natural force. We can drive a stone upward . . . into the air but it is yet true that all stones will forever fall.

Then the metaphor changes from a vertical to an inside-outside figure: "An individual is an encloser. . . . He encloses the world, as the patriot does his country, as a material basis for his character, and a theatre for action." The paragraph ends with electromagnetic and optical images. The soul "stands united with the Just and the True, as the magnet arranges itself with the pole; so that he stands to all beholders like a transparent object betwixt them and the sun and whoso journeys towards the sun, journeys toward that person" (W.III.95–96). The same figurative density produced by manifold mythological or scientific episodes results when the two idioms are compounded. In *Nature,* for example, Emerson uses the account of the physiology of perception in Brewster's *Life* of Newton (1831) to explain why we cannot consummate the "marriage" of intellect and devotion which is "the redemption of the soul": "The axis of vision is not coincident with the axis of things, and so they appear not transparent but opake" (CW.I.43).[7]

Fable affects the reader quite differently from metaphor. She or he spends more time within than between tropes, for a fable is not, like metaphor or self-paraphrase, instantly replaced. While "transition" does occur as we follow the fables' metamorphoses, this process is slower and messier than the metaphoric leap. Allusions tend to be more obvious, and we take more time to consider them. The difficult effects of multiplicity are nowhere better illustrated than in the Orphic poet's first utterance in *Nature.* This is not a coherent narrative, but a gathering of mythological fragments relating to a single plot, the "degradation" of "the universal man." The poet's theme unfolds in three explanatory allegories of increasing complexity which build to a kind of hyperbole of allusion.

We distrust and deny inwardly our sympathy with nature. We own and disown our relation to it, by turns. We are, like Nebuchadnezzar, dethroned, bereft of reason, and eating grass like an ox. But who can set limits to the remedial force of spirit?

A man is a god in ruins. When men are innocent, life shall be longer, and shall pass into the immortal, as gently as we awake from dreams. Now, the world would be insane and rabid, if these disorganizations should last for hundreds of years. It is kept in check by death and infancy. Infancy is the perpetual Messiah, which comes into the arms of fallen men, and pleads with them to return to paradise.

Man is the dwarf of himself. Once he was permeated and dissolved by spirit. He filled nature with his overflowing currents. Out from him sprang the sun and moon; from man, the sun; from woman, the moon. The laws of his mind, the periods of his actions externized themselves into day and night, into the year and the seasons. But, having made for himself this huge shell, his waters retired; he no longer fills the veins and veinlets; he is shrunk to a drop. He sees that the structure still fits him, but fits him colossally. Say, rather, once it fitted him, now it corresponds to him from far and on high. He adores timidly his own work. Now is man the follower of the sun, and woman the follower of the moon. Yet sometimes he starts in his slumber, and wonders at himself and his house, and muses strangely at the resemblance betwixt him and it. He perceives that if his law is still paramount, if still he have elemental power, "if his word is sterling yet in nature," it is not conscious power, it is not inferior but superior to his will. It is Instinct. (CW.I.42)

Despite the presence of a narrative impulse, this composite fable is quite unconcerned with narrative integrity. Emerson is more interested in playing many stories off each other than in telling a single tale. He compresses Nebuchadnezzar's fate into a simile, then continues the discourse on degradation in the second paragraph by way of the more elaborate cosmogonic fable beginning "A man is a god in ruins," which evokes the fall of the Titans or the dismemberment of Adam Kadmon and sustains the previous Biblical allusion by drawing on the New Testament Messiah. This paragraph provokes more questions than it answers. We expect the history of our ruin, but instead encounter an ironic defense of death ("the world would be insane . . . if these disorganizations should last") and the jarring association of "death and infancy." "Infancy" and "paradise" appear to be metaphors for or analogues of each other. As conflated mythic and euhemerist versions of man's history proliferate, our appreciation of their quantity and our uncertainty of their significance increase. The passage advances by way of another series of ad hoc projections of moral and mental states, freely borrowed from existing mythologies. The third paragraph displays the same associative, improvisational development.

The "god in ruins" reappears as the shrunken figure, the "dwarf," who inhabits the "house" of his former self. But again his history is confusing. Did the first man contain or was he contained by nature—was nature a vessel that he "filled," was it "externized" out of him, or were they "permeated and dissolved" in each other? Was there "universal man" alone or the universal couple suggested by "from man the sun, from woman the moon"?

Narrative and imagistic inconsistencies crop up in the scientific parables as well as the patently mythic ones. In the essay "Nature," Emerson strives to represent the interaction of thought and nature in terms of many natural processes:

> Here is no ruin, no discontinuity, no spent ball. . . . Nature is the incarnation of a thought, and turns to a thought again, as ice becomes water and gas. The world is mind precipitated, and the volatile essence is forever escaping again into the state of free thought. Hence the virtue and pungency of the influence on the mind of natural objects. . . . Man imprisoned, man crystallized, man vegetative, speaks to man impersonated. That power which does not respect quantity, which makes the whole and the particle its equal channel, delegates its smile to the morning, and distils its essence into every drop of rain. Every moment instructs, and every object; for wisdom is infused into every form. It has been poured into us as blood; it convulsed us as pain; it slid into us as pleasure; it enveloped us in dull, melancholy days, or in days of cheerful labor; we did not guess its essence until after a long time. (W.III.196)

The first sentence alone contains, synecdochically, three of Emerson's favorite explanations of the Fall of man: the myth of the Fall or "ruin" itself, "discontinuity" or the unaligned axes of eye and nature, and "spent" energy, entropy or the hypostasis of "Circles." Next, an elaborate conceit compares the transformation of water into ice and gas to the interchange of world and mind. As if these were not tropes enough, nature's history as "universal man" is packed into a catalogue: "Man imprisoned . . . crystallized . . . vegetative . . . impersonated." The distillation of the "essence" of "wisdom" reverses the ice-water-gas vaporization to describe the unrelated process of infusion. The paragraph concludes with a series which reminds us that any verb can "become typical . . . of Nature": wisdom "poured into us . . . convulsed us . . . slid into us . . . enveloped us. . . ." The vertical, parallel, inside-outside and action-reaction relationships simply are not congruent in this paragraph. Like the partial myths of degradation in the passage from *Nature,* its figures are the gestures of an imagination that sacrifices narrative sequence to its own power to "use" every available fable and to use them, in ways that we shall explore, against each other.

The enjoyment of this power can come very close to "the Comic." Indeed, if one attribute distinguishes Emerson's fables from his juvenile romances, it is the sense of humor that develops when critical detachment replaces sentimentality and confidence replaces self-pity. The imaginative exacerbation that multiplies metaphors or dilates them into fable also drives fable toward humor. We can observe this tendency in a passage on—appropriately enough—the "falsehood of exaggeration." After a spate of paraphrases, Emerson intensifies his prose by adding a fable with a slightly comic cast of characters.

> Nature sends no creature, no man into the world without adding a small excess of his proper quality . . . a little violence of direction in its proper path, a shove to put it on its way; in every instance a slight generosity, a drop too much. . . . Every act hath some falsehood of exaggeration in it. And when now and then comes along some sad, sharp-eyed man, who sees how paltry a game is played, and refuses to play but blabs the secret;—how then? Is the bird flown? O no, the wary Nature sends a new troop of fairer forms, of lordlier youths, with a little more excess of direction . . . and on goes the game again with a new whirl. (W.III.185)

The allegory of characters' "violence of direction" serves its argumentative purpose and then, with the appearance of the "sad, sharp-eyed man," "wary Nature," and the "troop of fairer forms," exceeds it. The fabulist is aware even as he speaks that his parable is a kind of cartoon. The rather strained avuncular playfulness of "how then? Is the bird flown? O no . . . on goes the game . . . with a new whirl" betrays a striving for effect. Parables planted in more relaxed passages of writing are peculiarly self-conscious, like conceits.

We sense that fable is an affair of set pieces, of conspicuous *tours de force*, because we know, both intuitively and certainly, that Emerson's fables are quotations. I use this term loosely to cover a variety of tactics, from direct quotation to the merest hint of allusion, from imitation to parody. Sufficient primary materials make it possible to prove that this is so; innumerable borrowings can be and have been traced through the journals and lectures to their eventual place in one or several essays. We would recognize the provenance of his fables even without this body of research, however, for his style proclaims its own allusiveness. He imitates the mannerisms of classical mythology, New Testament parable, Aesopian fable, moral *exempla,* and the adaptations of these modes in English and European literature. Indeed, his allegories are documentary evidence of stock responses, for he knows how, imagistically and rhetorically, to trigger our associations. With brilliant economy, he allusively evokes a mood, a landscape, plot, and atmosphere that he need not complete because readers familiar with the right clichés already have done so for themselves.

As the early journals show, he was enormously susceptible to archaic sonorities. His admiration manifests itself in exploitation. If language is a "dictionary of tropes," history is an encyclopedia of fables. The evocations of paradise, the Fall, and the Messiah in the passage from *Nature* are his way of heightening the Orphic poet's utterance; allusions are stitched together into the robe of eloquence. Even when he does not draw on Biblical plots, Emerson rises to the Bible's tones of prophecy and annunciation to bring about rhetorical climax. One recalls, in this connection, the closing paragraphs of "The Poet" (*W*.III.40–42). In the catalogue of flocks and shepherds, "the sunbright Mecca of the desert," and finally "this new yet unapproachable America" (*W*.III.71–72), he makes the rhetorical power of several mythologies serve his purposes. The impact on us of images from nationalistic, religious, and poetic literatures stems from our identification of those subjects with sublime sensations: altruism, communion, power, originality, transcendence. He plays upon our susceptibility. His allusions display literary greatness as sound and light shows illuminate the ruins of Rome and Athens for tourists. Peter Hughes, discussing the "stylistic compulsion" to allude, nicely captures the qualities of this kind of prose. He links it to "the developmental role in seventeenth- and eighteenth-century prose and verse of the commonplace books [one of the functions of Emerson's journals], collections of proverbs, and grammars." The "abbreviated recurrence" of axioms, aphorisms, and anecdotes, Hughes goes on, "out of context but everywhere" in educational literature, "had the effect of creating allusion without reference . . . a *revenant* rising out of every schoolbook."[8] Or, as Emerson himself puts it,

> Most of the classical citations you shall hear or read in the current journals or speeches were not drawn from the originals, but from previous quotations in English books; and you can easily pronounce, from the use and relevancy of the sentence, whether it had not done duty many times before. (W. VIII. 194)

Since allusion is the technique by which he constructs multiple fables, it is what carries Emerson beyond the sublime to parody. In the Orphic poet's speech in "The Poet," in the playful allegory of "exaggeration" in "Nature," and in the image of "babe-like Jupiters" at the end of "Intellect," the conventionality of allegory becomes part of his stylistic humor. The "Orphic poet" passage mimics Ovidian metamorphosis, the shape-changing that ensures escape or survival. Instead of mythological beings dissolving into a river or turning into a tree, Emerson imagines poems sprouting wings to avoid the mortality of their authors and to flee their critics. The trauma of the Ovidian moment vanishes in the irreverent adaptation that so enjoys its own facility. The second passage, from "Nature," is semi-automatic prosopopeia, featuring wary Nature and the sharp-eyed man. These are characters out of American folklore, like those of Melville's *Confidence Man,* done up in a fabulous way. The fable imitates the centuries of writers who established and then exhausted the conventions of classical allusion.

But the result of such easy personification is the far more inter-esting comedy of the "Intellect" passage. We recall that Emerson begins by marveling at "the calm & grand air" of the "cherubim" in Plotinus' writings. Suddenly the gap between the "grandees" ensconced in heaven and uncomprehending man below, between the language of moderns and that of sacred texts, strikes him as ridiculous. The mutual contemplation of round-cheeked gods in the clouds (a conflation of stock notions of classical and Christian sky-gods) and bewildered humans suggests cartoons of the newly deceased entering the pearly gates. Because we no longer under-stand or believe in such literal heavens, we invent, as Emerson has, anti-mythological fables that expose their conventions and artifices. For Emerson, as Bishop remarks, "irony is more serious than myth"; irony defends him against myth.[9]

We might expect Emerson's scientific and naturalistic illustra-tions to be exceptions to the rule of ironic allusiveness, since they are derived from works that are free from mythological mannerisms. At times, he seems to hope that, through science, he can make facts instead of fictions his analogues for moral truth. But he treats even science in an archaic manner that calls attention to its fig-urative status. In his plural allegories, metaphors drawn from phys-ics and physiology appear next to those from literary sources. He combines allusions to the fall of man with the vocabulary of optics or equates the charisma of gods and heroes with gravitational force. In such juxtapositions, the terms qualify each other. The earlier, mythological term gains in value when it is seen to foreshadow an empirical discovery. But at the same time, the physiology of per-ception appears to be as figurative an account of decline as the story of eating the apple. There are no facts, such passages tell us, unadulterated by fables; science is the myth of the nineteenth century.

This simultaneous elevation and devaluation of material should be a familiar phenomenon to us by now. It is the dynamic that acts on us strongly in the Knower, Doer, and Sayer paragraph (W.III.6), and, indeed, characterizes all repetition based on dis-continuous adjacency. The same logic at work in and on every sort of mythology is set forth in Emerson's account of a dream (his dream descriptions being some of his most interesting fables). A "pundit" tells him

> they mistake who seek to find only one meaning in sacred words & images, in the names of gods, as Jove, Apollo, Osiris . . . Jesus, & the Holy Ghost: for these symbols are like coins of different countries, adopted from local proximity or convenience. . . . [B]ut they all represent the value of corn, wool, & labor, & are readily convertible into each other, or into the coin of any new country. That sense which is conveyed to one man by the name & rites of Pan or Jehovah, is found by another in the study of earthquakes & floods, by another in the forms & habits of animals; by a third in trade, or in politics; by a fourth in electro-magnetism. (*JMN.*VII. 449–50)

This "dream" attempts to justify his substitution for each other of gravity, magnetism, and transparency or the pastoral landscape, Mecca, and America. It outlines the reasoning according to which, in the Orphic poet's fable in *Nature*, the Biblical Fall can be analogous to man's internal conflict between "thought" and "devotion," infancy can be paradise and vice versa, an Old Testament king can suffer the same alienation as the dwarf who cowers before his former image. Each myth refers us to another in an open-ended series, as in the serial metaphors discussed earlier. We can only tentatively extrapolate from the similarities among them to some ultimate reality for which they all stand. The belief that fables (and all figures) are grounded in or refer to facts yields to a more radical vision of fable as perpetual motion from one myth to another. There is no "corn, wool & labor" on which the value of the symbolic currency is based. The multiplication of mythologies—from those of Pan and Jehovah to trade, politics, and electromagnetism—is the ultimate inflation. In stating his theories of the relationship between the literal and figurative realms, seeking to define the status of writing in relation to nature and the mind, Emerson presents tentative ontologies of culture. Sometimes he claims that fable stands for an ascertainable objective truth; at other times, that mythologies imitate not reality, but each other, because we cannot express the thing itself.

One attitude is exemplified by the "perfect man" who "traverses the whole scale & sees & enjoys the symbol solidly" for a time. He "wears it lightly as a robe which he can easily throw off, for he sees the reality & divine splendor of the inmost nature bursting through each chink & cranny" (*JMN*.V.326). In this passage, literary symbols are ephemeral precisely because nature is not. This artist's playfulness arises from his sublime confidence that behind the surface of things exists a nearly palpable "reality" or "inmost nature." This optimism is tempered by slight hesitation in a journal entry on Zoroastrianism and Swedenborgianism:

> One would be glad to behold the truth which they all shadow forth. For it cannot but be truth that they typify and symbolize. . . . One sees . . . in them . . . the element of poetry according to Jeffrey's true theory—the effect produced by making everything outward only a sign of something inward. (*JMN*.IV.11)

He is convinced that religions signify a "truth" which he will soon discover. The reference to Jeffrey indicates how conventional it was, by 1832, to believe that "everything outward [is] . . . a sign of something inward." Fortunately, he expresses this facile doctrine of correspondence as desire, not fact, and so rescues it from banality. The optative mood of "One would be glad to behold" concedes that the truth is not yet visible. We hear the strength of his wish in the double negative, "it cannot but be truth. . . ." This construction skirts doubt as does a later equivocation: "Fact is better than fiction *if only we could get pure fact*" (*JMN*.VII.277; emphasis added). He has less patience with the fables of Calvinism than with more exotic doctrines. "[H]ow long is the society to be taught in this dramatic or allegorical style?" he demands after a "Sabbath in the country." "When is religious truth to be distinctly uttered—what it is, not what it resembles? . . . What hinders that instead of this parable the naked fact be stated?" (*JMN*.IV.91). If the tone is less genial here, Emerson's conviction that "naked fact" and "religious truth" can be known and "distinctly uttered" is even stronger.

He entertains several hypotheses about the nature of the truth that fable "shadows forth." Under the heading "Mythology," he subscribes to the popular belief that myth is the primitive fore-runner of modern science: "In reading the fables of Plutarch or Zoroaster . . . I feel that . . . these primeval allegories are globes & diagrams on which the laws of living nature are explained" (*JMN*.VI.227). From religious narratives, we can deduce natural law; "the avatars of Brahma will presently be textbooks of natural history" (*JMN*.IX.212). But this conviction dissolves when he actually turns his attention to "natural history." Myth may be translated into science, but science, he insists, must have "a right theory," must be "transcendental," "Symbolic" (*JMN*.IX.211), that is, mythical. The same recession into mythopoeia occurs when he momentarily grounds fable in the laws of the psyche:

> Trace these colossal conceptions of Buddhism & of Vedantism home, and they are always the necessary or structural action of the human mind. Buddhism read literally is the tenet of Fate; Worship & Morals, or the tenet of freedom are the unalterable originals in all the wide variety of geography, lan-guage, & intelligence of the human tribes.

The "structural action of the human mind" turns out to be a new mythology, not an empirical principle. Religion "read literally" translates into "the tenet of Fate" and "the tenet of freedom." The eternal contest between fate and freedom is an allegory of the structure of experience, not a literal representation, assuming the latter is even conceivable. Although Emerson does not succeed in reducing religion to psychology, perhaps the most interesting fea-ture of the attempt is that he acts as though he has. He anticipates the worst consequence of his initial line of reasoning. The passage continues:

> The buyer thinks he has a new article; but if he goes to the factory, there is the self-same old loom as before, the same mordaunts & colours, the same blocks even; but by a little

splicing & varying the parts of old patterns, what passes for
new is produced. (*JMN*.IX.311–13)

Repetition is the price of reducing culture to nature, mind, or any
other foundation. The danger of discovering a key to all mythologies
is monotony. Emerson's celebrations of movement and change strive
to avoid this result.

Myth takes a more dynamic psychological form as the projection
of desire. Religion reflects communal hopes, he proposes: "Men's
minds visit heaven as they visit earth, & hence the Turkish heaven
is a Harem; the Scandinavian, a hunting field; the Arabian, a place
of wheaten cakes & murmuring fountains" (*JMN*.II.54). Once he
conceives of history as a sequence of such projections, that spectacle takes on an independent existence. Objective correlatives—
culture, language, even thought—appear disassociated from our
experience:

> I fear the progress of Metaphys[ical] philosophy may be found
> to consist in nothing else than the progressive introduction
> of apposite metaphors. Thus the Platonists congratulated
> themselves for ages upon their knowing that Mind was a dark
> chamber whereon ideas like shadows were painted. Men de-
> rided this as infantile when they afterwards learned that the
> Mind was a sheet of white paper whereon any & all characters
> might be written. Almost every thing in language that is bound
> up in your memory is of this significant sort. . . . Life is
> nothing but the *lamp* of life that blazes, flutters, & goes out,
> the *hill* of life which is climbed & tottered down, the *race* of
> life which is run with a thousand Competitors. (*JMN*.II.224)

Emerson has frequently treated civilization as "the progressive
introduction of apposite metaphors," but here he suspects that it
is "nothing else." This position risks the related dangers of excess
and monotony. The feeling of being overwhelmed by metaphors
grows out of prior reductions; the sense that there are too many
myths originates in the belief that they are all alike. When myths
are viewed as effects of a single cause, they become equal in value
and identical in meaning. Devoid of unique content, religious ep-

ochs flow fantastically into each other from the point of view of the modern historian. The sheer quantity of myth proves that he has failed to make himself "master of the whole Fact," has been unable to penetrate to fact:

> With what good faith these old books of barbarous men record the genesis of the world. Their best attempts to narrate how it is that star & earth & man exist, run out into some gigantic mythology, which, when it is ended, leaves the beautiful simple facts where they were, & the stupid gazing fabulist just as far from them as at first. Garrulity is our religion & philosophy. (*JMN*.VIII.286)

Detached from a referent, fables proliferate and seem increasingly fictive. Wondering at the phantasmagoria of "cosmogonies," Emerson writes, "what ghosts & hollow formless dream-gear these theories are" (*JMN*.VII.352). The act of interpreting history is an exercise of power by the reader who can explain it in terms of God, mind, or nature. But when that reader loses—by losing faith in—his key to mythologies, the fables' revolutions accelerate. History appears to be as metaphoric and thus as unstable as language:

> Time is the principle of levity dissipating solidest things like exhalations. The monasteries of the Middle Ages were builded of timber, brick, & stone, so were the temples of Jove & those of Osiris yet they dance now before me late come into their globe like words or less. (*JMN*.V.399)

Some of Emerson's most characteristic strategies develop in order that boredom and unreality do not prevail. He understands how readings of myth can generate nihilism and knows, when he combats despair with power and motion, that this, too, entails risk. His first gesture is to put the modern individual in control of the past. He exhorts us to fight off paralysis, insisting that man, not time, is "the principle of levity"; he can choreograph the "dance" of history. But restoring the locus of control to man does not prevent unnerving figurative change. The powerful imagination reads history as metamorphosis. In Emerson's translation of Ernst Meyer's reply to Goethe, however, "The Idea of Metamorphosis" is an inestimable, but also perilous gift from above; it leads into the formless, destroys knowledge; dissolves it. It is like a centrifugal force & will lose itself in infinity if a counterpoise be not given it. (*JMN*.VI.300n., 301)

Transforming one fable into another generates anxiety about preserving one's identity against the threat of dissolution and formlessness. The scholar is both the master of mayhem and its victim.

The risks of this kind of mastery are entropy and scarcity. The "Genius" who can "toss every object in nature for his metaphor" (*JMN*.VIII.43) requires endless supplies of energy and raw material. Emerson, who never doubts man's right to make himself free at the expense of nature or culture, defines the imagination as "the use which the Reason makes of the material world." Nature "is made to serve," he declares. "It receives the dominion of man as meekly as the ass on which the Saviour rode," and the same can be said for religion, science, and literature. The interpreter "conforms things to his thoughts" and "impresses his being" on them, "subordinating nature for the purposes of expression" (*CW*.I.25, 31). The ultimate manifestation of his will to power over nature is the condition of transparency. It leaves him free from nature, not in it. Nature is rendered invisible by an annihilating second sight which looks through "translucid" facts (*W*.III.26). When the axes of vision and of things are aligned, the world appears "transparent" (*CW*.I.43). The poet "turns the world to glass" and substances "dislimn" under his gaze (*W*.III.20; VIII.18). It is not the eyeball, but what it looks upon, finally, that is transparent. Using history as fable has the same consequences as using nature for the purpose of "expression." The past "dissolves" or "dissipates," just as nature "dislimns," under the poet's eye. Even persons are subject to transparency, always the symbol of exploitation. In "Uses of Great Men," describing the transformation of our teachers from causes into effects, Emerson writes, "The opaque self becomes transparent with the light of the First Cause" (*W*.IV.35). "The marching intellect follows a scorched-earth policy," observes Packer in her discussion of this trope, "[it] devastates the countries it passes through."[10]

The implications of transparency are never articulated by Emerson. Do we suddenly see, behind a transparent surface, a world of Platonic ideas? Or, finding nothing beyond or behind nature, are we forced back on our own subjectivity? Melville makes the whiteness (transparency?) of the whale his symbol of such questions. Emerson, however, does not formulate them as questions. By not objectifying transparency, he is at least saved from Melville's impasse. Instead of trying to embody it, he represents transparency as a temporary condition that must always be reachieved. Its moment is too brief to see beyond. The desire not to confront a possible void points up the real danger in "an aesthetic of use," that is, "the anxiety of demand," the knowledge that "what can be used can be used up."[11] Nature must feel solid for Emerson's imagination to gratify itself in transitions from one object to the next. The artist needs things to transform, for only when exercising his metamorphic powers is he free. Transparency dematerializes nature and leaves the mind without anything to work upon. For the imagination's own sake, then, transparency cannot last.

These logical extrapolations of Emerson's arguments and metaphors, which have raised the issues of exhaustion and the withering away of nature, have taken us a long way from the subject of fable. However, the advantages and disadvantages of an aesthetic of use are the same regardless of what is being used. What I have tried to do is show how his imagination, which needs actively to control what it perceives, manipulates history until it becomes a phantasmagoria of fictions and manipulates nature until it becomes transparent. But a more important reason for following these tendencies to their most extreme conclusions is that we can better appreciate Emerson's strategic avoidance of the dangers implicit in his own poetics. After an analysis of Emerson's deconstructive tendencies, we begin again with a renewed awareness that virtually all his statements are figurative, even—perhaps especially—those about figuration. The particular approach to the interpretation of fable that he recommends, however, stops well short of perpetual figurative regression. The passages we are about to examine share a common plot, the triumph of the present reader over prior texts or over the past as text. Fable, he suggests, activates two faculties in the reader, Reason and the Understanding:

> Why must . . . the philosopher mince his words & fatigue us with explanation? He speaks from the Reason & being of course contradicted word for word by the Understanding he stops like a cogwheel at every notch to explain. Let him say, I *idealize*, & let that be once for all; or I *sensualize*, & then the Rationalist may stop his ears. . . .

> Fable avoids the difficulty, is at once exoteric and esoteric, & is clapped by both sides. (*JMN*.V.31)

Fable occupies a special ontological realm where it can evade the strict either/or categorization fostered by the bad Romantic habit of applying the Reason/Understanding dichotomy too strictly. It is both ideal and sensual, "esoteric" and "exoteric." Emerson re-iterates Coleridge's query, "Though not *fact*, must it needs be false?" (*JMN*.VI.329). Because "the world is enigmatical, every thing said & every thing known & done, & must not be taken literally but genially" (*JMN*.IX.351). The many connotations of "genial" extend from genius to generation and hint at a mood of cheerful, jovial, kindly sympathy. The word suggestively links humor and creativity, and implies that the relaxation of high seriousness frees us from excessive literalism. The genial reader simultaneously exercises Reason and the Understanding to apprehend literal and figurative meanings together.[12]

Emerson's interest in figurative meanings nevertheless is an expression of impatience, not tolerance. What first sounds like a liberal acceptance of multiple meanings quickly changes to something less generous. After listening to a Calvinist preacher expound obsolete doctrines, he comments, "though the whole is literally false, it is really true; only he speaks Parables which I translate as he goes" (*JMN*.IV.320). Elsewhere, he is more aggressive: "The poet writes fable, but I read truth in it: he rages or rests, he trifles now, & now is grand, but I remain single & firm, taking one even sense from the whole" (*JMN*.VIII.26). When Emerson hears a preacher who claims to speak the literal truth, he redeems the discourse by taking it figuratively. Conversely, when a poet intends "fable," he is still not satisfied, but must invent the truth which the fable represents. In both cases, the interpreter defines the meaning and value of what he reads by reversing the intentions of its author.

Although Emerson will reverse almost any position, his antithetical revisions most often involve the transformation of fact into fiction. He turns history into fable, which means that the historian becomes a critic. Emerson concurs with Carlyle's claims for the historian's role in making history:

> It is in no case the real historical Transaction, but only some more or less plausible scheme and theory of the Transaction, or the harmonised result of many such schemes, each varying from the other and all varying from truth, that we can ever hope to behold.

History does not come down to us as a system of " 'chains,' or chainlets, of 'causes and effects,' " Carlyle continues, but as a "Chaos of Being." The "Artist in History" creates meaning out of chaos. He interprets "that complex Manuscript, covered over with formless inextricably-entangled unknown characters."[13] Carlyle's historian is resigned to the necessity of being artistic in the face of the unknown. Emerson's (in "History") enjoys the fact that "Babylon, Troy, Tyre, Palestine . . . have passed or are passing into fiction" (CW.II.6). His self-serving motives are transparent:

> All inquiry into antiquity all curiosity respecting the pyramids, the excavated cities, Stone-Henge, Rome, Babylon, is simply & at last the desire to do away this wild, savage, preposterous *Then*, & introduce in its place the *Now*; it is to banish the *Not Me* & supply the *Me*; it is to abolish *difference* & restore *Unity*. (JMN.VII.111)

The geniality that apprehends fact and fable together conceals the aggressive conversion of fact to fable, the inversion by which "the student . . . esteem[s] his own life the text, and books the commentary" (CW.II.5). To turn facts into fiction is not to write fiction, but to read history as fiction. "[I]n the beautiful creations of the Grecian muse every fable, though related as religious truth and believed by the multitude as *history*, is, at the same time"— that is, in modern times—"a fine *allegory* conveying a wise and consistent sense" (*EL.*I.257).

Such passages present certain difficulties even after Emerson's antagonistic motives are made clear. He opposes the literal falseness of the preacher's statements to his own "really true" translation of them into parables. Truth and figurative meaning are allied in a way that seems to permit several versions of the truth. However, when Emerson contrasts his view, his "single and firm" perception of "one sense," to the poet's "fable," seeing through fables involves finding an integral truth. It requires the abolition of "differences" in favor of "Unity." To read allegorically is more "consistent" than to read historically; fiction is more reductive than fact. This seems like peculiar reasoning for an author like Emerson, whose style proves the multiplicity and inconsistency of fable. His defense would be that his one truth is precisely the heterogeneity of the self. I think, rather, that "truth" and "fiction" are words he employs to designate different phases of possession or "use." Anything he reads becomes, by virtue of that reading, "fiction"; the "truth" he discovers in this fiction is that only he can endow it with meaning, and, therefore, that he *is* its meaning. He deprives history of truth by interpreting it; then claims that it is true because *he* has done so. The montages of fables that exhilarate us need the prior critical reduction.

· CONCLUSION ·

ROMANTIC PROSE
AND THE ARTISTIC CRITIC

Emerson's treatment of genre, a major category of literary history, is analogous to his treatment of history in general. Both his ideas about genre and his own generic choices are characteristic of Romantic practice. However, suggesting his affinities with other Romantic writers should not turn into an attempt to bring them under a generic rubric. Romantic genres are not sets to which a work does or does not belong. Rather, as more and more scholars are pointing out, generic choices and thinking about genre constituted a critique of belonging.[1] These concluding observations about Emerson's affiliations, then, are meant not to draw the boundaries of Romantic prose, but to show that the aim of such prose, which is to frustrate such delimitation, has been realized so effectively that we are still recommending its program. For although, like the major German and English Romantics, Emerson rejects generic conventions, this tactic is not unique to nineteenth-century Romanticism. Seeking a way to operate outside existing categories is a seemingly perpetual attribute of literary change, or, at least, of the discourse about literary change produced by its participants.[2] One of the reasons why the concept of genre will probably survive is that it serves writers so well in their efforts to identify a past which they can then imitate or defy.[3] Regardless of whether one accepts genre as a generative principle integral to particular works of art, the fact remains that to Emerson and his contemporaries it represented real conventions and expectations.

The Romantics' efforts to evade the strictures of generic categories led them to imagine an art that, because it absorbed all sorts of discourse, was outside the bounds of any.[4] In a journal entry, entitled "Eloquence" and "Lyceum," Emerson describes this stance:

Here is all the true orator will ask, for here is a convertible audience & here are no stiff conventions that prescribe a method, a style, a limited quotation of books, & an exact respect to certain books, persons, or opinions. No, here everything is admissible, philosophy, ethics, divinity, criticism, poetry, humor, fun, mimicry, anecdotes, jokes, ventriloquism. All the breadth & versatility of the most liberal conversation highest lowest personal local topics, all are permitted, and all may be combined in one speech; it is a panharmonicon,— every note on the longest gamut, from the explosion of cannon, to the tinkle of a guitar. Let us try if Folly, Custom, Convention & Phlegm cannot hear our sharp artillery. Here is a pulpit that makes other pulpits tame & ineffectual—with their cold mechanical preparation for a delivery the most decorous,—fine things, pretty things, wise things, but no arrows, no axes, no nectar, no growling, no transpiercing, no loving, no enchantment. Here he may lay himself out utterly, large, enormous, prodigal, on the subject of the hour. Here he may dare to hope for ecstasy & eloquence. (*JMN*.VII.265)

Emerson's animus against "stiff conventions" arises from the fact that he associates method with prescriptions and limits imposed upon him and with the "exact respect" tradition requires from him. The way genre can come to symbolize literary authority is unusually clear in this passage, though I think that genre carries this meaning for many writers. Certainly Emerson's response to "Folly, Custom, Convention & Phlegm" was typical of his era. Instead of imagining a new genre, he calls for discourse that combines all known genres, all academic disciplines, all professions, and all forms of popular culture: "here everything is admissible, philosophy, ethics, divinity, criticism, poetry, humor, fun, mimicry, anecdotes, jokes, ventriloquism." His preference for the Lyceum arises from the association of writing with generic conventionality and of pulpits with a "cold, mechanical" and excessively "decorous" style. It is the outrageousness of secular public speech that appeals to him and that, in passages like this one, colors his writing. When Emerson characterizes himself as an orator, it is not so much because he associates speech with a more primitive language, but because speech is a free and undefined expanse outside the sharply demarcated territories of writing.[5] His choice is antithetical, part of the "sharp artillery" of his poetics. The sexual suggestions of the closing lines, the insistent passion of the catalogue which includes arrows, axes, nectar, growling, and transpiercing, and the strong sense of the body in "large, enormous, prodigal," splendidly conclude this celebration of a prolific fusion and confusion of genres.

Emerson's lists in this entry are gestures of acceptance and inclusion, but are critical and ironic, too. Philosophy, ethics, and divinity lose some of their sanctity by appearing in a series that gives equal time to mimicry, anecdotes, and jokes. Popular entertainments are dignified and academic pursuits mocked. Even the contiguity of "divinity" and "criticism" suggests a skeptical equivalence of value. Despite its impudence, however, this list implies that new works will be constituted out of fragments of old materials. A corollary to this openly intertextual program is that, while the prose "panharmonicon" will be an art of poetry, ecstasy, and eloquence, it will also be critical. The orator will create his speech by means of unlimited quotation. The resulting blend of invention and intellection will place art and criticism on equal footing.

The catalogues Emerson requires to describe this "panharmonicon" constitute a paradigm of the structure of much Romantic prose. A paragraph from *Walden*, for example, exhibits the same kind of organization:

The whole ground of human life seems to some to have been gone over by their predecessors, both the heights and the valleys, and all things to have been cared for. According to Evelyn, "the wise Solomon prescribed ordinances for the very distances of trees; and the Roman praetors have decided how often you may go into your neighbor's land to gather the acorns which fall on it without trespass and what share belongs to that neighbor." Hippocrates has even left directions how we should cut our nails; that is, even with the ends of the fingers, neither shorter nor longer. Undoubtedly the very tedium and ennui which presume to have exhausted the variety and the joys of life are as old as Adam. But man's capacities have never been measured; nor are we to judge of what he can do by any precedents, so little has been tried. Whatever have been thy failures, hitherto, "be not afflicted, my child, for who shall assign to thee what thou has left undone?"[6]

In a few lines, quotation is taken to the second power as Thoreau seeks to deflate by hyperbolic allusiveness the belief that everything has been done and said by someone else. In the course of a paragraph, he covers "the whole ground" of human writing, from Evelyn's book on aboriculture (which cites, in turn, Solomon and Roman law), to Hippocrates, Genesis, and the unidentified source of the final quotation, the Hindu classic, *Vishnu Purana*.[7] This series of references ranges from the mundanely practical to the sublimely moral, but each term is equally an excuse for the lassitude of the despairing Concord farmer, whose resignation Thoreau parodies. The liberating effect of such a catalogue is evident at the end of the next paragraph, where Thoreau exclaims, "We should live in all the ages of the world in an hour; ay, in all the worlds of the ages, History, Poetry, Mythology!—I know of no reading of another's experience so startling and informing as this would be."[8] In fact, he has just shown himself and us how to live in all the ages of the world in a paragraph. Thoreau's selection from the writings of others turns out to be the "startling and informing" reading, the fragmentation and recycling, that frees us from excessive respect for the written record.

The pervasiveness of "unlimited quotation" suggests that the experience of multiple influences is as problematic for Romantic writers as the anxiety induced by a single overpowering precursor.[9] These writers, particularly the American ones, fret more about tradition—the cumulative force of all great authors felt simultaneously—than about Wordsworth or Milton. The two difficulties are related. Worry about "the past" may be a screen for (and thus a later phase of) imaginative involvement with a single earlier writer. On the other hand, fixing on one influence may simplify a prior stage of more diffuse anxiety.

The multigeneric quality of Romantic prose had an effect on American fiction, as well as on nonfictional prose. One need only mention the preliminary sections of *Moby-Dick*, "Etymology" and "Extracts," to support the argument that Melville, too, aligns quotations or allusions in such a way as to create irony or undercut received knowledge. But within the novel proper, multiplicity has a more complex function. The mustering of legendary associations in "The Whiteness of the Whale" shows language to be inadequate to but evocative of the mysteries of experience. The multiple interpretations of the doubloon precipitate a hermeneutic *mise en abîme*. The whole work, constituted by Melville's imitations and parodies of genres—tragedy, sermon, scientific report, metaphysical tract, rhapsode, encyclopedia—can be read as self-deconstructing. But at the same time, the series of generic experiments makes possible the reader's shift of mood from skepticism to something like faith or pleasure in the "emotion of multitude."[10]

The mixture of genres in *Moby-Dick* is analogous to other structural phenomena in American fiction. The fact that it is only one of several kinds of heterogeneity is one reason not to describe Romantic prose primarily in generic terms. In the works of Hawthorne, for instance, the comparative perspective is an attribute of narration. Hawthorne's favorite device to render competing viewpoints is the narrator's quietly skeptical summary of communal speculations. In the "Conclusion" of *The Scarlet Letter*, he writes of the "letter" on Dimmesdale's breast, "As regarded its origin, there were various explanations, all of which must necessarily have been conjectural. Some affirmed. . . . Others contended. . . . Others, again . . . whispered. . . . The reader may choose among these theories."[11] The "theories" of Hawthorne's Puritans do not embody multiple idioms in the direct way that quotation does. However, they do contain the ostensible wisdom of different ages, sexes, and especially, social classes in a slice revealing the multitudinous mind of an imagined community. Hawthorne's critique of seventeenth-century New England and nineteenth-century America proceeds by way of such passages. Multiple points of view are presented with an ironic reticence which expresses the knowledge that theories of "origin," always "conjectural," depend on the reader's choice.

Although the structures of Poe's fictional prose do not, on the surface, resemble the serial arrangement of perspectives found in other writers, they are organized by precisely the same concerns. In the preface and closing note to *Pym*, Poe calls into question the conventional distinctions between authors and editors, fiction and nonfiction.[12] His sly insinuations of doubt about who writes what are a subtler version of the fun Carlyle had in *Sartor Resartus*, in which fragments by an absent author encounter the efforts of his suspicious commentator, through the mediation of the shadowy Hofrath. John Irwin has recently done for *Pym* what Elinor Shaffer did for "Kubla Kahn." He has shown, first, that the book is a tissue of borrowings from Romantic language theories, anthropological speculations, chronicles, and histories; and second, that this context leads to a radical redefinition of the relative status of events and interpreters, texts and authors. Indeed, in showing that *Pym* takes the form of analogous representations of essentially the same episodes (the overcoming of the vessel, the descent into the abyss), Irwin helps us to see that Poe's prose may, after all, be constituted through the same kinds of substitutions we have observed in other writers.[13]

The aims of such writing had been brilliantly articulated by Friedrich Schlegel, whose own novel, *Lucinde*, exemplifies them. His work was not a source for or influence on American intellectuals, but rather an analogous response to cultural fragmentation and comparative criticism. The purpose of "poetry," Schlegel announced, isn't merely "to reunite all the separate species of poetry and put poetry in touch with philosophy and rhetoric [though it implies all this]. It tries to and should mix and fuse poetry and prose, inspiration and criticism."

Such prose "can raise [poetic] reflection again and again to a higher power, can multiply it in an endless suggestion of mirrors," in which every subject matter appears analogous to every other. The heterogeneous work is an image of its author who is "able to attune himself at will to being philosophical or philological, critical or poetical, historical or rhetorical, ancient or modern."[14] Schlegel's antagonists, like Emerson's, are writers and critics devoted to preserving the stylistic status quo. And, like Emerson, his aggressiveness takes the form of fragmentation, a sign of what we might call intertextual consciousness. Fragments, he writes, are either inherited bits of history or modern compositions that imitate surviving pieces of the past. "Many of the works of the ancients have become fragments. Many modern works are fragments as soon as they are written." Modern discourse resembles "a collection of variants accompanied by a running commentary for which the original classical text has been lost."[15] Irony ("Witz") is his word for the state of mind that exposes the disunity of its own works in order to deny the integrity of the past.

The production of heterogeneous but repetitive texts is a sign of the Romantic preoccupation with self-consciousness, manifested, in the literary arena, as criticism. This trend was announced over and over. The "age in which we . . . have the honor to live deserves the humble but highly suggestive name of the Critical Age," Schlegel trumpeted playfully. "[S]oon everything is going to be criticized . . . and everything is going to become more and more critical, and artists can already begin to cherish the just hope that humanity will at last rise up in a mass and learn to read." "This age is emphatically critical," Margaret Fuller stated in the first number of *The Dial*. Coleridge presented himself as the first "philosophical critic," Carlyle cited criticism as one of the skills that enlightened German thinkers could offer the benighted English, and periodicals were established to carry out the new critical tasks.[16] Emerson articulated every writer's task when he meditated on the relative claims of "analysis" and "creation."

The resistance he encountered was also typical of Romantic criticism. The association of philosophical criticism with indecorous excesses, particularly with a kind of impudent mystification, was well established in the minds of its opponents. Francis Bowen, confronted with this development in Emerson's *Nature*, complained that "it gives a dictatorial tone to the expression of opinion, and a harsh, imperious and sometimes flippant manner to argumentative discussion."[17] For Emerson, as for Schlegel, Carlyle, Thoreau, the young Schleiermacher, Kierkegaard, and Nietzsche (to suggest some

of the major recurrences of this stance), refreshment demanded
the impolite and impolitic flouting of decorum. Even Coleridge,
despite his self-deprecating and conciliatory tone, violated convention in works that were major precedents for reflective nonfiction in English. *Biographia Literaria* and *Aids to Reflection* combined
seventeenth-century metaphoric extravagance with the difficulties
of German metaphysics, symptoms of the author's personal neu-
roses with literary arguments based on stylistic analysis, incessant
quotation with idiosyncratic commentary.

Literary criticism is still, or once more, being conducted in a
Romantic mode. Journals proclaim the advent of another "Age of
Criticism" as aggressive, lyrical, cryptic, and self-serving critics
exercise the licenses of authorship. Charges are made of bad manners—arrogance and obscurantism.[18] "Creative reading" takes the
form of recombinations of anthropological, psychological, linguistic, socio-economic, and gender theories of (to Americans) exotic
origin. It is assumed that the will to power, the instinct for play,
and erotic desire unconsciously shape critical texts as well as "literary" ones. And, in proper Romantic fashion, the critic's exac-
erbated self-consciousness gives rise to his need for the unconscious.
A prominent deconstructive critic describes the problematics of
reading in remarkably Emersonian terms. She writes, "It is only
by forgetting what we know how to do, by setting aside the thoughts
that have most changed us, that those thoughts and that knowledge
can go on making accessible to us the surprise of an otherness we
can only enounter in the moment of suddenly discovering we are
ignorant of it." A philosopher confronts the risks of repetition with
similar results: "We court danger in wanting to be freed from
categories; no sooner do we abandon their organizing principle
than we face the magma of stupidity. . . . But in concentrating on
this boundless monotony, we find the sudden illumination of multiplicity itself . . . suddenly, arising from the background from the
old inertia of equivalences, the striped form of the event tears
through the darkness and the eternal phantasm informs that sin-
gular and depthless face." The fact that critical theory has been
the cause and effect of a return to the study of Romanticism is the
most Romantic thing about it.[19] There is no way for us not to

know our sources and every reason to use them. The essential thing to be learned from Emerson, Schlegel, and, as I am about to suggest, Oscar Wilde, is that such uses are temporary and pleasurable.

Wilde offers one of the most cogent statements of the Romantic rationale for a heterogeneous, self-critical prose. The conjunctions among the theories of Schlegel, a German; Emerson, an American; and Wilde, an Englishman, writing over the course of a century, suggest the varied routes by which Romantic criticism has come down to the late twentieth century. Wilde's dialogue, "The Critic as Artist," is a witty summary of the Romantic poetics of prose. It features Ernest as straight man (the opposite of the protean hero of Wilde's drama) and Gilbert, who speaks for Wilde. Against Ernest's conviction that "the creative faculty is higher than the critical," Gilbert argues that the best part of artistic creation is critical. The artist's "instinct of selection," "that spirit of choice, that subtle tact of omission, is really the critical faculty in one of its most characteristic moods." Gilbert/Wilde resents the distinction between creation and criticism because it is used to devalue the latter; he attacks this tendency by equating criticism and invention. The critical faculty "invents fresh forms" because it turns against and away from existing styles: "Each new school, as it appears, cries out against criticism, but it is to the critical faculty in man that it owes its origin."[20]

Wilde's critic is antithetical, is, indeed, remarkably "Emersonian." He seeks out exposures to a variety of authors in order to know and define himself. These conflictual encounters bring into being the only critic "intense" enough to read properly:

> just as it is only by contact with the art of foreign nations
> that the art of a country gains that individual and separate
> life that we call nationality, so, by curious inversion, it is only
> by intensifying his own personality that the critic can interpret
> the personality and work of others.

The analogy between the critic's reading and the exposure to "foreign nations" is reminiscent of Emerson's stance as mediator of traditions. Wilde's critic is neither rational nor fair nor sincere, which is to say, he is ironically self-conscious about his own multiplicity: "[H]e recognizes that each mode of criticism is . . . simply a mood, and that we are never more true to ourselves than when we are inconsistent." It is no wonder that Wilde referred to Emerson, another critic-as-artist, as "that master of moods."[21] "Through constant change . . . alone," the critic "will find his true unity. . . . For what is mind but motion in the intellectual sphere? . . . What people call insincerity is simply a method by which we can multiply our personalities." The critic's athletic transformations liberate him from his own past and from his cultural past: "[He goes about] winning from the various schools the secret of their charm, bowing, it may be, before foreign altars, or smiling . . . at strange new gods. What other people call one's past . . . has absolutely nothing to do with oneself. When one has found expression for a mood, one is done with it." The smiling and bowing before "foreign altars," like Emerson's secret laughter at Wordsworth, precedes an almost instantaneous rejection, even a forgetting. Out of the experience of this alternation between ironic acceptance of others and delighted self-love, Wilde proclaims, in behalf of his—and our—tradition, "The artistic critic . . . is an antinomian always."[22]

NOTES

INTRODUCTION

1. The works of Harold Bloom offer us a theoretical vocabulary with which to approach the issue of literary influence among prose writers and, even more usefully, exemplary readings of the kind of rhetorical perturbations, figurative presences and absences, and discontinuities that provide textual clues to the dynamics of influence. His remarkable corpus, from *The Anxiety of Influence* (New York: Oxford University Press, 1973) to *Agon* (New York: Oxford University Press, 1982) responds to other influential works on the question of influence, particularly Eliot's "Tradition and the Individual Talent" (in *The Sacred Wood: Essays on Poetry and Criticism* [London: Methuen, 1920; University Paperbacks, 1960]) and Walter Jackson Bate's *The Burden of the Past and the English Poet* (New York: Norton Library, 1972). George Bornstein's studies also trace the dynamics of poetic influence in the Romantic tradition. See *Transformations of Romanticism in Yeats, Eliot and Stevens* (Chicago: University of Chicago Press, 1976) and *Yeats and Shelley* (Chicago: University of Chicago Press, 1970). Perry Meisel's study of Pater's influence on the criticism of Virginia Woolf, *The Absent Father*, is a fine example of the kind of study I am undertaking (New Haven: Yale Univerity Press, 1980).

2. Stephen E. Whicher, *Freedom and Fate: An Inner Life of Ralph Waldo Emerson*, 2nd ed. (Philadelphia: University of Pennsylvania Press, 1971), p. 21.

3. In my discussion of the higher criticism, I have relied heavily on Hans W. Frei's *The Eclipse of Biblical Narrative: A Study in Eighteenth and Nineteenth Century Hermeneutics* (New Haven: Yale University Press, 1974). Here I refer to pp. 158–62, 173–78. I have also been influenced by E. S. Shaffer's brilliant analysis of the literary ramifications of the higher criticism in England, *"Kubla Khan" and the Fall of Jerusalem: The Mythological School in Biblical Criticism and Secular Literature, 1700–1880* (Cambridge: Cambridge University Press, 1975).

4. Studies of the syncretic impulse in the literature of the American Renaissance include Dorothee Metlitsky Finkelstein, *Melville's Orienda* (New Haven: Yale University Press, 1961), pp. 13–24; H. Bruce Frank-

lin, *The Wake of the Gods: Melville's Mythology* (Stanford: Stanford University Press, 1963), pp. 1–16, 103–105; Robert Richardson, *Myth and Literature in the American Renaissance* (Bloomington: Indiana University Press, 1978), especially ch. 1, "The Two Traditions."

5. Hans Frei, *Eclipse of Biblical Narrative*, pp. 183–201, 290–306.

6. The standard work on the sublime is Samuel H. Monk's *The Sublime: A Study of Critical Theories in Eighteenth-Century England* (Ann Arbor: University of Michigan Press, 1960). Discussion of the sublime was transformed by Thomas Weiskel's *The Romantic Sublime: Studies in the Structure and Psychology of Transcendence* (Baltimore: Johns Hopkins University Press, 1976). Weiskel's ideas have been subtly extended by Neil Hertz in "Lecture de Longin," *Poétique* 15 (1973), 292–306 (recently retranslated in *Critical Inquiry* 9 [1983], 579–96) and "The Notion of Blockage in the Literature of the Sublime," in Geoffrey Hartman, ed., *Psychoanalysis and the Question of the Text*, English Institute Essays (Baltimore: Johns Hopkins University Press, 1978), pp. 62–85. I have found the latter essay particularly useful, since in it Hertz relates the Romantic sublime to the dynamics of literary criticism today. Frances Ferguson, in "The Sublime of Edmund Burke, or the Bathos of Experience," *Glyph: Johns Hopkins Textual Studies* 8 (1981), pp. 62–79, persuasively restores the category of the Beautiful to the structure of the Sublime.

7. The "hermeneutical sublime" is Thomas Weiskel's term for Kant's "mathematical sublime."

8. I am proposing a somewhat narrower definition of irony than Anne K. Mellor offers in *English Romantic Irony* (Cambridge: Harvard University Press, 1980), "The Paradigm of Romantic Irony," pp. 3–30. She identifies irony with a vision of a chaotic universe governed by continuous flux and unstable oscillations. According to Mellor, the Romantic alternately promoted and lamented this chaos, depending on the degree of his or her skepticism about synthesis and teleology. I would not identify irony with the mere perception of instability, but with a particular stance toward it. I do not include in Romantic irony the nostalgia for or hope of unity, though these moods are certainly closely related to irony.

9. Neil Hertz, "Blockage in the Literature of the Sublime," pp. 72–73.

10. Friedrich Schlegel, *Lucinde and the Fragments*, translated by Peter Firchow (Minneapolis: University of Minnesota Press, 1971), Critical Fragments #42, p. 148.

11. The phrase comes from the title of Tzvetan Todorov's *The Poetics*

of Prose, translated by Richard Howard (Ithaca, N.Y.: Cornell University Press, 1977). I extend the term to non-narrative prose.

12. Hans Aarsleff, *The Study of Language in England, 1780–1860* (Princeton: Princeton University Press, 1967), p. 29f. M. H. Abrams, *The Mirror and the Lamp: Romantic Theory and the Critical Tradition* (London: Oxford University Press, 1953), pp. 290–92.

· 1 ·

INVOCATIONS

1. Milman's *Samor* was published in New York in 1818 (*JMN.*I.7n.).

2. Harold Bloom, *A Map of Misreading* (New York: Oxford University Press, 1975), p. 173.

3. See, for example, Coleridge's *Biographia Literaria,* edited by J. Shawcross (Oxford: Oxford University Press, 1907), I, 9–10, 62–63.

4. Clearly, I take issue with Gay Wilson Allen's assertion that "Ralph lacked the competitive spirit, and for him sibling rivalry was either so faint or so well concealed that it appears to have been almost nonexistent," *Waldo Emerson* (New York: Viking Press, 1981), p. 39. Although one would not want to equate competitiveness and sibling rivalry, Emerson's anxiety about keeping up with his own generation was certainly intensified by the achievements of his brothers.

5. "Thoughts on the Religion of the Middle Ages" was published in *The Christian Disciple,* New Series IV (November-December 1822), 401–408.

6. Neil Hertz, "Blockage in the Literature of the Sublime," p. 78.

7. Ibid., pp. 62–73.

8. See Philip F. Gura, *The Wisdom of Words: Language, Theology, and Literature in the New England Renaissance* (Middletown: Wesleyan University Press, 1981), especially ch. 1 on Unitarian scriptural exegesis. See also Richardson, *Myth and Literature in the American Renaissance,* on the nineteenth-century boom in comparative mythology; Stanley M. Vogel, *German Literary Influences on the American Transcendentalists* (New Haven: Yale University Press, 1955); René Wellek, "Emerson and German Philosophy," *New England Quarterly* 16 (1943), 41–62, and "The Minor Transcendentalists and German Philosophy," *New England Quarterly* 15 (1942), 652–80. Richardson and Vogel append excellent bibliographies on German material in the Boston area with special reference to Emerson's exposure to it. I strongly suspect that Emerson's 1831 lectures on "The

Four Evangelists" (Houghton ms. bMSAm/1280.193) display his critical learning even more specifically than his journals or published works, and I plan to examine these documents.

9. Allen, *Waldo Emerson*, p. 85.

10. Letters of William Emerson, May 29, August 27, October 10, 1824, and January 17, 1825. Columbia University Microfilm.

· 2 ·
EXPEDIENTS

1. Allen, *Waldo Emerson*, pp. 168–71.

2. Joel Porte, *Ralph Waldo Emerson: Representative Man* (Cambridge: Harvard University Press, 1978), "Economizing," especially pp. 250–52.

3. Ralph L. Rusk, *The Life of Ralph Waldo Emerson* (New York: Charles Scribner's Sons, 1949), p. 150.

4. Henry F. Pommer, *Emerson's First Marriage* (Carbondale: Southern Illinois University Press, 1967), p. 116.

5. Ralph L. Rusk, *Life*, p. 152.

6. From Carlyle's review of *The Corn Law Rhymes* in *Collected Works*, edited by H. D. Traill, Centenary Edition (New York, 1896–1899), *Critical and Miscellaneous Essays*, I, 351.

· II ·
INTRODUCTION

1. As Mary R. Rucker has observed, scholars "have compared his essays to music, mosaics, circles and spiral staircases" ("Emerson's 'Friendship' as Process," *ESQ* 18:4 [1972], 235). To her catalogue, one can add the Unitarian sermon, the public lecture, nature or man's progress through it, and the faculties and operations of the mind. See Lawrence Buell, *Literary Transcendentalism* (Ithaca: Cornell University Press, 1973), chs. 5–6; Jonathan Bishop, *Emerson on the Soul* (Cambridge: Harvard University Press, 1964); and David Porter, *Emerson and Literary Change* (Cambridge: Harvard University Press, 1978), chs. 6–8.

2. William T. Harris originated the phrase in "The Dialectical Unity of Emerson's Prose," *Journal of Speculative Philosophy* 108 (1884), 195–202. Charles J. Woodbury found the origins of Emerson's order in the Socratic dialogues and the writings of Coleridge, *Talks with Emerson* (1890;

rpt. New York: Horizon Press, 1970), pp. 150–52. See also F. B. Sanborn, *The Genius and Character of Emerson* (1885; rpt. Port Washington, N.Y.: Kennikat Press, 1971), pp. 339–64. In our day, Walter Blair and Clarence Faust, "Emerson's Literary Method," *Modern Philology* 42 (1944), 79–95, have set forth more precisely the similarities between Emerson's idiosyncratic logic and Plato's image of a "twice-bisected line." Barry Wood (*Publications of the Modern Language Association* 91 [1976], 385–97) follows the lead of Sherman Paul (*Emerson's Angle of Vision* [Cambridge: Harvard Univerity Press, 1952], pp. 112–19) in asserting a connection between the structure of *Nature* and the dialectical system contained in Coleridge's discourses on method in *The Friend*. See also Richard Lee Francis, *American Quarterly* 19:1 (1967), 39–52, "The Architectonics of Emerson's *Nature*" and Gusthaaf van Cromphout, "Emerson and the Dialectics of History," *Publications of the Modern Language Association* 91:1 (1976), 54–64.

3. Whicher, *Freedom and Fate* (1971) and Porter, *Emerson and Literary Change*, p. 134.

4. Eric Cheyfitz' stated object is "to record [the] shifting imbalance of power" in *Nature* and other works (*The Trans-parent: Sexual Politics in the Language of Emerson* [Baltimore: Johns Hopkins University Press, 1981], p. xiii).

5. Quoted in George Willis Cooke, *An Historical and Biographical Introduction to Accompany The Dial*, 2 volumes (New York: Russell and Russell, 1961), I, 133.

· 4 ·
"THE AMERICAN SCHOLAR"
AND THE DIVINITY SCHOOL "ADDRESS"

1. Oliver Wendell Holmes' response to "The American Scholar" is quoted in the notes to the "Address" in the 1903 edition (W.I.110).

· 5 ·
"THE POET"

1. Bishop, *Emerson on the Soul*, p. 131.
2. Ibid., p. 184.
3. Hugh Blair, *Lectures on Rhetoric and Belles-Lettres*, edited by Harold

F. Harding (Carbondale: Southern Illinois University Press, 1956), II, 354–56.

4. James M. Cox, "R. W. Emerson: The Circles of the Eye," in *Emerson: Prophecy, Metamorphosis, and Influence,* edited by David Levin, English Institute Essays (New York: Columbia University Press, 1975), p. 70.

5. The source of this passage must be Spenser's Garden of Adonis, that other secret place which guards the mystery of metamorphosis. Emerson's reference to the moment as "here" also recalls Wordsworth's "here the Power so called" (*The Prelude* VI.11.592–616). Wordsworth, too, stops before the secret of the imagination and represents its mystery as a creative, unitary power: "like the mighty flood of Nile / Poured from his fount of Abyssinian clouds / To fertilize the whole Egyptian plain." "The Poet" and *The Prelude* describe encounters between the self and regenerative power in versions of the Renaissance allegory of a place where life originates.

6. *The Winter's Tale,* IV.iv.11.88–90. Joel Porte adduces the same scene in a discussion of Emerson's changing conceptions of nature and fate, *Representative Man,* pp. 226–28.

7. Paul de Man, "Intentional Structure of the Romantic Image," in *Romanticism and Consciousness: Essays in Criticism,* edited by Harold Bloom (New York: W. W. Norton, 1970), p. 71.

8. *Shorter Oxford English Dictionary,* 2nd ed. s.v. "demon." Geoffrey Hartman, *Beyond Formalism* (New Haven: Yale University Press, 1970), p. 319.

9. Entered in Emerson's journal a few months after his son's death, the first version of this passage is preceded and followed by meditations on that event: "This beloved and now departed Boy, this Image in every part beautiful, how he expands in his dimensions in this fond Memory to the dimensions of Nature" (*JMN.*VIII.205). Waldo seems to have vanished into the landscape that both reminds Emerson of his loss and veils a consoling "Spirit." Only the poor, hungry, and simple—those who have purged themselves of "fashion and covetousness"—earn a glimpse of the *genius loci.* (As usual in Emerson's value judgments, socioeconomic, moral, and aesthetic capacities are conflated. Wisdom discriminates against the residents of Boston and New York, who have grown jaded by consuming imported culture—"wine and French coffee" [*W.*III.29]). He is among the needy by virtue of the grief that has left him unsophisticated. However, the pain of Waldo's death is ameliorated by his ghostly return as the light of Wisdom. Cox's hypothesis that Emerson habitually converts the deaths

of family members into imaginative energy seems borne out by this passage, both in its original form and as it appears in "The Poet" (Cox, "The Circles of the Eye," pp. 71–73).

10. *Longinus on the Sublime,* translated by William Smith, p. 55. "For the mind is naturally elevated by the true *Sublime,* and so sensibly affected with its lively strokes, that it swells in transport and inward pride, as if what was only heard had been the product of its own invention."

11. See also *JMN.*VI.312; VII.30, 127; VIII.221.

12. Barbara Packer, "Uriel's Cloud: Emerson's Rhetoric," *Georgia Review* (Summer 1978), p. 326.

13. Barbara Packer, *Emerson's Fall: A New Interpretation of the Major Essays* (New York: Continuum, 1982), p. 15.

14. Vivian Hopkins, *Spires of Form: A Study of Emerson's Aesthetic Theory* (Cambridge: Harvard University Press, 1951), pp. 196–97.

15. Porter, *Emerson and Literary Change,* p. 194.

16. The conflated images of salvation, matrimony, and nature recur in Harold Bloom's description of the outcome of "The Internalization of Quest-Romance," a plot that this passage illustrates very neatly. In *Romanticism and Consciousness,* p. 71.

17. Kenneth Burke, "I, Eye, Ay—Concerning Emerson's Early Essay on 'Nature' and the Machinery of Transcendence," in *Language as Symbolic Action* (Berkeley and Los Angeles: University of California Press, 1968), p. 200.

· 6 ·

"QUOTATION AND ORIGINALITY"

1. T. S. Eliot, in *The Sacred Wood: Essays on Poetry and Criticism,* pp. 49–50.

2. Sigmund Freud, *Beyond the Pleasure Principle,* edited and translated by James Strachey (New York: W. W. Norton, 1961), p. 12.

3. Peter Hughes connects the problems of quotation, repetition, and modernity in "Allusion and Expression in Eighteenth-Century Literature," in *The Author in His Work: Essays on a Problem of Criticism,* edited by Louis Martz and Aubrey Williams (New Haven: Yale University Press, 1978), pp. 297–317.

· III ·
INTRODUCTION

1. My translation of Philippe Lacoue-Labarthe and Jean-Luc Nancy, *L'absolu littéraire: Théorie de la littérature du romantisme allemand* (Paris: Seuil, 1978), "L'exigence fragmentaire," p. 58.

· 7 ·
REPETITION

1. Edward W. Said, *Beginnings: Intention and Method* (Baltimore: Johns Hopkins University Press, 1975), p. 262. Said's meditation throughout this book on the relationships among discontinuity and repetition, seriality, and fraternity suggests that the structures I find in Emerson's prose are deeply embedded in our tradition.

2. John Burroughs, *Literary Values* (Boston and New York: Houghton Mifflin, 1902), p. 190.

3. H. H. Emmons, *Philosograms of Emerson* (Cleveland: Rex Publishing Co., 1930) and *Light of Emerson: A Complete Digest with Key-Word Concordance* (Cleveland: Rex Publishing Co., 1930?). Quoted from the title pages.

4. Warner Berthoff, *Fictions and Events* (New York: Dutton, 1971), p. 197.

5. Charles Feidelson, Jr., *Symbolism and American Literature* (Chicago: University of Chicago Press, 1953), p. 129.

6. The forewords to *The Journals and Miscellaneous Notebooks* describe this process in summaries of the material printed in each volume. For example, the foreword to Volume VI gives careful attention to Emerson's collection of quotations (*JMN*.VI.ix–xvi).

7. "Rendered 'the flowing philosophers' by Jeremy Taylor" (*JMN*. X.160n).

8. Lawrence Buell is the only critic who has recognized that repetition is Emerson's "most characteristic structural device." He divides Emerson's catalogues into "expository," "illustrative," and "symbolic" varieties. *Literary Transcendentalism*, "Catalogue Rhetoric," pp. 166–87.

9. Ibid., p. 176.

10. Frederick Crews, *Random House Handbook*, 2nd ed. (New York: Random House, 1977), pp. 175–76.

11. Porter, *Emerson and Literary Change*, p. 207.

12. Mary Edrich, "The Rhetoric of Apostasy," *Texas Studies in Literature and Language* 8 (Winter 1967), 553–56.

13. A. Bronson Alcott, *Ralph Waldo Emerson: An Estimate of His Character and Genius* (rpt. New York: Haskell House, 1968), p. 7.

14. Crews, *Random House Handbook*, p. 175.

15. Alcott, *Ralph Waldo Emerson*, p. 35.

16. Samuel Taylor Coleridge, *Aids to Reflection*, edited by James Marsh. 1st American ed. (Burlington, Vt.: Chauncy Goodrich, 1829), pp. 183–86.

17. Soren Kierkegaard, *Repetition: An Essay in Experimental Psychology*, edited by Walter Lowrie (New York: Harper and Row, 1964), quoted from *The Concept of Dread* in "Editor's Introduction," p. 21.

18. Jean-Pierre Mileur, *Vision and Revision: Coleridge's Art of Immanence* (Berkeley and Los Angeles: University of California Press, 1982), pp. 28–33.

19. Walter Benjamin, *The Origin of German Tragic Drama*, translated by John Osborne (London: NLB, 1977), p. 178. Thomas McFarland's recent study, *Romanticism and the Forms of Ruin: Wordsworth, Coleridge, and Modalities of Fragmentation* (Princeton: Princeton University Press, 1981), argues persuasively that the related notions of ruin, fragmentation, polarity, and the hope for a miraculous intuition of wholeness organize and define Romantic writing.

· 8 ·

DETACHMENT AND TRANSITION

1. Friedrich Nietzsche, *The Use and Abuse of History*, translated by Adrian Collins (Indianapolis: Bobbs-Merrill, 1949, 1957), p. 6.

2. Wallace Stevens, *The Collected Poems of Wallace Stevens* (New York: Alfred A. Knopf, 1954), p. 392.

3. Samuel Taylor Coleridge, *Biographia Literaria*, I, 202.

4. Gerald L. Bruns, *Modern Poetry and the Idea of Language: A Critical and Historical Study* (New Haven: Yale University Press, 1974), pp. 43–55.

5. Friedrich von Schiller, *Naive and Sentimental Poetry* and *On the Sublime*, translated by Julias A. Elias (New York: Ungar, 1966), pp. 111–12; *On the Aesthetic Education of Man*, translated by Reginald Snell (New York: Ungar, 1974), p. 39.

6. Friedrich Wilhelm von Schelling, "Concerning the Relation of the

Plastic Arts to Nature," translated by Michael Bullock, in Herbert Read, *The True Voice of Feeling: Studies in English Romantic Poetry* (New York: Pantheon Books, 1953), pp. 334, 342.

7. The lines of Emerson's poems seem to be formed by the same urge to intensify by compression. A complex thought is squeezed into the fewest possible words, which are forced out of their normal order to accommodate a surplus of meaning. The discontinuity of the poems is caused by the cryptic quality that results from compression rather than by the fissures between the repetitive expansions of the prose. In the former, discourse is forced to fit a space too small for it; in the latter, it is permitted such an unlimited expanse that gaps appear between parts. Is the poetic motto that precedes each essay a fragment requiring the more discursive prose to complete and explain it, or is the essay contained in—reduced to—its motto? Their inverse structures seem to require each other. For the reader, the gnomic motto is a puzzle. He turns to the essay for the relief of interpretation but finds that Emerson's prose is aphoristic and proverbial. It aspires, in other words, to the condensation of the motto.

8. Guillaume Oegger, *The True Messiah*, translated by Elizabeth P. Peabody (Boston: E. P. Peabody, 1842), rpt. in Kenneth Walter Cameron, *Young Emerson's Transcendental Vision* (Hartford, Conn.: Transcendental Books, 1971), p. 338.

9. Sampson Reed, *Observations on the Growth of the Mind* (Boston, 1826), rpt. in Cameron, *Young Emerson's Transcendental Vision*, p. 316.

10. *Wordsworth and Coleridge: Lyrical Ballads, 1798*, edited by W.J.B. Owen, 2nd ed. (London: Oxford University Press, 1969), p. 148.

11. Feidelson, *Symbolism and American Literature*, p. 150.

12. Monk, *The Sublime*, pp. 15–17, 26–27.

· 9 ·

FIGURATIVE LANGUAGE

1. John Locke, *An Essay Concerning Human Understanding* (Oxford: Oxford University Press, 1914), Book III, ch. ix, section xxii.

2. Abrams, *The Mirror and the Lamp*, pp. 290–92.

3. Quoted by Lois Whitney, "English Primitivistic Theories of Epic Origins," *Modern Philology* 21 (May 1924), 358. From Blair's *Critical Dissertation* (New York, 1810), I, 88.

4. Harold Bloom, *Kabbalah and Criticism* (New York: Continuum, Seabury Press, 1975), pp. 120–21.

5. Freud, *Beyond the Pleasure Principle,* pp. 46–47.

6. Wallace Stevens, *The Necessary Angel: Essays on Reality and the Imagination* (New York: Vintage Books, 1951), "Three Academic Pieces," I, 72–75, 80; "Effects of Analogy," p. 118. The similarity between Stevens' poetics and Emerson's corresponds to, if it does not account for, the extraordinary structural parallels in their repetitive works.

7. Packer, *Emerson's Fall,* pp. 73–74.

8. Hughes, "Allusion and Expression in Eighteenth-Century Literature," p. 309.

9. Bishop, *Emerson on the Soul,* p. 130.

10. Barbara L. Packer, "Emerson's Apocalypse of Mind," Ph.D. dissertation, Yale University, 1973, p. 207.

11. Bloom, *A Map of Misreading,* p. 173.

12. Samuel Taylor Coleridge, "On the Principles of Genial Criticism," in *Criticism: The Major Texts,* edited by Walter Jackson Bate (New York: Harcourt, Brace and World, 1952), p. 373. Emerson almost certainly did not read these essays, published in a Bristol newspaper in 1814. Nevertheless, the meaning Coleridge gave to the term "genial" gives us a way of measuring Emerson's tendency to dramatize as conflict what others imagined as reconciliation. Although Coleridge's "principles" included Pythagoras' definition of beauty as the reduction of many to one, he altered this dictum, emphasizing the critic's "simultaneous intuition of the relation of parts, each to each, and of all to a whole; exciting an immediate and absolute complacency," a pure pleasure entirely divorced from the will. Emerson, on the other hand, likes reduction and the pleasures of the will.

13. Thomas Carlyle, "On History," *Collected Works, Miscellaneous Essays,* II, 88–90. Carlyle's model for the historian is clearly the higher critic, who studies "that complex Manuscript," the Bible, seeking to "harmonize" the Gospels into a "more or less plausible scheme" but is still confronted with the text's uninterpretable "Prophetic" residue.

Conclusion

1. Philippe Lacoue-Labarthe and Jean-Luc Nancy, *L'absolu littéraire,* of which an excerpt is translated in *Glyph: Johns Hopkins Textual Studies* 7 (1980), 1–14; also Jacques Derrida, "The Law of Genre," translated by Avital Ronell, in the same issue of *Glyph,* pp. 202–29. The papers in this issue were presented at the Strasbourg International Colloquium on Genre in 1979.

2. Thus David Porter's *Emerson and Literary Change* quite properly focuses on the meaning of Emerson's generic choices, though without taking into account the influence and context of other Romantic prose writers. Michel Beaujour argues provocatively that Lacoue-Labarthe and Nancy's category of absolute literature is not a Romantic development, but that the idea of a "universal genre" is a venerable notion "bound up with the Renaissance belief that there existed a forgotten short-cut to knowledge and power." "Genus Universum," *Glyph* 7, pp. 15–31.

3. Claudio Guillén writes, "It is a mistake to assume that poetics is intended primarily for scholars and aestheticians. The traditional target of poetic theory has been the writer." *Literature as System: Essays toward the Theory of Literary History* (Princeton: Princeton University Press, 1971), "The Uses of Literary Genre," p. 122. Jonathan Culler also ascribes the usefulness of genre to its function in the dynamics of reading and writing: *Structuralist Poetics: Structuralism, Linguistics, and the Study of Literature* (Ithaca: Cornell University Press, 1975), pp. 135–37, 147–48. Other reconsiderations of the uses and history of genre theory include Gerard Genette's influential "Genres, 'types,' modes," *Poétique* 32 (1977), 389–421; and Paul Hernadi, *Beyond Genre: New Directions in Literary Classification* (Ithaca: Cornell University Press, 1972).

4. Philippe Lacoue-Labarthe and Jean-Luc Nancy, "Genre," *Glyph* 7, pp. 3, 10–11.

5. The association of the primitive with freedom from institutional constraints is habitual in Romantic poetics. We can hardly separate, for example, Wordsworth's animus against poetic diction from his praise of rural man in the prefaces to *Lyrical Ballads*.

6. Henry David Thoreau, *The Annotated Walden*, edited by Philip Van Doren Stern (New York: Bramhall House, 1970), pp. 151–52.

7. Thoreau, *The Annotated Walden*, pp. 151–52.

8. Ibid., p. 152.

9. I do not, with this distinction, want to reduce Bloom's vision of literary influence to a series of one-to-one relationships between writers. Virtually all of his readings take the form of a wide-ranging meditation on a multitude of earlier texts, though for the later poet, he argues, these tend to be felt through the work of a single writer.

10. Richard Brodhead borrows Yeats's phrase (for Shakespeare) in his brilliant description of the effects of generic multiplicity in the fictional works of Emerson's contemporaries: *Hawthorne, Melville and the Novel* (Chicago: University of Chicago Press, 1977), pp. 14–17, 195–203.

11. Nathaniel Hawthorne, *The Scarlet Letter: A Facsimile of the First*

Edition, edited by Hyatt H. Waggoner and George Monteiro (San Francisco: Chandler, 1968), pp. 314–15.

12. Edgar Allen Poe, *Selected Writings of Edgar Allen Poe,* edited by Edward H. Davidson (Boston: Houghton Mifflin, 1956), pp. 247–48, 405–407.

13. John T. Irwin, *American Hieroglyphics: The Symbol of the Egyptian Hieroglyphics in the American Renaissance* (New Haven: Yale University Press, 1980), especially chs. 4 and 11.

14. Friedrich Schlegel, *Lucinde and the Fragments,* Athenaeum Fragment #116, p. 175; Critical Fragment #55, p. 149. It is unlikely that Emerson was familiar with the *Athenaeum* itself. However, he probably did encounter some of the material that had appeared there in the collected works of Auguste and Friedrich Schlegel, Novalis, and in various reviews and translations. From the Boston Library Society, he borrowed two volumes of one of the Schlegels in 1821, then, in 1824, "Schlegel on Literature." In 1835 he withdrew Volume I of what must have been F. Schlegel's *Sämmtliche Werke,* a volume containing *Geschichte der alten und neuen Litteratur,* from the Boston Athenaeum; in 1836, Novalis' *Schriften* (probably two volumes in one containing the fragments, among other works); in 1845, Schlegel's *Lectures on the History of Literature;* in 1851, Novalis' *Schriften* again. He owned Novalis' *Henry of Ofterdingen* (Cambridge, 1942), F. Schlegel's *Philosophy of History* (London, 1835), and A. W. Schlegel's *Course of Lectures on Dramatic Art and Literature.* On the whole, he seems to have been well acquainted with the later works of the Schlegels and less familiar with the earlier productions of the *Athenaeum* group, which are closer to his own works in spirit. My source for this information is Stanley M. Vogel, *German Literary Influences on the American Transcendentalists,* pp. 167–81.

15. Friedrich Schlegel, *Lucinde and the Fragments,* Athenaeum Fragments #24, p. 164; #216, p. 190.

16. Friedrich Schlegel, "On Incomprehensibility," *Lucinde and the Fragments,* p. 261. Margaret Fuller, "A Short Essay on Critics," *The Dial* 1:1 (1840) (rpt. New York: Russell and Russell, 1961), 5. Samuel Taylor Coleridge, *Biographia Literaria,* I, 62. Thomas Carlyle, "State of German Literature," *The Dial* 3:1 (1842), 13–16; "Le plus ancien programme systématique de l'idéalisme allemand" in Lacoue-Labarthe and Nancy, *L'absolu littéraire,* pp. 53–54; Samuel G. Ward, "Criticism," *Aesthetic Papers* (Boston: Peabody, 1849), pp. 5–24.

17. Review of Emerson's *Nature* reprinted, with Christopher Pearse Cranch's parody of such reviews, in Perry Miller, ed., *The Transcenden-*

talists: An Anthology (Cambridge: Harvard University Press, 1950), pp. 173–78, 300.

18. M. H. Abrams, "How to Do Things with Texts," *Partisan Review* 46:4 (1979), 566.

19. Barbara Johnson, "Nothing Fails Like Success," *SCE Reports* 8, *Deconstructive Criticism: Directions* (Fall 1980), p. 15. Michel Foucault's review of Gilles Deleuze's *Difference et repetition* and *Logique du sens*, in *Language, Counter-Memory, Practice: Selected Essays and Interviews*, edited by Donald F. Bouchard (Ithaca: Cornell University Press, 1977), pp. 188–89. To mention only a few of the affinities between current literary theory and criticism of Romantic writings, we have the work of de Man and Derrida on Rousseau, of Lacoue-Labarthe and Nancy on the *Athenaeum*, of Lacan on Poe, of Hartman on Wordsworth. The latter, in the preface of Bloom et al., *Deconstruction and Criticism*, p. ix, remarks, "Since the era of the German Romantics . . . and of Coleridge . . . we have not seen a really fruitful interreaction of these 'sister arts [philosophy and literary study]'. Yet the recent revival of philosophic criticism . . . is like a new dawn that should not fade into the light of common day. The important place taken in these essays by Romantic poetry is also worth noting: perhaps we have begun to understand what kind of thinking poetry is, especially Romantic poetry that was often held to be intellectually confused or idle." See also Kenneth Dauber, "Criticism of American Literature," *Diacritics* 7:1 (1977), 55–66.

20. Oscar Wilde, "The Critic as Artist," *The Portable Oscar Wilde*, edited by Richard Aldington (New York: Viking Press, 1946), pp. 69–73.

21. *The Letters of Oscar Wilde*, edited by Rupert Hart-Davis (New York: Harcourt, Brace and World, 1946), p. 169.

22. Oscar Wilde, "The Critic as Artist," pp. 93, 114, 118, 134–35.

INDEX

aggression. *See* antagonism and aggression

Alcott, Bronson, 170–71

alienated majesty, dynamics of, 82, 101, 110, 149, 151, 190, 207. *See also* influence

allegory, 91–92

allusion, 18, 104, 203, 216; and fable, 211–12, 215, 217. *See also* quotation

America, literary culture, 101, 103–104. *See also* nationalism

antagonism and aggression, 12, 14, 25–26, 36, 95, 100, 107; and prose style, 10, 13, 53, 98, 107, 116, 171; in interpretation, 11, 42, 79, 234; theory as, 90–93, 96; toward nature, 95. *See also* interpretation

authorship, collective, 143–46, 150–52

Beaujour, Michel, 250

Benjamin, Walter, 174

Bible, 46, 110, 139; allusions to, 24 (Abraham and Isaac), 118 (Nativity), 138 (Flood); Gospels, 59–60, 108–109. *See also* higher criticism

Bishop, Jonathan, 115, 217

Blair, Hugh, 119–20, 197

Blake, William, 118

Bloom, Harold, 143, 202–203, 239, 245, 250

Bowen, Francis, 234

Brodhead, Richard, 250

Buell, Lawrence, 246

Burke, Kenneth, 139

Cameron, Kenneth Walter, 33

Carlyle, Thomas, 181; first meeting, 69–72; on history, 226, 249; *Sartor Resartus*, 233

catalogues, 122, 124

Channing, William Ellery (1780–1842), 66

Channing, William Ellery (1818–1901), 117

Cheyfitz, Eric, 76

closure, 112–13, 136–37, 139–40

Coleridge, Samuel Taylor: Emerson's visit, 66–68, 70–72; influence, 43; on criticism, 26, 249; on imagination, 182–83; on Trinity, 171; prose style, 235

comparative method, 40, 88; and history, 103; and literature, 9, 143–44, 232; and religion, 9, 44, 106, 108, 144. *See also* higher criticism

correspondence, theory of, 197

Cox, James M., 244–45

criticism: attacked, 85–86, 100, 115; attitudes toward, 3, 17, 26–27, 93; genial, 249; nineteenth-century, 5, 103, 234; present theories of, 235, 252; quotation as, 148–50. *See also* higher criticism; interpretation

"Criticism," 1841 journal entry, 192–94

Dante, 193–94

deMan, Paul, *see* Man, Paul de

De Quincey, Thomas, 148

De Wette, Wilhelm L., 42

detachment and transition (metaphors), 175–94; and intellect, 161,

detachment and transition (*cont.*):
165; and irony, 136; and metaphor,
202; and naming, 124; and quotation, 148; and repetition, 167, 173.
See also fragments and fragmentation; prose style; "Transition,"
1847 journal entry; transitions

Eliot, T. S., 194
Emerson, Charles Chauncy (brother),
30
Emerson, Ellen Louisa Tucker (first
wife), 47, 50, 57–58
Emerson, Mary Moody (aunt), 7, 35
Emerson, Ralph Waldo: at Jardin des
Plantes, Paris, 85; composition and
revision, 158, 160–66, 168, 176–
78, 193–94, 246; desire for greatness, 25–27, 30–32; in England,
66–72, 97; journals and journal-
keeping, 4, 17–18, 150–51, 160,
162–63; marriage, 57–59; ministry, 50, 97; reading, 251; relation
to brothers, 30, 32, 241; resignation from ministry, 44, 48–49, 60–
61; schoolteaching, 30; works:
"American Scholar," 97–102;
"Art," 181; "Character of Socrates" (Bowdoin Prize essay), 27–30;
"Comic," 8, 135, 184; Divinity
School "Address," 97, 104–13,
204; "English Literature," lecture
on Bacon, 157, 177; *English Traits*,
67, 70; "Experience," 11–14, 18,
183; "Fate," 183–84; "Four Evangelists" (lectures on Gospels), 59;
"History," 226; "Indian Superstition," 33–34; "Intellect," 133–34;
"The Lord's Supper," 61–66, 104–
105, 203–204; "Memory," 180;
"Natural History of Intellect,"
165–66, 188–89; *Nature*, 85–96,
189, 195–97, 234; *Nature*, "Prospects," 146, 186, 211–13, 216;

"Nature" (essay), 213–14, 216;
poetry, 248; "Poet," 102, 114–40,
166–67, 169–73, 190, 195, 198–
99, 205, 244; "Powers and Laws of
Thought," 192; "Present State of
Ethical Philosophy" (Bowdoin Prize
essay), 17, 27, 29–30; "Quotation
and Originality," 141–53; *Representative Men*, 152; "Self-Reliance,"
52, 177; sermons, 10, 50, 59–61;
"Swedenborg, or The Mystic," 131,
205–206; "Thoughts on the Religion of the Middle Ages," 35, 39;
"Trust Yourself," 51–52, 60
Emerson, Waldo (son), 244
Emerson, William (brother), 30, 43–
44
energy (metaphor), 177–81, 187
English literature, 137, 152
essays, subject matter, 10, 76–77
essay structure, 87, 126, 141, 242;
and Emerson's development, 113,
140; dialectical unity, 75–76; paradigm, 77–78; speaker's roles, 83–
84, 114. *See also* prose style

fable, 208–27; and religion; 33; defined, 196
figurative language, 195–227; and influence, 56; conceptions of, 9; of
Jesus, 64–65, 108–109. *See also*
fable; interpretation; irony; metaphor; symbols
fragments and fragmentation, 74, 177,
181, 233, 247; and irony, 183; and
repetition, 157, 160; of past, 81; of
sources, 104. *See also* detachment
and transition; prose style
French Revolution, 29
Freud, Sigmund, 180, 207

genre, 228–30, 233, 250
German literature, 71, 152
Germany, 43

Library of Congress Cataloging in Publication Data

Ellison, Julie K.
Emerson's romantic style.

Includes bibliographical references and index.
1. Emerson, Ralph Waldo, 1803–1882—Style.   2. Romanticism—United States.   3. Influence (Literary, artistic,
etc.) I. Title.
PS1644.E43   1984   814'.3   84-42582
ISBN 0-691-06612-4 (alk. paper)